WHEELS ON FIRE

Wheels on Fire

*The Amazing Inside Story
of the DaimlerChrysler Merger*

DAVID WALLER

Hodder & Stoughton

Copyright © 2001 by David Waller

First published in Great Britain in 2001
by Hodder and Stoughton
A division of Hodder Headline

The right of David Waller to be identified as the Author of
the Work has been asserted by him in accordance with the
Copyright, Designs and Patents Act 1988.

10 9 8 7 6 5 4 3 2 1

British Library Cataloguing in Publication Data
A CIP catalogue record for this title is available from
the British Library

ISBN 0 340 77036 8

Typeset by Palimpsest Book Production Limited,
Polmont, Stirlingshire
Printed and bound in Great Britain by
Mackays of Chatham PLC, Chatham, Kent

Hodder and Stoughton
A division of Hodder Headline
338 Euston Road
London NW1 3BH

For Jane

CONTENTS

LIST OF ILLUSTRATIONS

Photographs by permission of the author.

29. Jürgen Scrempp, Robert Eaton and Richard Grasso.
30. The DaimlerChrysler share certificate with the portraits of the firm's founders: Gottlieb Daimler, Karl Benz and Walter P Chrysler.
31. Eckhard Cordes, Rudiger Grube, Lydia Deininger and Jürgen Schrempp.
32. Karl-Heinz Zimmermann, Jürgen Schrempp, Lydia Deininger and David Coulthard, Jürgen Hubbert and Norbert Haug.
33. Schrempp with US President Bill Clinton.
34. Jürgen Schrempp, Katsuhiko Kawasoe and former US President George Bush.
35. Jürgen Schrempp.
36. Jürgen Schrempp and Gerhard Schröder.

FOREWORD TO THE UK EDITION

The idea for a book about Daimler-Benz first occurred to me back in the early 1990s when I was a young reporter working for the *Financial Times* in Frankfurt.

The company exerted a powerful fascination. It was not merely the mystique of its Mercedes-Benz cars nor the sheer scale of the largest industrial group in Europe. It was the company's historic role at the centre of German industry and at the heart of Europe's largest economy. All of which combined to make Daimler-Benz a formidable story, its dramas played out on a heroic stage.

I left Germany in 1994, a time when Daimler-Benz was at a crossroads, torn between the forces of modernisation and of conservatism. The modernisers wanted to open up Daimler to the international capital markets. They were prepared to challenge the ruling orthodoxy which had taken the company down a disastrous diversification path. To them the traditionalists appeared dangerously arrogant and complacent in the face of mounting challenges.

Back in the UK, I watched as the drama unfolded. I saw how the modernisers won through in the person of Jürgen Schrempp (who took over as CEO in May 1995) and how this led to an epochal restructuring of the company. The story came to symbolise the revitalisation of the German economy – the breakdown of the old social market system in the wake of reunification with East Germany and the growing assertiveness of German industry on the international stage.

It was also a tale of leadership. I followed how Schrempp stopped the bleeding and restored the company to health – and then seized the initiative in the auto industry by pushing through the historic merger with Chrysler Corporation. Schrempp had the force of globalisation on his side, but none of this would have happened without his firm grip on the tiller. This iconoclastic, unorthodox CEO adroitly took a company with limited strategic options and gave Daimler the chance of becoming the world's leading automotive group.

After the Chrysler deal I revived my plans to write a book. It would centre on the drama of the DaimlerChrysler merger, but it would place the transaction in its broader context. Telling the story from the European point of view for the first time, it would show how the swiftly executed deal followed years of careful planning. It would be a portrait of a deal but also of Schrempp, the man behind the deal. It would take the reader as close to the events themselves as one could possibly be without having been there oneself. It would describe the titanic battle now taking place in the automotive industry – and show how DaimlerChrysler has emerged with the potential to be one of the industry's handful of global leaders.

So, at least, this is how the story appeared when I prepared the German edition of this book. During the second half of 2000, however, the cyclical decline of the US auto industry intensified, dragging down the Chrysler Group's earnings and the DaimlerChrysler share price. Even if the underlying logic of the deal remains as compelling as ever, the ending of the story is thus less straightforward or happy than it initially seemed.

The book could not have come about without the support of Jürgen Schrempp who granted me unprecedented access to him and to DaimlerChrysler. The only condition that he imposed was that he could check the quotations attributed to him. I have also had the benefit of talking to many independent commentators and analysts as well as dozens of executives within the company. I thank all those to whom I have spoken without whose insights this could never have come into being. However, the judgements contained in this book are ultimately mine – so I take full responsibility for what appears in the following pages.

London, 29 November 2000

INTRODUCTION

Seventeen Minutes That Changed the World

12 January 1998

The black Mercedes-Benz S-Class leaves Wayne County airport, heading north towards the Detroit suburb of Auburn Hills. In the back of the chauffeur-driven car, its prominent passenger knows that this trip to Michigan could be a defining moment in the history of the automotive industry.

Jürgen Schrempp, the chairman of the board of management of Daimler-Benz, holds a slim briefcase on his lap. Schrempp has brought the battered brown leather case with him on his private plane from his office in Stuttgart in south-west Germany. The documents and charts inside the briefcase show the logic of a merger the dimensions of which have never been seen before in the 115-year-old automotive industry. Schrempp is certain that the deal will fly, but will his counterpart buy in?

The German executive, wearing his favourite blue suit and a signal-red tie, is looking tanned and healthy after a short break in the sunshine of South Africa. His heavy twelve-cylinder Mercedes is making its way towards Chrysler's headquarters in the leafy outskirts of Motor City. He glances out of the blackened rear windows and catches sight of the Ford Motor Corporation's Dearborn headquarters. Schrempp knows he can only fight competitors such as Ford by changing the rules of the game. He has the new game-plan in his briefcase, and Chrysler will play a crucial role in the game.

What is the best way to broach the subject of a deal, the CEO of Daimler-Benz asks the slight, dark-haired woman sitting next to him in the back of the car? Should I come straight to the point or go into a huge amount of detail? Lydia Deininger, Schrempp's assistant, knows that he has made up his mind already. His gut tells him he should skip the detail and stick to a broad-brush presentation; a few sentences outlining the rationale for what could become the biggest cross-border merger in industrial history.

Arriving at Chrysler's imposing corporate headquarters forty minutes later, he is shown to the chairman's office on the fifteenth floor. He follows his instinct and the meeting with Bob Eaton is over almost before it has begun. Schrempp leaves behind the contents of his briefcase. On the way back to town, he and Lydia stop off at the Fox and Hound steakhouse, an English-style country-house hotel complete with log fires and sumptuous leather furnishings.

It was a short visit to the Chrysler headquarters, lasting no more than seventeen minutes, but the consequences were profound. It set in motion a sequence of events which would culminate ten months later in the merger of Daimler-Benz AG with Chrysler Corporation to create DaimlerChrysler AG.

Thursday, 7 May 1998

At 5 a.m. Jürgen Schrempp goes for a jog around London's Hyde Park, accompanied by his bodyguard. Tired after a punishing travel schedule between Germany and the US, he is nevertheless supremely excited. Less than four months after his initial conversation with Eaton, the deal will be announced later today.

The thought of finally being able to go public after months of secrecy fills him with elation. It will be the biggest cross-border merger of industrial companies in history, creating a global giant with $155 billion in sales, a market capitalisation of around $100 billion and anticipated profits of $7 billion for 1999.

The merged company will fuse the mystique of the Mercedes-Benz marque, synonymous with speed, luxury and engineering excellence since the birth of the motor car, with the emotionally charged Chrysler brand. Chrysler, the smallest but most profitable of the big three American car producers, is a symbol of Americana and a dominant force in the fast-growing mini-van and sports utility vehicles segment of the US market. The company is a byword for pluck and entrepreneurial bravado, having hauled itself back from the brink of bankruptcy several times since the Second World War. Now, Chrysler is one of the most profitable and innovative car companies in the world.

The new group will manufacture cars and trucks in thirty-four countries, selling its products in a further 200 countries, more than the United Nations has member states.

With 442,000 employees, DaimlerChrysler will create jobs, not shed them as is usual in conventional deals. It is a merger of equals and a merger for growth, Schrempp will reiterate to journalists, politicians, analysts and investors hundreds of times in the next twenty-four hours.

From a strategic point of view, the deal is audacious. Here are two of the world's leading auto manufacturers seizing the initiative in the final round of the industry's global consolidation. Many have predicted such a move, but the endgame for the overcrowded industry has until now failed to materialise. At one fell swoop, the new company will become one of the handful of giants which will determine the course of the automotive industry in the twenty-first century. The merger of Daimler and Chrysler creates one of the world's big three automotive companies alongside Ford and General Motors (measured in terms of sales). The new company will be a $100 billion rival to Toyota for the number one slot in terms of market capitalisation. It will be more than twice the size of Volkswagen, its closest European rival.

It is the first time that two big regional leaders have merged from a position of strength. The traditional pattern for the auto industry has been that the strong buy the weak, as when BMW bought Rover in the UK or Ford acquired Jaguar. The industry is beset with overcapacity but national pride and managerial egos have traditionally stood in the way of groundbreaking transactions. This deal is different. Here is the verdict of Nick Snee, automotive analyst at the J.P. Morgan investment bank: 'The formation of DaimlerChrysler changes the landscape of the automotive industry,' he tells his clients on the day. 'Daimler-Benz has captured one of the industry's most attractive prizes and staked out its claim on the global market . . . perhaps doing permanent damage to the global ambitions of its rivals.'

The transaction is bold from a technical point of view, too. It is to be the first sizeable transatlantic stock-for-stock merger. No cash changes hands, only the exchange of shares for shares. A simple enough proposition in theory, but in practice a minefield of complications. Many who subscribed to the compelling strategic logic of the deal found it difficult to believe that it could be implemented in practice, so profound were the obstacles encountered along the way. It will have taken just 200 working days from the start of negotiations to closing, a record for a transaction of this size and complexity.

At the time, it is the sheer panache of the deal that impresses people as much as anything else. The two companies have got to the point of announcing a deal, a difficult process at the best of times, without a single leak. Had there been any hint of what was afoot, the deal could well have been thwarted. In the absence of any advance notice, the sheer scale and boldness of the deal is overwhelming.

For Schrempp, who has dreamed of such a move since before he took over as CEO of Daimler-Benz in 1995, the day goes by in a flurry of activity. First he makes courtesy calls to other captains of German industry and politicians such as Helmut Kohl, then Chancellor of Germany, and Gerhard Schröder, then Prime Minister of Lower Saxony but soon to be Kohl's successor.

Schröder congratulates Schrempp warmly. The two men have known each other for a long time. Schröder instantly sees the political mileage in a merger where jobs are created and where a German company is the dominant partner. Closely involved in the auto industry through his role as a member of the Volkswagen supervisory board (VW is the biggest employer in his home state of Lower Saxony), he also understands the strategic logic of the deal.

By comparison, the call to Kohl is awkward. The German Chancellor has been tied up in meetings all morning. He is in Strasbourg negotiating with Jacques Chirac over the choice of president for the nascent European Central Bank. He and Schrempp do not get to talk until mid-afternoon, by which time the Chancellor has had himself briefed on the implications of the deal. Schrempp senses that the statesman is disgruntled. He would like to have been told earlier in the process. He didn't find it very amusing to be caught out when President Chirac of France came up to him first thing and asked about the big transatlantic merger. He knew nothing about it. The risk of telling him ahead of the announcement had been too great.

The same obsessional degree of secrecy has applied on the American side too. Later that day Bob Eaton, the Chrysler Chairman, calls Robert Rubin, US Treasury Secretary; Alan Greenspan, chairman of the Federal Reserve; Dennis W. Archer, the Mayor of Detroit; and John Engler, the Governor of Michigan.

At midday, Schrempp and Eaton are driven in separate cars to the press conference at the London Arena to the east of the City. Preparations have been under way for the past week. More than 300 journalists attend, including nearly forty who have flown in from Germany this morning; another 170 listen in from abroad. Schrempp and Eaton conduct twenty-one interviews with key reporters from around the world. From 2.15 to 3.45

they are the focal point of another conference call, this time with analysts and investors. There are 690 participants, all eager to know more details of the extraordinary transaction. Later that day nearly 100 journalists phone in from the US for a separate North American conference call.

Schrempp and Eaton give twenty interviews to US cable channels. Eaton has no problem giving the identical spiel a dozen times in a row, but by the end of the exercise Schrempp is exasperated and tells his communications chief that he will never do interviews like that again. He likes to see the whites of the questioner's eyes: that way there is a chance of a debate. Talking to an impersonal TV camera is no fun.

Schrempp and his entourage stay overnight in London. The next morning shortly before six they are whisked to Luton airport where a private jet takes them to Frankfurt. At the Steigenberg Hotel close to the airport Schrempp and Eaton host a conference for 110 German analysts and investors. Then there is time for a quick call to Erwin Teufel, Prime Minister of the state of Baden-Württemberg in south-west Germany where Daimler-Benz employs 125,000 people, before getting on the company Gulfstream 5, this time to the US.

On the eight-and-a-half-hour flight to New York, Schrempp has a chance to digest the headlines in Friday's papers. The initial reaction to the deal is one of astonishment and euphoria. 'It is a historic marriage,' says Germany's *Handelsblatt*. 'Forget globalisation the buzzword,' comments the *Wall Street Journal*, 'say hello to globalisation the reality.' 'The ideal motor marriage,' is the appreciative headline in the *Financial Times*. Only the staid *Frankfurter Allgemeine Zeitung* newspaper fails to be caught up in the mood of excitement, commenting sourly that 'the idea is an adventure with an uncertain outcome'. The share prices of both companies rise by nearly 10 per cent, a strong vote of confidence from the world's financial markets.

Schrempp also reads some of the letters of congratulation that have started to flood into his Stuttgart office. One of the first to arrive is from Jack Welch, chairman of General Electric

Company of the US. In a four-line note Welch explains that he is travelling. 'I woke up this morning to see the two of you [Schrempp and Eaton] on CNBC. Congratulations on what looks to be a tremendous pioneering deal.'

The note from Welch is especially pleasing for Schrempp, who consciously adopted Welch as a role model during 1995 and 1996, difficult years when Schrempp had just taken over as CEO of Daimler-Benz and was fighting to restructure the ragbag of businesses he had inherited from his predecessor. His style was so tough that Germany's unions gave him the nickname Neutron Jürgen. This was a deliberate echo of the nickname 'Neutron Jack' Welch, applied to the American manager in the early stages of his career at GE. ('Neutron' because the people were all sacked but the factories were left standing.) The unions meant it as an insult, but Schrempp always felt honoured by the comparison.

Arriving in New York at 2 p.m., they are taken straight from the plane to the Waldorf-Astoria Hotel on Park Avenue where Schrempp meets up with Bob Eaton to give an interview to Alex Taylor, automotive correspondent of *Fortune* magazine. Immediately afterwards Schrempp and Eaton give a presentation to 150 analysts and investors. The stars of Wall Street, usually an unemotional bunch, give Schrempp and Eaton an unprecedented standing ovation. They, like virtually everyone else when first hearing about the deal, are overwhelmed with shock and excitement.

When the conference is over, Schrempp checks his quotes which will appear in three leading German newspapers over the weekend: the *Bild am Sonntag*, the *Welt am Sonntag* and the *Spiegel* magazine. He is driven to the airport and flies back across the Atlantic with some of his closest colleagues and advisors, including his assistant Lydia Deininger; Manfred Gentz, the Daimler finance director; Rüdiger Grube, a senior strategist; and Christoph Walther, the jovial head of corporate communications. They sing along to a CD of the songs of the tenor Andrea Bocelli, arriving back at home in Stuttgart early on Saturday morning. Not surprisingly, Schrempp is tired out. It has been one hell of a week.

On the plane to New York, Schrempp takes a call on his satellite phone. The call comes from Bernd Pischetsrieder, the CEO of BMW and old friend of Schrempp's from his days in South Africa. Pischetsrieder has rung to congratulate Schrempp on the deal.

'Tell me, Bernd, is there anything I can do for you?' Schrempp asks towards the end of the conversation.

Schrempp has noted that the front page of today's *Financial Times* carries two stories about consolidation in the global automotive industry. Across the top of the page is the *FT*'s first story about the DaimlerChrysler deal. Lower down is a report stating that Volkswagen has trounced BMW in the battle to take control of Rolls-Royce Motor Cars Ltd, the UK manufacturer of luxury cars.

For those putting the finishing touches to the negotiations with Chrysler in the past week or two, it has been a relief to know that the automotive press, and the two big German competitors, have been distracted by their tussle over Rolls-Royce. That and the strict code of secrecy imposed on all those involved in the negotiations have helped preserve a total media blackout until the day before the merger agreement is signed.

The juxtaposition of the two headlines is telling. By comparison with the Chrysler deal, the Rolls-Royce transaction is small beer, worth a mere £430 million ($718 million). It is also strategically far less significant. The Rolls-Royce deal eventually struck by the Germans gives BMW and VW a nice brand-name in one small, admittedly prestigious, segment of the market. It does nothing to secure the future of either company.

For Jürgen Schrempp and the Daimler-Benz team, there is a further irony to this news report. If they hadn't played their cards right, they might well have ended up like Rolls-Royce – a manufacturer of luxury cars at the end of a strategic cul-de-sac, with no choice left but to sell out to the higher of two foreign bidders. There but for the grace of God go we, was Schrempp's unspoken thought as he caught a glimpse of the contrasting headlines.

This scenario is not widely appreciated inside Daimler-Benz, let alone outside the firm, on the very day that it is announcing its remarkable transatlantic deal. And yet it is true that the Chrysler deal is driven as much by strategic weakness as by strength. Mercedes-Benz, the jewel in the Daimler-Benz crown, is running out of options. In just a few years' time, it will reach the limit to its growth. The brilliance of the DaimlerChrysler deal is that the Germans have turned a position of relative weakness into one of leadership. In 200 days Daimler has passed from being a potential Rolls-Royce to being one of the strongest auto companies in the world.

There are two reasons for this. One is the transformation already wrought on Daimler-Benz by Schrempp between 1995 and 1997. As we shall see, the group was in no fit state to merge or take over anyone in the early years before this transformation was completed.

And the second reason is the mystique of the Mercedes-Benz brand, a rare enough story in itself.

PART 1

A Tale of Two Icons

CHAPTER 1

The Star Is Born

A brief history of Daimler-Benz and the Mercedes-Benz brand

The factory is as clean as an operating theatre. There is barely a sound as computerised machine tools align themselves over the engine frame before jabbing home a bolt or a component with unerring precision. Every day the plant at Bad Cannstatt on the outskirts of Stuttgart produces nearly 2,000 V6 and V8 engines which are shipped around the world to be installed under the bonnets of Mercedes-Benz passenger vehicles. This is German engineering at its most advanced.

Two miles from this factory is a wooden greenhouse standing in a public park. Respectable ladies wearing elegant loden coats walk their well-behaved dogs around the network of gravel paths. They pay little attention to the greenhouse, ignorant of the historic significance of the modest building or of the very paths on which they are walking. The quiet pathways were the test-tracks for the first spluttering motor-bicycles and spindly motorised vehicles out of which evolved the modern car.

Here, in 1886, Gottlieb Daimler and his assistant Wilhelm

Maybach developed their fragile motorised carriage. At the same time, 100 kilometres north in the city of Mannheim, Karl Benz was putting the finishing touches to his Patent-Motorwagen, the first patented motor car. The two men never met during their lifetimes and their names only came together with the formation of Daimler-Benz AG in 1926.

Benz, the son of a locomotive driver, had since he was a child wanted to build a vehicle that could be driven without the need for railway tracks. Daimler wanted to do this too but his ambitions went further. He grasped the revolutionary power of motorisation, sensing the impact that motorised mobility would have on human society. He predicted, correctly, that it would change people's lives by giving them the freedom to move about, quickly and independently. He did however underestimate the size of the potential market that he was busy creating. He reckoned that the European market would be saturated once 5,000 vehicles had been sold. He believed the constraint to growth would be a shortage of chauffeurs.

In due course, the company he founded would adopt the three-pointed star as its trademark. Now one of the world's most recognisable brands, the corners of the star signified the entrepreneur's desire to create a transportation company '*zu Lande, zu Wasser und in der Luft*' – on land, at sea and in the air. Before the end of the nineteenth century his company was selling engines for boats and the first flying-machines as well as manufacturing buses and lorries. During the course of the next 100 years the company that bears his name would evolve into Germany's largest, most prosperous and most powerful industrial group.

Born in 1834 in Schorndorf outside Stuttgart, Daimler rose from humble beginnings to wealth and professional eminence. His father was a pub landlord and he trained as an apprentice weapons maker before qualifying as an engineer. Daimler worked closely with Nikolaus August Otto at the Deutz engine factory in Cologne, helping to pioneer new technology such as the revolutionary four-stroke engine. At the time, this was a powerhouse of innovation, the world's first factory dedicated to the production of gas engines.

Daimler had a gift for seeing the commercial application of new technology, for turning ideas into marketable reality. '*Nicht aber die Idee, sondern die gute Ausfuehrung ist das Hauptmoment,*' was his motto: 'The idea isn't enough, the most important thing is to put it into practice.'

In 1882, aged forty-eight, Daimler decided to return to his native Swabia and bought a villa and its parkland in the spa town of Cannstatt. Together with Wilhelm Maybach, another refugee from the Deutz factory and a designer of great brilliance, they converted the greenhouse into a workshop and began their pioneering work.

Maybach was the younger of the two by ten years. Orphaned at an early age, he came from a long line of blacksmiths and had been inventing machines since adolescence. If Daimler was the visionary, Maybach was the man who would convert the vision into prototypes and patents.

Working amid conditions of total secrecy, they were raided one night by the local constabulary. The gardener, aggrieved at being locked out of the greenhouse, reported them to the police as he suspected they were counterfeiters. Nothing was found. To the local police, they were '*tüftlers*' or '*dickköpfige Spinner*', eccentric mechanics who took pleasure in harmless experiments.

Daimler and Maybach developed a 212cc engine shaped like a clock, a triumph of miniaturisation and an ingenious appropriation of Nikolaus Otto's ideas. Powered by petrol and delivering a mighty 1 bhp, this engine was installed in a sturdy bicycle frame and in 1885 the world's first motor-bicycle was created. Maybach took the contraption on its maiden journey, a two-kilometre stretch from Cannstatt to Untertürkheim.

In the spring of the following year, Daimler ordered a coach from a Stuttgart firm. Again, it was a hush-hush operation. He told the manufacturer that this was a present for his wife. Once it arrived at the greenhouse, a slightly more powerful version of the clock engine was mounted to the rear. Power was transferred to the wheel axle by means of a belt. It had two speeds, slow and fast. This was the world's first four-wheel car.

Meanwhile, Karl Benz decided to take his own vehicle for a test drive. He had limited faith in his invention and jumped off the vehicle seconds into its maiden voyage. Like many engineers of that era, he was fearful of explosions, a common enough hazard in early experiments. It took his wife to prove the resilience of his creation. In 1888 Bertha Benz told her husband that she and their two sons would be making a trip to visit her mother in Pforzheim eighty kilometres away. She didn't tell him that she would be taking the car. Driving the second of her husband's three-wheelers, she and her sons had an epic journey. The sons got out and pushed every time the car approached a hill, they stopped at every chemist's shop for fuel. Bertha had to use her hat-pin to clean out the clogged-up intake manifold and for the first time in history a woman's stockings were applied to a failing engine – this time when the ignition cable sheared.

The epic journey strengthened Benz's resolve and gave his company some much needed publicity. Benz & Cie went from strength to strength. In 1900 he sold 603 cars, making his the biggest automobile factory in the world.

The history of the automotive industry would have been very different if the early cars had been named after Frau Benz. It is difficult to imagine Janis Joplin singing in her yearning, expressive way: 'I wanna buy me a Bertha Benz.' It does not have the same resonance as Mercedes-Benz.

The marque derives its name from Mercedes Jellinek, the daughter of Emil Jellinek, a raffish German-born, Jewish businessman with a taste for speed and fine living. Mercedes was a lovely blonde child born in Vienna in 1889. Her importance for the story is solely that her father was obsessed with her name, which means grace in Spanish. Jellinek built a Villa Mercedes on the outskirts of Vienna before commissioning another one with the same name in Nice. Before too long he had a boat named after Mercedes – in 1903 it would win a race down the Seine from Paris to the sea. In 1900 the name was applied to cars for the first time. Two Mercedes cars entered the Speed Week in Nice, where aristocrats and moneyed businessmen gathered in the hot Riviera sun to test their prowess in a variety of racing challenges.

In the same year he completed an ambitious deal with the Daimler factory, undertaking to buy thirty-six cars in return for 555,000 Goldmarks and the exclusive right to market the cars under the Mercedes name in the Austro-Hungarian Empire, in France, Belgium and the US. The order underwrote the success of the Daimler enterprise while bringing fabulous riches to Jellinek.

He had a strong practical interest in the vehicles he bought and worked closely with Maybach to design better and faster cars. After the 1900 races, when one of the prototype Mercedes was involved in a fatal accident, his feedback to Maybach was to build a car with a motor at the front and a lower centre of gravity. The result was a lighter, faster, more stable machine that was the sensation of the 1901 Nice Speed Week. Mercedes cars dominated the competition, winning the long-distance race, the one-mile speed trial and the hill-climb.

The glamour of the Mercedes brand today dates back to this early event. From 1901 onwards, the Mercedes car would be associated with speed, performance and style.

The fledgling German automotive industry developed in a different direction from that of the US, where before the decade was out Henry Ford was to put his Model T into mass production. The US had a fast-expanding middle class, the natural customers for the early motor cars, while Germany was a young nation which had come late to industrialisation. The middle classes were not well enough established to provide a mass market for the car. Other German companies such as Adam Opel targeted the bourgeoisie, but Daimler focused on the pan-European super-rich. With the exception of the British royal family (who prefer Rolls-Royces), most monarchs of the twentieth century have had Mercedes as their official cars. The first Mercedes-Benz entered the collection of the Holy See under Pope Pius XII in 1930 and a specially adapted Pope-mobile is now on display in Mercedes' carriage museum at Untertürkheim.

From the earliest days, racing provided the forcing ground for one technical innovation after another. The style and speed of racing cars such as the first S-Class cars of the 1920s or the legendary Silver Arrow of the late 1930s or the W196 of the post-war years rubbed off on the models developed for ordinary customers. Numerous victories on the racetrack served to reinforce the cars' elite image and publicise their superior performance. David Coulthard and Mika Häkkinen, driving for McLaren-Mercedes in the current Formula One series, are aiming to repeat the successes of legendary world champions such as Rudolf Caracciola and Juan Manuel Fangio. Indeed, Häkkinen has been twice world champion in a Silver Arrow.

For Benz and the rival Daimler-Motoren-Gesellschaft, the First World War meant in the first instance an expansion of production and employment as they geared up for military production. After the war, however, reparations and the miserable economic and political climate took their toll. Daimler and Benz were forbidden to manufacture aircraft engines, by now an important part of their total business. In a desperate attempt to fulfil unused capacity, Daimler embarked on an early diversification. Products from the early 1920s include furniture and typewriters, the latter adorned incongruously with the Mercedes star.

It is in these days of rampant inflation that the Deutsche Bank enters the picture. The bank was founded in 1870 by Georg von Siemens on the eve of the modern German era. In the following year the German Reich came into being, following Bismarck's victory in the Franco-Prussian War. Von Siemens and his co-founders wanted to finance the growth of industry within the new Germany. As his name suggests, von Siemens was a scion of the family that had founded the great electrical engineering company.

From the very earliest days Deutsche Bank was closely associated with German industry. In 1887 von Siemens and the Deutsche Bank helped Emil Rathenau found the Allgemeine-Elektricitäts-Gesellschaft, a company set up to exploit the new electrical technology pioneered by Thomas Edison in the US. (Ironically, in 1985 AEG would be acquired by Daimler-Benz and ten years later dismantled and closed down by Jürgen Schrempp.) Deutsche Bank helped found the company, backed Daimler's decision to buy it and ultimately sanctioned its inglorious end.

Deutsche Bank's role was not unlike that of J.P. Morgan's in the US in the years before the Glass-Steagall Act. Morgan acted as power-broker to governments and US industry alike. The difference is that the Deutsche Bank preserved its power throughout the twentieth century, while the influence of the House of Morgan was drastically curtailed by the depression-era legislation.

Outside the bank's Frankfurt headquarters there is a granite statue which speaks volumes for Deutsche's own understanding of its role in Germany. The smoothly polished folds of stone wrap around and inside each other in unending curves. The title of the statue: *Continuity*. In a troubled century, Deutsche Bank has been a bastion of stability.

Nowhere is this more the case than with Daimler-Benz, a company which was formed in 1926 when Daimler and Benz forged a merger. The instigator of this deal was Emil Georg von Stauss of the Deutsche Bank who wanted to promote consolidation of Germany's troubled automotive industry. Von Stauss, who would achieve notoriety in the next decade as an enthusiastic Nazi and 'political banker', wanted to hammer together the two best car companies in Germany which between them controlled 30 per cent of the market. From this time on, the

9

chairman of the Deutsche Bank management board has doubled up as chairman of the Daimler-Benz supervisory board.

After two years working together in a joint venture agreement, Daimler and Benz signed their merger contract in 1926. The document specified that the Benz name should never be dropped from the company's name, a provision that would become pertinent in the closing stages of Daimler's negotiations with Chrysler so many years later.

The two companies made expensive, uncompromising cars. Daimler's motto was: '*Das Beste oder Nichts*', 'The very best or nothing at all.' Benz formulated a similar philosophy in a slightly different way: '*Vom Guten das Beste*', 'Of all that's good (only) the best.' The former rivals were well matched.

In the late 1920s a young author and political activist living in Munich had an unexpected success with his first book. Like many people in a similar position before and since, he decided to celebrate his new prosperity by buying a prestigious car. So when he received his royalty cheque he commissioned a top-of-the-range four-litre Mercedes. The man who placed the order was Adolf Hitler, and the book was *Mein Kampf*. The car was delivered on 29 January 1929.

This was not Hitler's first car from the Mercedes-Benz stable – he bought a Benz in 1924 – nor would it be his last. Months before the outbreak of war in 1939 Daimler gave him a splendid Type 770 Cabriolet, a touring model, for his fiftieth birthday. Although he could not himself drive, Hitler was fascinated by cars in general and had a high personal regard for Mercedes-Benz cars in particular.

Shortly after Hitler took power in January 1933, he outlined his plans to revive the German auto industry. The sector had been badly hit by the world economic crisis and the number of people employed by Daimler-Benz fell by half in the five years to 1932. It was undoubtedly part of the dictator's early appeal to German industry as a whole that he delivered on his promises. He slashed taxes on cars and the industry boomed as a result.

In 1933 alone 70,000 jobs were created by car manufacturers and production jumped by 54 per cent. Along with its domestic rivals, Daimler experienced a dramatic increase in sales. It took on thousands of workers, expanded its capacity, and started making money again. In 1935 Daimler paid long-suffering shareholders their first dividend since the merger of Daimler and Benz in 1926.

Hitler was obsessed with the idea of a car for the common man – what would become the Volkswagen. The car was designed by Ferdinand Porsche but the German car manufacturers could not agree on how to move to production. At Hitler's desired price of Reichsmark 900 per car, no one was going to make money on these machines. Jakob Werlin, an old friend of Hitler's and a Daimler board director, helped out the Nazi leader. Daimler's factory at Untertürkheim built the first thirty prototypes, then known as 'strength through joy' cars, or KfD-Wagens (*Kraft durch Freude Wagens*). A new company was set up to build the cars for the mass market. Based in Wolfsburg, this was the forerunner of the modern Volkswagen AG.

Daimler-Benz played an active role in the militarisation of the country in preparation for war, under discussion from the earliest days of the Nazi regime. Daimler invested heavily in its truck factory at Marienfelde near Berlin, and in 1935–6 it built an entirely new factory at Genshagen to the south of the German capital which would be a dedicated facility for the mass production of aircraft engines. The factory was deliberately sited in deep woodland, its 100 workshops dispersed over a wide area so they would be difficult to identify from above. The planners knew this was not the most efficient way to build a factory, but they wanted to minimise the risks of aerial bombardment. War was already on the agenda.

The year 1939 was set to be the best in Daimler's history, with more cars and trucks produced than ever before. But, like the rest of German industry, Daimler had made a pact with the devil. In September 1939 the private sale of cars was forbidden.

Thereafter Daimler's production would be entirely given over to the requirements of the war. The companies' factories worked flat out producing trucks for the front and engines for tanks, speedboats and aircraft.

From 1939 onwards, the company made increasing use of forced labour, supplementing its own depleted workforce with thousands of prisoners of war, civilians from occupied countries and political prisoners transferred from concentration camps. At plants such as Untertürkheim, Sindelfingen, Mannheim and Berlin–Marienfelde, these starved and maltreated unfortunates made up more than a third of the labour force. They worked and lived in conditions of desperate danger and squalor, subject to the constant threat of air-raids and beatings by guards. As the war progressed, and the prospect of victory diminished, they were given the tasks of building underground caverns to which much of the company's productive capacity was transferred.

The period 1933 to 1945 was a dismal chapter in Daimler's history, as it was for the German nation and its people. At this distance it is worth remembering that Daimler-Benz was by no means alone in co-operating enthusiastically with Hitler's regime. Virtually all Germany's big banks and industrial companies threw their weight behind the Nazi leader right from 1933. The use of forced labour was commonplace. And speaking out against the regime was not an option, as the fate of Hermann Köhler recalls. This director of the Deutsche Bank's Stuttgart branch and member of Daimler's supervisory board dared to voice public criticism of the Nazis. He was executed in the autumn of 1943.

Half a century later, Daimler-Benz was at the forefront of German industry's attempts to make amends. In the late 1990s the company made the biggest contribution to a compensation fund for former slave labourers. And at the time of writing, Manfred Gentz, Daimler's chief financial officer (CFO), heads the foundation which is co-ordinating the efforts of German industry to make restitution.

*　　*　　*

At the end of the war, 70 per cent of the buildings at the Untertürkheim plant had been flattened; the figure was 80 per cent at Gaggenau and 85 per cent at Sindelfingen. The Berlin factories were destroyed. Mannheim was relatively untouched, with only 20 per cent damage.

What was left of the workforce set about clearing up the rubble and had soon created orderly paths through the ruins. Yet Daimler's management and the occupying armies of the US and France found it difficult to believe that anything would ever be manufactured at any of the Daimler plants again. 'The company had practically ceased to exist,' was the sombre verdict of the 1945 Annual Report when it was finally published six years later.

And yet Daimler-Benz did rise quite literally from the ashes. Painstakingly, the company hauled itself back into business. Key components were dug out of the ground where they had been buried to protect them from bomb attacks. According to some estimates, the damage was not as bad as it seemed: the underground caverns had served their purpose and perhaps only 15 per cent of key machine tools were destroyed. Plans for new models were revived.

Production of cars rose from 214 in 1946 to 1045 in 1947 and 17,417 in 1949, while the number of trucks produced rose sixfold to 6,000 in the same period. In May 1949 the company launched three new vehicles at the International Export Fair in Hanover: a 3.5 tonne truck and two versions of the 170 S-Class. The models proved immensely popular at home and abroad. Steadily, Daimler regained old ground and by 1951 it employed around 32,000 people, as many as before the war.

Appropriately enough, James F. Byrnes, US Foreign Secretary, chose Stuttgart to give the historic 1946 speech in which he urged Germans to work hard and live modestly with the aim of rebuilding German industry for peaceful purposes. Daimler, together with hundreds of other Swabian engineering companies, would take him at his word. But beyond hard work, the real impetus to Daimler's post-war revival came two years later, from factors well beyond its own control. The launch of the Marshall Plan in 1948, under which the US channelled investment into defeated Europe, ensured that the country would not turn into a land of rubble and swineherds as some in the US had hoped. In the same year Ludwig Erhard, Germany's great post-war Economics Minister, introduced the Deutsche Mark. The new currency restored confidence to the battered German economy and rapidly became the cornerstone of the country's past-war prosperity.

In February 1953 Germany's respectability as a member of the international community was confirmed by the London Debt Accord, which opened the way to the convertibility of the D-Mark and re-established Germany's international creditworthiness. (The German delegation was led by Hermann Josef Abs, soon to be chairman of Daimler's supervisory board.) For the mass of ordinary Germans, equally symbolic events were the country's victory in the 1954 football world championship and the double victory of the German team in the 1954 Formula One championship. With Juan Manuel Fangio at the wheel of a Mercedes-Benz W196, Mercedes-Benz took first place while Karl Kling took second place, balm for the soul of the German nation.

From this point, Daimler's growing prosperity mirrored that of Germany as a whole. Turnover was DM502 million in 1950, DM3.7 billion in 1960, DM10.5 billion in 1970, DM31 billion in 1980 and DM85 billion a decade later. Over the same period the number of cars and trucks produced rose from 42,200 to 842,000 and staff numbers climbed from 31,000 to 377,000.

Daimler's tough post-war CEOs took the best of their inheritance to build Germany's richest, most powerful company. They maintained the company's reputation for engineering excellence and innovation while successfully extending the Daimler franchise around the globe. Daimler opened assembly plants and distribution networks in North and South America and Asia. By 1956 it sold its cars and trucks in 127 countries through nearly 1,400 representative offices. Having chosen to concentrate exclusively on the top end of the passenger car market, Daimler's new models captured the imagination of successive generations of wealthy customers. Cars such as the wing-doored 300 SL sports car and the 1972 S-Class saloon added to the mystique of the three-cornered star. The cars led the field in terms of safety and innovation: for example in the late seventies Mercedes introduced airbags and ABS braking systems after nearly twenty years of research.

The quality of the Mercedes car allowed Daimler to charge higher prices than its competitors. This fed through into high margins, profits and reserves. By 1985 the group's reported pre-tax profits were DM6 billion. This did not tell the full story, as Daimler took advantage of Germany's flexible accounting rules to shield profits from shareholders and the taxman alike, building hidden reserves of cash which nourished an aggressive investment programme. The company became financially self-sufficient.

It seemed that Daimler-Benz could never again find itself as vulnerable as it had been in the late 1920s and 1930s.

Every year throughout the eighties, Deutsche Bank and Daimler-Benz would go through a ritual designed to demonstrate the car manufacturer's independence from its largest shareholder.

Daimler's board of management would summon the bank's senior officials to Stuttgart and ask them to demonstrate that the bank was a financially solid institution. At issue was the DM5–6 billion of cash that Daimler-Benz had accumulated, the surplus from its extraordinarily successful post-war expansion. Daimler would politely ask whether Europe's most powerful financial institution was a safe place to keep the cash on deposit.

With equal courtesy, Deutsche Bank would explain why it was good for that amount of money, a sizeable sum of course, but a mere fraction of its total balance-sheet wealth. In the end the two sides would invariably agree that the money should stay on deposit at the Deutsche Bank, and that the bank would pay Daimler a market rate of interest on the deposit. Deutsche Bank could not expect to charge that little bit extra to Daimler, despite being the owner of more than a quarter of the company and the main influence on its strategy for more than half a century.

The story illustrates the subtle antagonism between Daimler and Deutsche, a feature of their relationship for decades. Daimler has always been keen to demonstrate its independence, while the bank has pulled the strings at the highest level for the entire post-war era.

Since time immemorial Deutsche Bank has used its dominant position on the supervisory board to influence Daimler's strategy and to determine the choice of chief executive. Until the early eighties this functioned smoothly. For example Joachim Zahn, CEO from 1965 to 1979, was a Deutsche Bank protégé who carefully built up the company's prestige and husbanded its prosperity. When he stepped down in 1979, he was replaced by Gerhard Prinz who was to last only four years in the job: tragically, he dropped dead of a heart attack on his exercise bicycle. Werner Breitschwerdt was appointed his successor, a controversial decision as influential directors at both the bank and the company were in favour of Edzard Reuter instead. Reuter was the up-and-coming finance director and head of planning, a visionary who wanted to take Daimler out of its automotive heartland into the fast-growing businesses of the future. His father was Ernst Reuter, the socialist politician who achieved international fame as Mayor of Berlin during the city's 1948–9 blockade. His autobiography tells of the shock of returning to the ruins of Berlin in the immediate aftermath of the war. Like Alfred Herrhausen, one of his backers, Reuter devoted his life to rebuilding his country, spending the best part of thirty years with Daimler-Benz. He made Breitschwerdt, a traditional Swabian engineer, look like a backwoodsman.

Alfred Herrhausen took over as 'speaker' of Deutsche Bank's management board (equivalent to a UK or US CEO) and as chairman of the Daimler-Benz supervisory board in July 1985. He occupied an office at Daimler's Stuttgart headquarters from which he planned a radical overhaul of Daimler's management. Breitschwerdt was encouraged to resign and Reuter was appointed in his place. At the same time Herrhausen brought on board Helmut Werner as head of the truck division. Werner, the genial former chief executive of the Continental tyre company, was seen as a potential successor to Reuter. In due course he would be appointed head of Mercedes-Benz where he presided over a revitalisation of the core car company.

These were fateful decisions for Daimler-Benz which can only be properly understood in the light of Herrhausen's personality and special standing in German business and society. He was a cool, ascetic man who was passionate about philosophy. He transcended humble origins (his grandfather was a butcher) to become an international ambassador for modern Germany.

As chief executive of Deutsche Bank and chairman of the Daimler-Benz supervisory board, he was Germany's most powerful businessman and the embodiment of post-war German success. This made him vulnerable to attack. At 8.34 on the morning of Thursday, 30 November 1989 he was assassinated in a bomb attack as his chauffeur-driven S-Class Mercedes pulled away from his Bad Homburg home. Herrhausen was killed outright, but his chauffeur survived the attack. The insignia of a red star and a Kalashnikov rifle left at the side of the road marked out the assassination as the work of the Red Army Fraktion, left-wing terrorists who for decades conducted a brutal campaign against Germany's post-war business and economic leaders.

The murder punctured the mood of carefree optimism that had swept through Germany since the Berlin Wall's demise the previous month. According to the sick logic of the terrorists, aiming to wound the fabric of that republic months before the historic reunification with East Germany, there could not have been a better target.

Although chairman for little more than four years, Herrhausen had a profound impact on Daimler-Benz. He was the chief supporter of Edzard Reuter, CEO of Daimler-Benz from 1987 until Jürgen Schrempp took over in 1995. Herrhausen and Reuter were co-architects of the plan to transform Daimler-Benz into an 'integrated high-technology company'.

With hindsight, the strategy developed by the two men proved a disaster for the company. By 1995 Daimler-Benz was on its knees. It is tempting to speculate what would have happened if Herrhausen had lived. Would Herrhausen have recognised the failure of the strategy? Would he have done anything about it? Could he and Reuter have made it work?

There is no answer to these questions.

Herrhausen's successor was Hilmar Kopper, a chain-smoking Prussian. Kopper, down-to-earth and plain-speaking, marked the beginning of his term by moving out of his predecessor's office at Daimler's Stuttgart headquarters – being CEO of Europe's biggest bank was a full-time job, he maintained. The relationship between Kopper and Reuter would never be harmonious.

CHAPTER 2

The Chrysler Story

From Walter P. Chrysler to Lee Iacocca

In 1908 a thirty-three-year-old engineer fell in love on a visit to Chicago.

The object of Walter P. Chrysler's affections was not flesh and blood, but rather an ivory and red Locomobile touring car on display at an auto show. For four days in a row, Chrysler skulked around at the show, his gaze transfixed by the lines of the Locomobile. He determined to have the machine at any price, quickly securing a loan of $4,300 towards the $5,000 price of the dream car.

Chrysler shipped his new possession home to Kansas, lavishing as much care on the machine as if it were indeed a new bride. When he got home, he stripped it down, taking the car and its engine to pieces and reassembling them time and time again before he took the car for a drive. Chrysler was obsessively interested in finding out how the car worked. He wanted to know exactly how each component operated and how it was manufactured.

Chrysler decided there and then that the future of transportation lay not with railroads, where he had made his living since the age of seventeen, but with cars. In 1910 he left his job at the American Locomotive Company in Pittsburgh to join Buick, part of the General Motors fold. Chrysler prospered: over the next decade he became president of Buick and a GM vice-president. By 1920, he had amassed a big enough fortune to resign from the company and endure a spell of early retirement. He was fed up with working with William C. Durant, the legendary founder of GM.

He was lured back into the industry with a formidable $1 million a year pay package and the task of turning round the heavily indebted Willys Overland. The company survived to manufacture the famous Jeep, and after various changes of ownership was absorbed into the Chrysler Corporation many decades later. In 1921 Chrysler became chairman of Maxwell and Chalmers, two ailing manufacturers. He sorted them out, merged them together in 1923, and started producing cars bearing his name. A couple of years later, he took control of the company. From then on it was known as the Chrysler Corporation.

The first Chrysler car was launched in January 1924 at the New York auto show. The official event was for cars in production only, so Chrysler unveiled the low-slung prototype in the lobby of the Commodore Hotel. The publicity stunt paid off. With a top speed of 70 mph and equipped with innovative hydraulic brakes, the six-cylinder Model 70s proved an instant success and around 20,000 vehicles were sold in the first year. Over the next four years the number of cars produced and the range of models available expanded rapidly. By 1927 Chrysler was America's seventh biggest auto manufacturer, producing 182,000 cars.

The following year Chrysler acquired Dodge Brothers, a financially troubled maker of robust vehicles, and launched the low-priced DeSoto and Plymouth brands. By the time of the Great Crash of October 1929, Chrysler had joined the ranks of the 'Big Three' US auto manufacturers alongside Ford and General Motors.

In the same month that the stock market imploded, Chrysler closed out on the eponymous skyscraper at the junction of 42nd Street and Lexington Avenue in mid-town Manhattan. For just eleven months, this seventy-seven-storey edifice was the tallest building in the world; in May of the following year the Empire State Building was completed, taller by 204 feet. Crowned with a 185-foot steel spike, the company's 1,046-foot headquarters were adorned with hubcap friezes and stainless-steel gargoyles. 'Bizarre, fantastic and exotic, it grasps the attention of the passer-by,' gushed a contemporary account, 'as well as the amazed interest of the countryside and distant seafarers for miles around.'

The building was daring and original, qualities which were associated with the early Chrysler cars and would characterise the vehicles for many decades to come. Such is its symbolic resonance that in early 2000 many DaimlerChrysler executives had tears in their eyes when Jürgen Schrempp told a town-hall meeting in Auburn Hills that some head office functions based in Detroit would in due course be moved back to the building in New York. The move may foreshadow the creation of a 'virtual' headquarters for DaimlerChrysler in the US – but a formal transfer of the company's HQ from Stuttgart is unlikely given Daimler's German heritage.

The building was also a monument to the success of Walter Percy Chrysler himself, an archetypal American entrepreneur who through hard work and ingenuity hauled himself up from the obscurity of the Kansas plains to success and riches. He was a beefy, direct man who during his railroad years had learned how to pack punches and utter outrageous curses. By the late 1920s the crudeness was a thing of the past: standing proudly in his double-breasted jacket next to the latest phaeton or coupé to bear his name, the photos show him exuding sleek good health and self-assurance.

There is something Germanic about his solid demeanour, and indeed he was of German descent. Diligent researches by the DaimlerChrysler archivists have proved that his family name was originally Kreissler. The entrepreneur's forebears emigrated from Worms in Rheinland-Palatinate to the US in the nineteenth century.

Unlike many businessmen who prospered in the heady years of the Roaring Twenties, Chrysler did not come unstuck in the Great Depression that followed. He was disciplined as well as driven, and his flair for design was matched by good business sense. He kept on investing in innovative technology throughout the lean years. His trio of top engineers – Carl Breer, Fred Zeder and Owen Skelton, inevitably dubbed the Three Musketeers – produced one innovation after another. These included the 'Floating Power' engine mounting system which isolated engine vibration from the main frame of the vehicle; automatic spark control; rustproof bodies; and the world's first one-piece curved safety-glass windshield. Then came the snub-nosed 1934 Chrysler Airflow. With its teardrop profile, a steel safety-cage construction and a host of other innovations, it was ahead of its time when it was launched and flopped with the consumer. Gradually, however, it came to set the standard for safety and comfort throughout the industry. In retrospect, it was arguably the first modern car and its styling is echoed in the 1990s generation of 'cab forward' Chryslers and the pug-nosed PT Cruiser.

While many US car companies were forced into bankruptcy during the thirties, Chrysler went from strength to strength. It was the only auto manufacturer to have bigger sales in 1933 than in 1929. By 1940 it had 25 per cent of the market and had displaced Ford as the second largest auto company in the US after GM.

Walter Chrysler died in 1940. The passing of this patriarchal figure, together with the US entry into the Second World War in December 1941, marked a turning point for the company.

Like the rest of American industry, Chrysler was obliged to abandon production of cars for the consumer in favour of matériel for the allied forces. Its factories turned out trucks, engines for ships and planes, tanks, rockets, as well as tugs and radar systems. The most famous of all Chrysler products was the thirty-two-ton M-4 Sherman tank, the main combat vehicle of the US army and its allies. Chrysler produced 18,000 of these agile, reliable machines. In addition it supplied 500,000 Dodge trucks. Meanwhile, Willys Overland, which joined the Chrysler fold only in 1987, produced the Jeep. Willys manufactured more than 368,000 vehicles for the US army during the course of the war.

The value of the equipment produced by Chrysler during the war was $3.4 billion out of a total of $29 billion provided by the auto industry, a share that belies the emotional impact of Chrysler's products. A generation of Americans would associate the company's tanks and trucks with the heroic struggle to liberate the world from the Axis powers. The Jeep also became a symbol of freedom. The company and its products acquired an iconic status that is exploited by its marketing men to this day.

With the return to peacetime conditions, Chrysler emerged as a less adventurous company than it had been before the war. Under K.T. Keller, Chrysler became a byword for conservatism. Keller insisted that his cars should be tall enough to get into with a hat on. In an age when the hat was no longer an essential sartorial requirement, Chrysler's cars quickly acquired a reputation for being boxy and old-fashioned compared to Ford and GM's sleek new models. Sales plummeted and by 1954 market share had declined to a worrying 13 per cent, the lowest since the war.

It is from this point that we can chart an enduring feature of Chrysler's recent history: a propensity to swing from boom to bust. The North American auto industry has always been a cyclical business, with lean years following years of plenty with dependable regularity. From now on, Chrysler could be relied upon to outperform in the good years and underperform in the bad ones, a recipe for perennial instability.

In 1955 the company's fortunes revived dramatically with

the introduction of the Chrysler 300, a brutishly powerful 300-horsepower vehicle whose 'Forward Look' styling harked back to the contours of the Airflow twenty years before. Under design chief Virgil Exner, Chrysler launched a succession of aggressively styled, muscular cars which restored the company's fortunes. And yet with the dawn of the next recession in 1958 Chrysler was once again vulnerable. While sales for the industry as a whole dropped by 31 per cent, Chrysler's output dropped by 48 per cent. By 1962 the company's market share had dropped to a perilously low 8.3 per cent.

'My wife's divorcing me. My girlfriend is pregnant, my son has been expelled from Yale, and now I've just been promoted to vice-president at Chrysler.' The joke signalled the depths to which Chrysler had sunk (quoted in David Halberstam's *The Reckoning*).

With the arrival of the autocratic Lynn Townsend as chairman, the company staged a superficial recovery. Market share and earnings climbed in line with the nationwide boom in car sales. However, Chrysler was storing up grave problems for the future. Townsend exhausted Chrysler's resources on an ill-fated attempt to build an international network, buying into a succession of second-rate companies such as Rootes of the UK, Simca of France and Barreiros of Spain. Production for the home market was focused on big, gas-guzzling cars, a misjudgement on the eve of stringent clean air legislation and the 1973 oil shock.

The engineering pizzazz of the past evaporated in a company that was now run by accountants. Sales figures overestimated the real level of demand, and tens of thousands of unwanted cars were parked on vacant lots throughout Michigan. Years later, the sight of one such 'sales bank' outraged Lee Iacocca. When he joined Chrysler in late 1978 he had to drive past acres of unsold cars on his daily journey to work. Weeds were growing between the cars, snow covered the vehicles throughout the winter, and to cap it all the land on which excess stock had to be parked was rented from arch-rival Ford.

By 1970 Chrysler had nearly $800 million of debt and was more heavily indebted in relation to its assets than GM or Ford. When Penn Central went bankrupt in 1970 with debts of $1 billion, the spotlight turned to Chrysler: would it be the next to go? For a perilous few months the company faced a growing liquidity crisis as it was shut out from the commercial paper market. Only determined financial diplomacy helped reopen the credit lines. Chrysler staggered on and in 1971 managed to finance the purchase of a 35 per cent stake in Japan's Mitsubishi Motors Corporation. For the next two years it posted record sales, before crashing down to earth in 1973 with the imposition of the oil embargo by the Organisation of Petroleum Exporting Countries.

The OPEC embargo set the scene for a dire decade. Legislative pressure on the auto industry intensified as the government struggled to find ways of reducing US dependency on Middle East oil. The Big Three were obliged to invest heavily in fuel efficiency and small car technology. At the same time, demand for cars was blighted by one recession after another.

Chrysler suffered more acutely than Ford or GM. It was smaller and less financially robust than its competitors and thus less able to absorb the costs of the new regulations. And, unlike GM and Ford, it did not have any cushion to protect itself against the recession in the US market. The two bigger companies had prosperous international operations, while Chrysler's international network merely added to its woes. The heavily loss-making Rootes in the UK was kept afloat only with a substantial injection of aid from the British government. In 1978 Chrysler abandoned its attempt to be a global company, selling off its factories in the UK, Spain and France to Peugeot-Citroën for a total of $430 million in cash and shares.

Chrysler's problems were exacerbated by poor management and lousy engineering. On 2 November 1978, the day that Lee Iacocca joined the company, Chrysler reported a quarterly loss of $159 million, the worst in its history.

*   *   *

The impact of Lee Iacocca on Chrysler – and on America as a whole – is the stuff of legend. Here, briefly, are the facts.

Iacocca was born on 15 October 1924 in Allenstown, Pennsylvania, the son of first-generation Italian immigrants. His father Nicola was an enterprising businessman who ran a hot-dog emporium known as the Orpheum Wiener House. The tight-knit Iacocca family weathered the depression years and young Lee (christened Lido) graduated from high school in 1942. A childhood bout of rheumatic fever left its scars and meant that he was ruled ineligible on medical grounds to fight in the war. Instead of joining up, he went to university to study mechanical and industrial engineering. In 1946 he joined Ford Motor Company.

Iacocca quickly found his métier in the sales and marketing side of the business. He rose rapidly through the ranks, bursting to national prominence in April 1964 with the launch of the Ford Mustang. With its sleek, feline styling, consciously echoing the shape and pace of European racing cars, the Mustang was an instant triumph. Not only did it look good, at a sales price of under $2,500 it was eminently affordable. It captured the mood of post-war America at its most prosperous and self-confident, and it propelled Iacocca to the top of the auto industry. He (and the car) were featured on the covers of both *Time* magazine and *Newsweek* in the same week. In early 1965 he became president of Ford's car and truck group. In 1970 he was promoted to be president of the entire company.

According to any conventional measure of business achievement, his tenure at the top of Ford was highly successful. The two years before his forced departure brought in record earnings. But Ford was not a conventional company: it was still controlled by the founding family whose whims had to be heeded at least as much as the bottom line. Iacocca's independent management style, not to mention his penchant for high living and a prodigious salary, antagonised Henry Ford II, Ford's chairman and the grandson of the company's founder. By 1975 Ford had started intriguing to have Iacocca removed.

Iacocca fought to retain his position, surviving increasingly humiliating attempts to undermine his authority. The final blow fell on 13 July 1978. Ford summoned Iacocca to his office and unceremoniously dismissed him from the company that had been his life for thirty-two years.

The way Iacocca told the story in his bestselling autobiography, the sacking was the result of an epic battle between a drunken reactionary and a visionary upstart who had the pluck and foresight to challenge the Ford family's authority. Others thought that Iacocca, through his own arrogance and egocentricity, brought it upon himself. Whatever the rights and wrongs of the case, it made Iacocca available to the ailing Chrysler. And it made sure that when Iacocca accepted the invitation to join Chrysler, he was burning with a preternatural zeal to prove – to himself, to Henry Ford, to Detroit and the world at large – that he was still a force to be reckoned with in the auto industry.

The fifty-four-year-old Iacocca joined as president and chief operating officer with the promise that he would take over the chairman's job from John J. Riccardo in 1980 at the latest. In fact, Riccardo left early and in September 1979 Iacocca was appointed chairman and chief executive.

Chrysler was in far worse shape than Iacocca had imagined when he took the job. Morale was appalling, the balance sheet was shot to pieces, the plants were dirty and dangerous. In his autobiography, Iacocca admitted that he would not have joined Chrysler 'for all the money in the world' had he known what lay ahead.

Iacocca's first step was to hire in a team of former colleagues from Ford to shake up Chrysler's inbred management culture. But in the short term this could do nothing to revive the company's market share – down to 8 per cent – nor could it reverse the company's worsening financial position. In the summer of 1979 Chrysler drew down an emergency credit line, sowing seeds of panic among the banks who were collectively owed several billion dollars. Losses for the second quarter of

1979 exceeded $200 million. There was no way to undertake the $2 billion extra investment required if Chrysler were to meet the federal government's increasingly tough clean air and safety regulations.

Following the fall of the Shah of Iran, oil prices had risen sharply and the auto industry had plunged once again into severe recession. The success of Japanese imports made matters even worse. Chrysler was staring catastrophe in the face.

The solution was to turn to Washington for aid. Iacocca's pleas for a state bail-out unleashed a passionate ideological debate about the wisdom of rescuing a private-sector concern. In opposition, the Republicans were against it, while Jimmy Carter's Democratic administration was open to persuasion. Iacocca mobilised a grass-roots campaign of 2,000 dealers and workers who stepped up the pressure on Congress.

They deployed every argument they could think of. Chrysler would not survive a conventional bankruptcy. Chrysler was the largest employer of African Americans in the US. It was the biggest employer in the city of Detroit. The company was a victim of unfair trade practices at the hands of Japanese importers. Washington was responsible for Chrysler's plight because of the burden of legislation it had imposed . . . and so on.

As the cash began to dwindle, support for a rescue mounted. It would, however, be a bail-out with strings attached. Chrysler would not get the outright cash injection it was lobbying for, rather the state would underwrite further loans. And, Congress made clear, Chrysler would only get this if it delivered a series of concessions – from employees, dealers, management, suppliers, creditors and lenders. In December 1979 Congress passed the Chrysler Corporation Loan Guarantee Act. The legislation, which provided $1.5 billion in loan guarantees, was signed into law by President Carter on 7 January 1980. Chrysler did not receive any funds until the middle of the year by which time the banks had finally agreed to restructure the company's $4.5 billion debt.

During the next two years Chrysler racked up cumulative

losses of nearly $2.2 billion and tottered on the verge of collapse. The country was mired in recession, interest rates were high, consumers were not buying new cars. Iacocca fought ferociously to keep the company afloat. He took the hatchet to costs, slashing the break-even point by 50 per cent and chopping inventories by $1 billion. On one summer's day in 1980 he sacked 3,000 of the company's 6,500 engineers. By the end of 1981 half the company's white-collar jobs had been eliminated. Iacocca was obliged to make monthly trips to Washington to report on the company's progress. He had to ask for permission every time the company wanted to spend $10 million, a humiliating reverse for a man used to gadding about the globe in a Ford company jet.

And yet the roots of the company's spectacular recovery were in place. Even before Iacocca joined Chrysler, his former Ford colleague Hal Sperlich had been pushing for investment into a small car platform. This was counter-cultural for Chrysler, traditionally a manufacturer of gas-guzzling muscle-cars, and for the Big Three as a whole. Detroit had long resisted government pressure to produce smaller cars, refusing to believe that this was what the customer wanted. But with fuel prices rising, a sea change in customer preferences was imminent. Iacocca found the funds for the K car platform recommended by Sperlich. (There was no special significance in the letter K – it was standard practice for manufacturers to assign a letter to new production lines. A platform is the engineering base for chassis and body construction.) The programme provided the basis for a series of small, fuel-efficient front-wheel-drive cars. The first of these – the Dodge Aries and the Plymouth Reliant – were launched in the autumn of 1980.

There were the usual engineering flaws and it took more than a year for the new models to gain acceptance. By early 1982, however, they were the motor of Chrysler's recovery. As the economy recovered, Chrysler's profits rebounded. By 1983, its fortunes had staged a dramatic revival. Chrysler earned record profits in the first quarter and had enough cash to pay back $400 million of the $1.2 billion owed to the government. In July 1983 Iacocca went to Washington and paid back the remainder of the loan eight years early.

For Iacocca, this was a very personal triumph. He had staked his own reputation on Chrysler's recovery in as direct a way as possible: from the autumn of 1980 he had appeared in the television advertising for the company's new generation of vehicles. 'If you can find a better car . . . buy it,' was his battle cry. The public responded to the challenge, buying the cars and helping to rescue a battered icon of Americana. His virtuoso TV performances, coupled with his picture on the front page of *Time* magazine in March 1983, made him one of the country's most famous businessmen. Iacocca's autobiography, published in 1984 and a bestseller for thirty-seven consecutive weeks, told his life story as a parable of the American dream and took his fame to further heights.

By now, Iacocca had another success behind him: the mini-van. This was the revival of an idea Iacocca and Sperlich had toyed with at Ford, but had never been able to get off the ground at their old employer. The concept was to meld the fuel economy of a station wagon with the spaciousness of a van. It was an entirely new category of vehicle, one which Iacocca hoped would prove attractive to families as a means of ferrying around kids and relatives and shopping.

The hunch proved correct and when the first mini-vans were launched in January 1984 they proved spectacularly popular. Built on the K car platform, they had the feel of a car, but the utility of a small van. Insatiable demand for the new Dodge Caravans and Plymouth Voyagers drove Chrysler's profits to record levels. First quarter earnings exceeded those for the whole of the previous year and for 1984 profits were $2.4 billion – the best result in Chrysler's history. From worrying where the next cent would come from, Chrysler found itself awash with cash.

If invested wisely, there was a chance that Chrysler would be able to free itself from the endless post-war cycle of boom and bust. If squandered, Chrysler would be back on its knees the next time there was a recession.

PART 2

Preparing the Ground

CHAPTER 3

How to Destroy DM100 Billion in Ten Years

The story of Daimler-Benz's disastrous diversification in the ten years to 1995

In the summer of 1993 a cheeky young financial journalist asked the chief executive of the Deutsche Bank how long Edzard Reuter was going to carry on being chief executive of Daimler-Benz.

Hilmar Kopper, who had yet to kick his sixty-a-day habit, took a deep drag on his Marlboro before giving a terse reply. 'Herr Waller,' he said, 'Edzard Reuter will remain chief executive of Daimler-Benz . . . for as long as I want him to!'

With this remark, Hilmar Kopper put one or two things straight. He made it clear that the jury was out on Edzard Reuter. He made it even clearer that the decision on Reuter's fate would be taken by the Deutsche Bank and no one else. And he let it be known that further questions on this delicate issue would be distinctly unwelcome.

Behind the scenes, the question was being asked with growing urgency. Daimler-Benz had become a machine for destroying value, for swallowing up cash. The more sales the company generated, the less money it made. The more money earned by the Mercedes-Benz car business, the more would ploughed into on the group's ill-fated diversification into aerospace and electrical engineering.

It is difficult, in the light of the ensuing débâcle, to remember that Herrhausen and Reuter were not entirely misguided.

After the 1978–9 oil crisis, Daimler's strategic planners took a cool look at the core car business. They recognised that the industry suffered from overcapacity and was vulnerable to the ups and downs of business cycles. Competition was intensifying, even at the top end of the market dominated by the Mercedes brand. Why not secure the company's future by investing in industries with better growth prospects? The funds for this would come from the cash-rich Mercedes-Benz car and truck business. Reuter, head of planning and finance director in the early 1980s, articulated this strategy in a paper presented to the board in August 1984. The new areas of expansion would be aerospace, electrical engineering and software services. The plan was to replicate the prestige and prosperity of the Mercedes brand in these new sectors so that ultimately they would feed back innovation and cash to the car business. Accordingly Daimler embarked on a prodigious acquisition spree.

The first step came in 1985 when Daimler paid DM550 million to take majority control of MTU (Motoren und Turbinen Union), a venerable manufacturer of aircraft engines. Reuter recognised that MTU was no more than a toehold in the world aerospace market. It was essential to build a stronger position. Next came the purchase of a 68 per cent stake in Dornier GmbH, Germany's second biggest aircraft manufacturer, followed by the acquisition of Messerschmitt-Boelkow-Blohn GmbH (MBB). MBB was Germany's largest aerospace company and through its subsidiary Deutsche Airbus the German shareholder in the European Airbus consortium. It was also Germany's biggest defence contractor, the systems leader on lucrative assignments such as Jaeger 90 and the Eurofighter project.

MBB was owned by a mix of private companies and regional

governments and not surprisingly the negotiations were complex and protracted. Throughout 1989 Reuter battled to put together a deal, facing fierce opposition from the Dornier minority shareholders, from the IG Metall engineering union and from his own supervisory board. Herrhausen was distinctly cool about the whole project. The purchase of a 50.01 stake in MBB for DM1.9 billion was not completed until December 1989, less than a month after his death at the hands of terrorists.

In 1985 Daimler also branched out in a totally different direction, buying a majority stake in AEG, the electrical engineering group which made everything from fridges and kettles to automation systems, trams and computer chips. AEG was an historic company and Reuter's aim was to restore it to its former glory as a serious rival to Siemens. It was an enormous enterprise with 72,000 employees and DM11 billion of turnover. In 1986, though, AEG did not have market leadership in any of the market segments in which it operated. The DM1.6 billion deal, the biggest in the country's history at the time, meant that Daimler-Benz leapfrogged Siemens to become Germany's leading industrial group.

The acquisitions continued until the early 1990s. In October 1992 Daimler bought Fokker, the Dutch manufacturer of commuter aircraft. This was supposed to be the strategic masterstroke for Daimler's regional aircraft business but it quickly went pear-shaped. In July 1991 Daimler paid DM1.5 billion for a 34 per cent stake in Cap Gemini Sogeti, Europe's largest software developer. The aim was to extract synergies with debis, Daimler's new IT and financial services division. This did not deliver its initial promise and was eventually sold at a profit.

The companies acquired in the early years had a number of features in common. They were proud and traditional with distinctive corporate cultures, making them difficult to integrate into Daimler-Benz. Daimler compounded the problem by not making a clean job of the acquisitions. Daimler left in place troublesome minority shareholders who made the most of their power to cause trouble and frustrate rational business decisions. And it was an indulgent parent, reluctant to take the knife to costs and implement the kind of root-and-branch restructuring the companies desperately needed.

They all turned out to face grave competitive and structural challenges. AEG never managed to establish leadership in any of its businesses. The defence industry collapsed with the fall of the iron curtain and the end of the cold war. And in the early 1990s aerospace plunged into a deep cyclical trough.

Reuter's strategy was in keeping with the spirit of the times. Conglomerates were fashionable and the diversification had the blessing of top management consultants such as McKinsey & Co. Moreover the big US car companies were pursuing a similar strategy at the time. General Motors bought Hughes Aircraft in 1985, Chrysler bought Gulfstream, and Ford moved into financial services.

'In '85 and '86 . . . no one could predict what was to happen in 1990 with the breakdown of communism and the German reunification,' Manfred Gentz told a reporter from *Institutional Investor* magazine in late 1995. 'This dramatically changed the aircraft and the defence business, while the field of electrical technologies is now completely different. When the whole political scenario changed, so did the terms of trade for our business.' When asked whether Daimler would repeat the diversification, the Daimler-Benz director asserted: 'I think the answer is that we were right to broaden our basis.'

Reuter's diversification was well intended, as well as à la mode. The aim was to reduce the group's risks, to make it more secure. But the opposite happened. The new companies absorbed cash and management attention, to the detriment of the core Mercedes-Benz business. 'Every year the car business has been denied funds of DM1.5–2 billion which but for the losses on the newly acquired businesses would have flowed to Mercedes,' lamented a group of senior managers in a letter of complaint delivered to Kopper in August 1992. 'That is enough to completely refit a factory or to invest in new car products.'

By the early 1990s Mercedes was suffering. Its new tank-like S-Class was poorly received and the model cupboard was bare. Annual sales had stagnated at fewer than 600,000 for five years in a row. 'It was a company that had lost its way,' recollects Bob Lutz, the former Chrysler president who in the early 1990s was head of Ford's European operations. 'It had become slow, sluggish and arrogant, producing cars that were further and further away from what people wanted.'

The poor performance of the acquisitions could be sustained for as long as the core car business carried on generating cash. In the early years Daimler was nourished by windfall profits generated by Mercedes' North American operations. The strong dollar fed through to high D-Mark earnings. Later on, in the early nineties, Mercedes was bailed out by Germany's post-reunification boom. But in 1993 the recession caught up with Mercedes-Benz and the car and truck division plunged into losses for the first time in fifty years. The outside world caught a glimpse of the looming problems in September 1993 when Daimler-Benz published its figures under US accounting rules for the first time. The company reported a loss of nearly DM1 billion for the first six months of the year. For the full year the loss was nearly DM2 billion.

There was another signal that all was not well at Daimler-Benz.

Keith Hayes, the plain-speaking auto analyst from Goldman Sachs, has a favourite trick when he comes in to speak to senior managers at Daimler-Benz. He often puts up a slide showing two sharply diverging lines. 'Imagine this is your pension,' Hayes says. The managers look more carefully at the chart. It represents the appalling share price performance of one company when compared to the stock market as a whole. 'This, gentlemen, shows the Daimler-Benz share price relative to the German market for the ten years to 1995.' The managers gulp in disbelief. It is indeed a very sad story.

By any measure, the performance of the Daimler-Benz shares in the decade to 1995 was dire. The market went up while

Daimler's share price went nowhere. If investors had wanted their portfolio of shares to do better than the market as a whole, all they had to do was own the other twenty-nine companies in the DAX index of Germany's thirty biggest stocks and not own Daimler shares. Only two companies did worse than Daimler, one of which was the near-bankrupt Metallgesellschaft. The other was Deutsche Babcock, an engineering company. Not very distinguished company for Germany's proudest industrial group.

While the share price fell, the company grew its sales. In the decade to 1995 group sales more than doubled from DM50 billion in 1985 to DM120 billion in 1995. But the value of the company on the stock market halved over the same period, from DM68 billion to DM34 billion. And during this time Daimler is reckoned to have invested a staggering DM70 billion in its new acquisitions, including the money spent on these companies and the losses they subsequently made. Crudely, therefore, around DM100 billion of capital was destroyed in the decade to 1995.

Does the stock market justly reflect the performance of a company such as Daimler-Benz? Edzard Reuter didn't think so. The owlish intellectual, a highly cultivated man with a passion for music and show-jumping, was a passionate advocate of a long-term approach to doing business. He contended that Daimler-Benz was in a privileged position when compared to Anglo-American competitors. As a German company, it was liberated from the short-term performance pressures imposed by stock market investors. And when the profits failed to materialise, he gave the impression that he had the right vision for Daimler-Benz's future but that no one else could understand it.

But stock markets are very efficient processors of information. Share prices reflect all known data about a company's future profitability, rising or falling in line with the company's ability to generate free cash flow, that is, cash above and beyond that which needs to be reinvested and so is available to be paid out to shareholders as dividends. The markets may misread the situation for a year or two, but as the 1980s passed into the 1990s the Daimler-Benz share price was sending an unequivocal signal: there was a rottenness at the core of the company. Daimler was becoming bigger and bigger, but it was becoming steadily less profitable. It was absorbing cash and destroying value. This was the market's unemotional verdict on Edzard Reuter's attempt to create an integrated high-technology company.

From the Anglo-American perspective, it is extraordinary that Reuter and his management team could have remained in place for so long. In the US and the UK there is a 'market for corporate control'. In other words, if management does a bad job, shareholders will gang up on the CEO and replace him with a candidate of their own. The management is like a tenant in a house. The owner can come along and give the tenant notice to quit. The mechanism for this is the takeover bid.

In Germany, such bids are extremely rare. Managers have traditionally enjoyed a high degree of job security, protected from bidders by the walls of Fortress Germany, the network of interlocking shareholdings and directorships that have been a feature of the German business landscape from the very beginnings of the industrial era. The first successful unfriendly takeover bid for a German company from abroad took place only in 2000 when Vodafone, the British mobile telephone company, took over its rival Mannesmann.

By the early 1990s Daimler-Benz had become a topsy-turvy world in which the normal rules of economics were inverted. Conventional business wisdom says that management allocates capital to those investment projects that will lead to positive returns. If there is a choice of competing projects, the investment will be channelled into the project that promises to generate more profits in relation to the risks undertaken. At Daimler-Benz, the more money you lost, the more head office would send you cash. This was the consequence of a bizarre accounting system which worked as follows.

Business divisions – there were thirty-five of them in 1995 – were expected to provide quarterly reports to head office. Until 1996, this consisted of a forecast of what profits were going to be for the year compared to plan. There were two serious flaws in this approach. First, the yardstick used to measure profit was *Betriebsergebnis*, which could loosely be translated as 'operating profits before book-keeping adjustments'. The flexibility to make these adjustments gave the divisional barons unlimited scope to manipulate the numbers – for example by channelling subsidies from one subdivision to another or by releasing provisions that could artificially inflate profits. In 1993, for instance, the Mercedes-Benz division probably reported a small profit at the *Betriebsergebnis* level. Analysts suspect that this was only possible because passenger cars came to the rescue of an appalling performance in the European trucks business. The numbers bore no resemblance to what the company would eventually report to the outside world. They gave head office management little idea of the underlying economics of the businesses – and made it very difficult for them to take properly informed investment decisions.

The second flaw in the financial reporting system was the planning round. Early in the year, the divisions got together with head office to devise a detailed plan. After three months they reported how they were measuring up to the plan. The story was always the same: it's early days, of course we'll make it. Another three months later the divisions reported once again that they were on track. If they weren't, no one bothered to probe too deeply because the hallowed holiday season had arrived. It was only in the autumn when everyone had come back from holiday that problems came to light. The full picture would only emerge in October and November, by which time it was too late to take corrective action.

It was like someone taking a jump across a river. For most of the year, the feet were running in the air. Then in October or November they would crash into the water. The mechanism for communicating this state of affairs to the management board of Daimler-Benz was bizarre. All the divisions had to do was to notify the board that they were falling short of their plan (a process called *Abmeldung*). Instead of being fired, demoted or in any way chastised for their failure, the managers knew that everything would be all right. They knew that head office would transfer the cash they required to make up the deficit. Here, German tax law compounded the absurdity. Unless head office transferred the cash, the loss in the division could not be deducted from the group's total earnings for tax purposes.

'I used to lie awake wondering what the hell was going on,' recalls Hilmar Kopper, who as chairman of the supervisory board was responsible for overseeing Daimler's performance. 'It wouldn't have been so bad if it had been just me who was in the dark, the problem was that management hadn't the faintest idea either.'

This behaviour was sanctified by tradition. For decades Daimler-Benz had been an astonishingly rich company. Until the Reuter era, successive post-war CEOs had salted away billions. These reserves of fat engendered a deep-seated complacency. It was the arrogance born out of affluence. By the time Schrempp took over in mid-1995, the affluence had gone, the reserves were run down. Only the arrogance remained.

On the evening of 28 April 1995 Edzard Reuter invited a handful of select journalists to a private briefing over dinner following the annual press conference earlier in the day. Reuter liked to use such informal occasions to put a gloss on the official statements that were for general consumption. By this time Schrempp had been CEO-in-waiting for nearly a year and Reuter would be stepping down in a matter of weeks.

There was one issue on Reuter's mind: he wanted to be appointed successor to Hilmar Kopper as chairman of the supervisory board. Kopper offered Reuter the job early in 1994. 'I told Mr Reuter that he could be my successor if we could announce as soon as possible that Jürgen Schrempp would take over from him as CEO,' Kopper says now. Deutsche Bank was mulling over its own strategy. Over time, it wanted to reduce its portfolio of industrial holdings and use the cash to strengthen its core banking business. The bank wanted to prepare itself for a position of less influence at Daimler-Benz – and what better way to do this than by reducing its visibility at the helm of the supervisory board? Under the circumstances it was appropriate for Reuter to become the first non-Deutsche Bank chairman of Daimler-Benz since 1926.

The announcement of Schrempp's appointment was duly made in June 1994. Two months later, Kopper changed his mind about Reuter. He was on holiday in France when he heard that Reuter wanted to put himself forward for his father's old job as Mayor of Berlin. Kopper was furious: he felt at the very least Reuter should have communicated this to him directly rather than through the front page of a newspaper. He had fought a battle with some of his supervisory board colleagues to secure Reuter's position, and now he felt let down. And, given the scale of the problems beginning to emerge at Daimler, Kopper did not think it possible for a man to combine the role of chairman with high public office. The very fact that Reuter was thinking about this suggested to Kopper that Reuter had underestimated the scale of Daimler's future challenges. Not only that, it appeared to Kopper that Reuter obviously preferred a political position to one of the hottest seats in German industry.

'I had given my promise to Reuter, but I felt released from this promise by virtue of Reuter's action,' Kopper says. He did not communicate this change of heart to Reuter, waiting in vain for Reuter to tell him about his political ambitions. In April 1995 Reuter still held out hopes of becoming supervisory board chairman. With a month to go before he stepped down, he had been offered an ordinary directorship on the supervisory board but nothing more. It was clearly vexing him, and he lined up Jürgen Schrempp and other board directors to join him for the private press briefing. Reuter's aim was to secure Schrempp's on-the-record backing for the top job.

'It was clear by this point that whatever promises had been made, Hilmar Kopper had decided that it just wasn't going to happen,' recalls Schrempp. 'Once Reuter got wind of this he started his own lobbying campaign. He asked me to come to make sure the journalists knew what a very good relationship we had and he wanted me to make a statement saying that I insisted he would become the chairman.'

Schrempp had no objections to this in principle, but told Reuter that he was not going to come out in public against a major shareholder. Late in the afternoon he asked Reuter to stay away from the subject, saying that a squabble in the newspapers would not help his campaign. Reuter agreed that he would hold his tongue.

At the dinner the starter was barely finished before the inevitable question came. 'Are you going to be the next chairman?' he was asked.

'I am not going to comment on this question,' Reuter replied. There was a short pause. 'But they gave me all these promises,' he continued, launching into a tirade of complaints about Deutsche Bank's behaviour. 'I simply can't rely on them,' he lamented.

After the dinner was over Schrempp and Reuter drank a glass of schnapps together. 'I'm sure you know what you're doing,' said Schrempp, 'but can you please explain to me why you said all that stuff.'

'I just had to get it off my chest,' was the reply.

The next day the newspapers were full of headlines about the looming conflict between Reuter and Deutsche Bank. Worse, it was clear that Kopper and Reuter hadn't talked to each other properly for some months, evidence that the channels of communication between the CEO and his chairman had broken down. On the eve of the Schrempp era, Reuter had just dashed whatever faint chance he may still have had of becoming chairman of Daimler-Benz.

CHAPTER 4

Out of Africa

The life and philosophy of Jürgen E. Schrempp

In the summer of 1999 Jürgen Schrempp gave a speech at the Mansion House in the City of London. Attended by the Lord Mayor in his antiquated rig-out of robes, gold chain and knee-breeches, Schrempp surveyed the audience of the great and the good of the City of London, industrialists and bankers, with a degree of scepticism. Schrempp enjoys the trappings of power that come with his job, but he is allergic to all manifestations of pomp and circumstance.

Accordingly, when he discovered that an hour of his schedule had been set aside for a guided tour of the Mansion House, one of London's architectural gems, he was delighted. He ducked out of the tour and instead went to the bar at the Dorchester Hotel where he had a beefburger and chips. As he enjoyed his meal, he remembered with a chuckle that Chancellor Kohl once did something similar on a visit to Salzburg, disappearing off to a café for a piece of gateau rather than face an audience with Margaret Thatcher.

Schrempp has unpretentious tastes. His favourite meal is a steak or a beefburger, accompanied by a glass of light white wine at lunchtime or a robust Brunello di Montalcino or Barolo over dinner. While Edzard Reuter, Schrempp's predecessor as CEO of Daimler-Benz, fraternised with philosophers and politicians and devoted his spare time to horse-riding, Schrempp's favourite hobby is mountaineering. Once a year he joins Reinhold Messner, the world-famous mountaineer, and a small group of friends for a highly competitive climbing holiday in the Alps. He gives up alcohol and intensifies his jogging schedule for a month in advance to ensure that he is on form.

His friends include grandees such as Lee Kwan Yew, President of Singapore, George Bush, the former US President, and Jim Wolfensohn, the president of the World Bank. He spends his holidays with the likes of Nikki Lauda, the former racing driver and airline entrepreneur, Messner, the mountaineer, and Ben Willekens, president of the Art Akademie in Munich. But when his schedule allows he spends time with less exalted friends and acquaintances, including a group of architects and photographers from Stuttgart, the barman at the St Regis Hotel in New York and various buddies who he met during his career in and outside the company.

His own background is modest. He was born in 1944, the second of three sons. His father was a low-ranking administrative official at the local university. Too young to remember the war itself, he suffered privations as a child in the aftermath of the German defeat. He and his family often did not have enough to eat. Supper would consist of a bowl of cherries or apples or a plate of potatoes. His mother put a lock on the fridge because if the three Schrempp boys had raided it between mealtimes there would have been nothing left for dinner. This early experience of hardship is something he shares with Hilmar Kopper, the Deutsche Bank chief who remembers trading cigarettes with the occupying American troops in exchange for food.

If his early life was materially very restricted, Schrempp grew up in a warm and loving family environment. He was especially close to his father, a keen amateur soccer player and

48

coach who became honorary chairman of Sport Club Freiburg, the local football team which subsequently climbed its way into the Bundesliga, the German first division. He played for the soccer club at youth levels and still follows their fortunes keenly, cheering their victories and cursing their defeats. He was also close to his grandfather, who instilled into the young Schrempp a passion for chess, explaining to him the importance of strategy and tactics in achieving your ends in life. This is a lesson that Schrempp took very much to heart.

As a teenager, Schrempp would often discuss his choice of career with his father. There were two possibilities. The first was to become an engineer and invent a dream car. The second was to become a trial lawyer, indulging his love of debate. In the end, he was obliged to abandon his hopes of becoming an advocate. At high school he was good at maths and sciences but had problems learning French. This held him back one year and he did not fancy falling further behind. He dropped out of high school at the age of fifteen, enrolling as an apprentice mechanic at the local Mercedes-Benz dealership.

'I never forget that I started my career under a truck,' he says now. He took the decision after long consultations with his father, but it wasn't easy for him at the time. He spent his days up to his elbows in the engines of Mercedes-Benz trucks and no matter how hard he tried he could not scrub the oil off his hands. It rankled that when he went to dancing lessons in the evenings the oil was still there.

'All the other guys were at high school or on the way to university and there was I the only blue-collar worker,' recalls Schrempp. 'I immensely disliked this . . . this cannot be the purpose of life, I said to myself.'

He looks back on these early days with mixed emotions. He is glad that he escaped the constraints of life as a manual worker – yet he is proud that this is where he started. His experience under a truck gives him credibility with the workforce and at all stages in his career it has helped him forge good working relationships with the unions.

He enrolled as one of the first students at the fledgling Technical University of Offenburg and completed an engineering degree over three years. He had a particularly good relationship with his professors, with whom he used to travel on the train from Freiburg to Offenburg. He turned down a scholarship offered to him by Daimler, insisting he wanted to retain his independence. Indeed, when at college he helped develop an engine for Mercedes' arch-rival BMW.

He supported himself by playing the trumpet at weddings or in the cellar bars of Freiburg, playing jazz and dance tunes on an instrument that he bought with a loan from his father. To this day, Schrempp keeps a trumpet on an open shelf next to him in his office, and when he is in a very good mood he is known to pick up the silver instrument – a present from the Club of 300SL drivers – and play his favourite tunes.

His trumpet-playing drew Schrempp to the attention of Karlfried Nordmann, the head of the Freiburg Mercedes dealership and the future president of Mercedes-Benz North America. Nordmann was a bemedalled former fighter pilot, an exciting role model for the young Schrempp. Schrempp played the trumpet for a gathering of fighter aces from all around the world. His performance went down so well with the Americans, British and Germans who gathered for this riotous reunion that Nordmann lent him his car for the weekend. Schrempp had his first exhilarating experience behind the wheel of a big Mercedes. Nordmann, who was soon promoted to Mercedes head office, became Schrempp's mentor, persuading him to sign up with the Stuttgart company after he had finished his studies and his military service. In 1970 Schrempp joined the export service department in Untertürkheim.

Initially, it was a let-down. Schrempp joined the world's most famous automotive company with high hopes. His ambition to invent a new car was intact. Instead he found himself in a clerical office without a desk of his own. A quick pep-talk with Nordmann one morning got him back on track. He soon found himself enjoying his job. He was put in charge of Africa and was responsible for co-ordinating the field and the Stuttgart-based technical and production departments. If there was a technical problem in Namibia or South Africa, he had to sort it out. It was a period of what he calls 'continuous constructive fighting', a telling phrase which gives an early insight into Schrempp's character. He found himself relishing the cut and thrust of combative business life. He enjoyed getting to grips with problems and fighting his way to a solution. His love of constructive argument remains with him to this day.

This first job gave Schrempp a taste for adventure. He was constantly meeting engineers and marketing men who visited head office with tales of Africa. Having felt the constraints of provincial southern Germany, Schrempp liked what he heard of open spaces and life beyond the confines of head office. He lobbied for a job in Africa. Finally he got the offer early in 1974. 'Anything is better than sitting in a small village just outside Stuttgart,' his wife said when he told her about the opportunity. Schrempp told the story to journalists decades later and it cost him a couple of bottles of wine and an apology to the Mayor of the village of Klein Heppach.

Schrempp, his wife and two young sons flew down to South Africa in mid-July 1974, days after Germany beat France in the final of the World Cup. The plane was full of singing German supporters on their way back to the Cape. It was Schrempp's first long-distance flight and an extremely uncomfortable one, with no separate seats for the two kids. Leaving Stuttgart behind him, the world was opening up for Schrempp.

He returned to head office only in 1987. By that time, he was a very different person: a man of the world, internationally experienced, ready for promotion to the very top. But for two years in the US, he spent the entire time in South Africa. The country had a profound impact on his personality and on his view of the world. He loves South Africa deeply, for its scenery, for its people, for its sounds and smells, for its wine. He owns a game farm deep in the bush and has recently bought a plot of land on the coast near Cape Town. The screen-saver on his personal computer shows an aerial photograph of Cape Town. As chairman of SAFRI (the South Africa Initiative of German Business), he is actively involved in the promotion of the country's wellbeing and in April 1995 he was appointed by Nelson Mandela to be South Africa's Honorary Consul General to the German states of Baden-Württemberg, Rheinland Palatinate and Saarland. The South African flag hangs behind his desk, face-masks and spears hang on the wall of his office, further reminders of the African connection. In more relaxed moments, he talks about retiring down there or going off to do what he feels he would love to do, namely run his own business. It is where he goes for Christmas or New Year, even the odd hastily snatched weekend when his travel schedule allows it.

Schrempp and his family took to South Africa immediately: he was a young man who had landed the right job at the right time in his life. It suited his gregarious nature, and it nurtured his growing independence. He was appointed service manager in 1975 and travelled the country getting to know dealers and customers. He climbed steadily through the ranks of the organisation and in 1980 he joined the board of Daimler-Benz South Africa. 'By then I knew every road in South Africa, every dealer, every journalist who mattered, every fleet manager and his grandmother,' he recalls fondly. It was like an extended family and the friendships forged at this time have lasted.

Schrempp's business mentor was Morris Shenker, chairman of Daimler's South African operations. Shenker, a diminutive, feisty former second-hand car dealer from the eastern Cape, was a practising Jew whose family had suffered at the hands of the Nazis in Poland. He is one of Schrempp's few acknowledged role models. Schrempp grew to revere the man and was honoured to be a pall-bearer at his funeral.

'He was highly respected but immensely disliked at the same time,' says Schrempp, looking for the secret of Shenker's appeal. 'He was totally independent. When he talked to people back in

Stuttgart he said I need this and that and didn't take any bullshit from middle management.'

Schrempp learned to look on head office with a critical eye. 'With every kilometre's distance from head office your wellbeing increases,' he said at the time. He referred to the Untertürkheim headquarters complex as 'Bullshit Castle'. In fact, the jibe was originated not by Schrempp but by a head of the North American operations. Yet Schrempp and his band of brothers adopted the phrase and used it all the time. It came back to haunt him much later when the very first measure he implemented as CEO was to slash the number of employees at the new head office in Stuttgart Möhringen. 'Out in the field we found it funny,' he says. 'In 1995, I must admit, it was pretty demoralising.

'I have nothing against bureaucracy *per se*,' he says now, 'but in Germany there are always so many teams and committees. It's cumbersome but it's cosy at the same time. If you ever have a problem, you have to go to someone, then someone else, and so it continues. You're never really responsible personally for anything, it's always a team decision.'

In South Africa, it was different. 'I was able to take decisions on the spot. If you had a problem, you got together with two or three people over dinner and sorted it out. You could take your decision, stand by it and move on without consulting great numbers of people. I liked it immensely.'

In 1982 Schrempp was called back to Stuttgart to discuss a secret project. He was taken directly from the airport to see Gerhard Prinz, Daimler's then CEO. He was offered the job of president and CEO of Euclid, a US manufacturer of heavy-duty off-road trucks used primarily in the open-cast mining industry. Initially, he was reluctant to take on the assignment. 'I'm too young for the job,' Schrempp told his CEO. 'What happens when I go into the office of some big-shot lawyer or mine owner? They'll laugh at me. I'm only thirty-eight after all!'

'If people laugh at you when you go in, that's fine,' said

Prinz. 'If they're still laughing at you when you leave, it won't be because of your age.'

Schrempp took the job and moved to Cleveland, Ohio. As he and his family arrived on the plane, they looked down on a landscape blighted by smog and pollution. 'Do we have to live here?' his wife asked Schrempp.

He immediately saw that Euclid was in deep trouble. The deep US recession made it difficult to sell the company's trucks to the domestic construction industry. Exports were throttled by the strength of the US dollar. Euclid was fighting tough competitors such as Komatsu and Caterpillar. Furthermore, the strategy that led to the acquisition of Euclid had been undermined by the purchase of Freightliner in 1981. The Freightliner deal took Daimler-Benz fairly and squarely into the on-road truck market. There was no strong rationale for staying in the off-road segment as well. It would have taken many millions to establish a strong competitive position. It was not worth throwing good money after bad, Schrempp reasoned. Daimler-Benz should sell Euclid.

As Schrempp's colleagues back in Stuttgart saw it, there was one flaw in the argumentation. They agreed with his analysis of the market and the financial position, but he had apparently ignored one sensitive issue. Euclid was the CEO's baby. Dr Prinz had made his career on the back of the acquisition of Euclid and could not be expected to sanction the sale of the company. 'You want to tell Prinz that we need to kill his baby,' was the bemused reaction of Gerhard Liener, then head of Daimler's truck division. 'Let's play for time.'

'That's not my style,' said Schrempp. 'I'm going to see Prinz and I'll tell him the way it is.'

'Then you're going on your own,' said Liener.

In the CEO's office, Schrempp spoke uninterrupted for half an hour. Prinz, far from being angry, listened intently as Schrempp outlined the case for a disposal. When Schrempp had finished, Prinz asked lots of questions. 'I think you've got a point,' Prinz said at last, bidding the young manager prepare the case in more detail. A couple of weeks later, Prinz flew to Chicago to hear a longer presentation recommending the disposal.

'Jürgen, you're right, we have to sell the company,' said Prinz at the end of the meeting. 'But do me a favour, can we do it quietly? You know this is tough for me.'

'Are we going to get the M&A [mergers and acquisitions] department involved?' said Schrempp.

'You don't normally ask the frog to take the water out of his own pond,' replied the CEO.

The sale was orchestrated by Schrempp with minimal assistance from Stuttgart. It was finally concluded in December 1984.

Schrempp had his first taste of Anglo-American short-termism. After he had signed the contract with owner Clark Equipment of the US, he had a conversation with Euclid's new CEO.

'I'll turn this round in a matter of three of four months,' said the new owner.

'Okay,' Schrempp said, somewhat perplexed. 'You're more experienced than I am, tell me your secret.'

'Seeing as you're moving out, I don't mind telling you,' the American replied. 'It's pretty straightforward. We'll cut 70 per cent of the company's research and development expenditure. The profits'll go up immediately.'

'If you do that you won't have a company,' Schrempp countered. 'In three or four years you won't have any products at all, you won't be able to compete.'

'I won't be around in three or four years,' said the American, 'so who the hell cares?'

For Schrempp, who has always had a strong emotional attachment to the companies he works for, even when he is in the process of selling them off or closing them down, this was a shock to the system.

There was a second shock. On the day that the deal was done, he and Liener went for a drink in New York's Plaza Hotel. At around midnight, it suddenly dawned on him that he was out of a job. 'I had just restructured myself out of existence,' he recalls.

'If you are doing your job properly you have to be prepared to sell your job; it's the hardest thing of all.'

In truth, Schrempp was far from being unemployed. The sale marked him out as Daimler-Benz's restructuring expert and he had the chance to take over the group's ailing bus business in Mannheim. He turned this down. There was a position in Turkey, which again he turned down. In the end he was posted back to South Africa, this time as CEO of the group's entire operations in the country.

It was his dream job, but the political climate had changed for the worse in the years that he had been away. P.W. Botha's regime had not delivered and the shutters had come down on the country. The struggle to end the apartheid system had intensified and there was formidable pressure on Western businesses to disinvest. The banned African National Congress wanted to turn the screw on the government and urged foreign investors to pull out. Many US and UK businesses withdrew from South Africa completely or set up schemes whereby they transferred their assets to puppet companies which could easily be reacquired should political circumstances change. Schrempp did not toe the line. He was a vociferous critic of apartheid and yet a passionate supporter of continued investment. This combination of views was very unusual. It got him into trouble at home in Germany as well as in South Africa.

In Stuttgart, his conservative colleagues asked him whether he knew who his customers were. It was left unsaid that the number of Mercedes-Benz cars sold in the African townships was rather limited. 'Would you give speeches criticising communism if you were posted to Moscow?' he was asked.

'I can't answer that, they might shoot me,' Schrempp replied. 'Anyway I'm not in Moscow, I'm in South Africa and I have to look at myself in the mirror every morning.'

The debate came to a head when Schrempp asked for more capital to expand his operations. The management board of

Daimler-Benz was in favour, but the labour representatives on the supervisory board were fiercely against what they saw as an endorsement of the racist regime. Schrempp got his funds only when the chairman of the supervisory board exercised his casting vote. He did not leave it there, however. Together with Franz Steinkühler, then head of the powerful IG Metall union and a Daimler supervisory board member (he later resigned after admitting insider dealing), Schrempp developed a ten-point Code of Best Practice for German companies wishing to remain in South Africa. 'My idea was that we treat people there as we treat them in Europe,' recalls Schrempp, 'rather than do some deal that simply preserved the status quo until we were allowed to come back.

'Virtually the only legal way for the blacks to express themselves politically in those days was through their unions,' says Schrempp. 'I was strongly of the opinion that we could change things for the better by engaging the unions in dialogue over their working conditions. I didn't embarrass them by saying out loud that they had implored us to stay.'

Schrempp was one of a handful of executives who visited future President Thabo Mbeki in Lusaka, helping to forge contact between the outlawed African National Congress and the business community. Schrempp's outspoken criticism of the apartheid regime won him many friends within the ANC, however much they disapproved of his stance on disinvestment. Back in Germany, it raised Schrempp's profile, confirming his reputation as a man who knew his own mind and was not afraid to fight for an unpopular point of view.

By the time he was called back to Stuttgart in 1987, Schrempp was a contender for greater things. He had rough edges, it was true, but he had proved himself as a motivational leader. He appreciated the broader political environment in which a private sector enterprise operated, a quality which appealed to Edzard Reuter. His experience at Euclid showed he was capable of taking tough decisions and grappling with complex situations. He had proved himself outside Daimler's German heartland. He was already a potential leader of the Daimler-Benz group.

He became a deputy member of the Daimler-Benz management board, working as number two to Helmut Werner, the head of the trucks division. Ten years later, they would engage in a ferocious battle over the structure of the company. Schrempp won that fight, the necessary precursor to the merger with Chrysler, and Werner left the company. At the time, however, the two men were the best of friends. They flew round the world together on business trips and filled their spare time playing tennis, skiing or racing trucks on the Nürburg Ring racetrack. They were inseparable to the point that Schrempp was initially very reluctant to accept his next promotion, to head up Daimler's newly created aerospace division.

Reuter offered him the job over a glass of local Trollinger wine at his house in Stuttgart, teasing Schrempp by saying that the position could be a stepping-stone to becoming CEO of the entire group. 'I don't want to become CEO,' insisted Schrempp, 'and I don't want to be head of the aerospace division either.'

Schrempp agreed to go and see Alfred Herrhausen at the Deutsche Bank in Frankfurt. 'I won't say no to Herrhausen,' Schrempp told Reuter.

'Mr Herrhausen, I just can't abandon my truckers,' Schrempp said to his chairman. 'Helmut and I, we make such a good team. He's the chief locomotive driver and I'm the deputy. We've come out of the station and we're just stoking up the engine; soon we'll be running at full steam.'

'It's more difficult to build a locomotive than to drive one,' countered Herrhausen, pointing out that the aerospace division did not yet exist. He appealed to Schrempp's love of challenge and complexity. Schrempp took the post, seen by his peers as the most difficult job in the entire Daimler-Benz group.

Schrempp, now forty-five years old, moved to Munich and to a new world. He knew nothing about aerospace and defence and the learning curve was vertiginous. He inherited a ragbag of businesses ranging from passenger and military aircraft to engines and defence systems such as anti-aircraft missiles and spy satellites. Almost immediately, he found himself leading negotiations with the German government over the acquisition of MBB, the country's leading defence contractor. The move into the defence industry was highly controversial. Traditionalists complained that Daimler-Benz was deserting its core business as a car and truck manufacturer. Left-of-centre politicians accused Daimler of a sinister plot to recreate the arms giant that had played such an ugly role in Germany's past. Herrhausen saw the opportunity to build a pan-European defence company, a vision ultimately fulfilled only in 1999 with the creation of the German-French European Air and Defence Company (EADS). The unions tried to block the acquisition. It was voted through the supervisory board on the slenderest of majorities (11–9 in favour).

The business challenge was immense. In creating Daimler-Benz Aerospace (DASA), Schrempp had to fashion a rational business structure out of a group of fiercely independent businesses that had competed with each other for decades. The job was made harder by the 'cost-plus' culture prevailing in the defence side of the business. Normal commercial considerations were irrelevant as these businesses made money by charging the government a fixed fee of 10 per cent of outgoings. He set about rationalising the companies with negligible respect for Germany's conventional culture of consensus. Legal structures were dissolved, workers were fired and factories were closed. Schrempp became a hate figure, subject to regular death threats from terrorists and verbal attacks from unions, politicians and the media. Even his colleagues took against him, a trucker in the airline business, a Badener in Bavaria. Amid a maelstrom of constructive conflict, Schrempp was in his element.

The German defence industry was structured as a national job-creation scheme, with a factory in each of the country's sixteen Länder. Noting that the business was losing money and that Germany's defence budget was being cut, Schrempp resolved to close six of the factories. The first to be shut was at Lemwerder in Lower Saxony. This, critics lamented, was the first time that Daimler-Benz had ever closed down a manufacturing plant in its entire history.

'The sentiment at the time was that a company of the size and profitability of Daimler-Benz had a responsibility to keep the factory going,' recalls Manfred Bischoff, then Schrempp's CFO. For the first time, Schrempp began to formulate a doctrine designed to reconcile the demands of shareholders with the interests of society at large. 'Only a profitable company can be a social company,' is how he put it.

Politicians, fighting to keep factories alive, were not interested in the nuances of the stakeholder-shareholder debate. On one occasion he and Edzard Reuter met eight regional prime ministers. 'How much money do you want to keep the factories open?' he was asked.

'There's nothing you can give me,' responded Schrempp, 'but you have it in your power to make sure that I don't do anything more drastic.'

He developed a good working relationship with Gerhard Schröder, then Prime Minister of Lower Saxony and the future German Chancellor.

On one occasion, Schrempp persuaded Schröder to give a press conference in support of the Eurofighter programme. This was contrary to party policy but helpful for jobs, as Schröder recognised. On another, they got together on a Friday night in a Munich restaurant to hammer out the details of a factory closure in Schröder's home state. They forged a compromise whereby Lower Saxony took over the plant in return for a cash payment equivalent to the cost of shutting it down: Schröder saved some jobs and Schrempp stuck to his plan.

Schrempp respected the fact that Schröder kept his word. They became good friends and talk to each other on a first-name basis, unusual in the formal world of German business and politics. When Schrempp can do a favour to Schröder, he will do so – as when the merger of large parts of the German and French defence industries in 1999 (through the EADS deal) gave

Schröder a prominent platform to demonstrate the closeness of Franco-German ties.

Although Schrempp's style was outwardly adversarial, behind the scenes he was more conciliatory. He met Aloysius Schwarz, the tough chairman of the DASA works council, on a regular basis. Before each conversation they would agree whether they were having a formal or an informal meeting. If the latter, Schrempp would outline what he planned to do and the two men would work out ways of making the restructuring more palatable to the workforce. This didn't stop the public protests, but it formed the basis of an excellent working relationship between Schrempp and the workforce.

'What I did was highly unpopular but I did it on the basis that I could still be eye-to-eye with our labour representatives,' Schrempp recalls. The good personal rapport with union bosses would be vital in 1993–5, when the situation at DASA deteriorated. In that period Schrempp cut more than 22,000 jobs, nearly a quarter of DASA's total workforce. Despite sabre-rattling on both sides, the rationalisation took place without a single day's strike action. The rationalisation measures were agreed after consulting with unions under the German system of *Mitbestimmung*, or co-determination.

The system was imposed on German industry by the allies after the war. It was refined in 1975 by Helmut Schmidt's socialist government which strengthened labour representation on supervisory boards.

For a company the size of DASA or Daimler, this organ consists of twenty directors in total, ten representing shareholders and ten from the workforce. The chairman holds a casting vote and runs what is known as the Präsidium, a subcommittee of four directors who deal with personnel issues such as appointments to the management board and salary levels for top executives. There is also an informal subcommittee of shareholders' representatives (the so-called capital side of the board) which gets together with the management board to discuss business strategy and investment. Likewise, the employee side of the board gets together unofficially in a committee called the *Arbeitnehmervorbesprechung*. The full board meets once a quarter on average and tends to rubber-stamp important decisions.

The system is baroque, highly political, and far from transparent. And yet it has worked well for Germany. Labour and capital work together more productively than in rival economies. There are tried and tested procedures for avoiding conflict, and processes for resolving deadlocks. Although the result is not always sweetness and light, the system encourages co-operation rather than confrontation.

'In 1993 people told me not to do a tough restructuring because I might not get the votes from the labour representatives when it's coming up to choose the next CEO of Daimler,' recalls Schrempp. 'In due course they were 100 per cent behind me despite cutting tens of thousands of jobs at DASA because of the way I did it. I did it on a tough basis but took into account that occasionally I had to make deals – in terms of severance, timing, presentation. I never compromised in terms of not doing it but tried to cushion it . . . so when I continued as CEO I adopted the same approach.'

In the late summer of 1993 Schrempp was walking with Edzard Reuter in the garden of the latter's condominium on the shores of Lake Constance. Reuter confided to his protégé that he had recommended him as his successor as CEO.

'Let's remove that from the agenda,' said Schrempp. 'I'm not interested.'

This was only partly in jest. Schrempp was busy restructuring DASA. He wanted to fulfil Herrhausen's dream and turn DASA into Europe's most powerful aerospace business. He was toying with the idea of completing the job at DASA before moving on to set up his own business.

Reuter told him that Deutsche Bank was also behind the decision, although Schrempp knew that the decision had not been finalised.

Schrempp's vigorous way of getting to grips with DASA had drawn him to the attention of Hilmar Kopper. The banker was impressed by Schrempp's decisiveness and the clarity with which he communicated often unpopular decisions. 'He's a tough, hard-line type of guy,' recalls Kopper. 'Despite that he had won the trust of the unions. They sensed his fundamental honesty. There were no false promises, no salami tactics. He presented the worst-case scenario and just got on with it.'

Problems at Fokker, the Dutch manufacturer of regional aircraft acquired by Schrempp in 1992, enhanced rather than diminished Schrempp's standing in Kopper's eyes. Kopper was impressed at the way Schrempp faced up to the consequences of the acquisition and set in motion a rationalisation plan.

By 1993, it had become a two-horse race. One candidate was Jürgen Schrempp. The other was Helmut Werner, Schrempp's former boss and by now chief executive of Mercedes-Benz. Werner was the crown prince, anointed by Herrhausen as Reuter's successor-in-waiting. He was a much-liked manager credited with a swift revitalisation of the Mercedes marque. The two men preserved cordial relations, meeting regularly at Stuttgart restaurants to discuss their plans.

Reuter was originally due to retire in 1996 but Kopper decided to bring forward the changeover to 1995. Early in 1994 Kopper communicated his decision to Werner at the world show-jumping championship held in Aachen: Schrempp would be getting the job. He told Schrempp at the Helsinki meeting of the Bildeberg conference of CEOs and government ministers. 'Yes, I'd like to do that,' Schrempp said when the offer came. 'As if it were the most natural thing in the world,' recalls Kopper.

It was a deliberate decision to break with tradition. 'I did not want to continue in the old mould,' says Kopper, 'where the culture was "we've always been good and we always will be."'

There was a lot to be done. It was time for a fresh start.

*   *   *

Schrempp, a tall, fit man with craggy features and a penetrating gaze, has an imposing presence, exuding restless mental and physical energy. He is a powerful public speaker, his oratory rising to a crescendo and falling back with the rhythms and cadences of powerful classical music. ('It's like Elgar,' was the verdict of one investment analyst after hearing Schrempp extemporise to a roomful of top executives at the exclusive Cliveden Hotel near London.)

If he wants to persuade you of something, he will grasp your arm and subject you to a barrage of arguments. He will not let go until you concede his point. In meetings he is quite likely to take to his feet and embark on a staccato monologue to explain his point of view, complete with a full range of body, hand, facial and head gestures. He grabs the flip-chart, taking possession of it as if it were his partner in some wild Latin dance, turning from one page to the next in a frenzy. He is proud of his performance with the flip-chart. 'I can negotiate like hell with one of these,' he says.

Schrempp lives by three informal rules for success in business. First: be healthy. Hence he takes plenty of exercise, spending most Saturday mornings when he is at home in his private gym. When in London or New York he tries to keep himself fit with a quick pre-dawn jog around Hyde Park or Central Park. Friends said they had never seen him so frustrated as when a knee injury prevented him from taking his daily exercise.

Schrempp's second rule is that people should have a good time. He loathes protocol events, but he loves getting together with colleagues for informal brainstorming sessions where the line between business and fun is blurred.

He celebrated his fiftieth birthday on a plane coming back from Japan with a keg of beer supplied by Jürgen Weber, the chairman of Lufthansa, specially for the occasion. It was a rowdy party as Schrempp had three birthdays in the course of one journey as the plane flew from one time zone to another. Fellow first-class passengers were treated to the unusual sight and sound of Schrempp, Edzard Reuter and Helmut Werner singing lively folk-songs.

When he was at DASA, he and his staff would often decamp to a favourite restaurant on a Friday afternoon, spreading their papers across the tables and getting through business in an atmosphere of increasing jollity. In Munich he used to host impromptu gatherings at his Bavarian *Stübli*, a room furnished in cosy south-German style. Shortly after he took over from Reuter as CEO, he had a *Stübli* built next to his new office, and this is still the scene of much informal brainstorming.

Every year at the Davos International Economic Forum, Schrempp has a private party in a restaurant halfway up a mountain. Invitations to the so-called Bergführer event are much coveted, precisely because it is so different from all the other receptions in Davos. It is informal and there is not a glass of champagne in sight. Schrempp normally wears a jumper while some smart guests don their Bavarian Tracht waistcoats and breeches. It starts with a glass of glühwein outside in the snow. During dinner, Schrempp gives a serious speech; one year it looked at the reality of globalisation in the wake of the DaimlerChrysler deal, another it examined the responsibilities of business leaders to future generations of management. Afterwards, there is a lively debate which as the hours pass gets livelier still. Around midnight the singing begins. Schrempp and his friends gather around a microphone and bellow out folk-songs. The party tends to conclude at around 4 a.m. A few hours later, Schrempp and colleagues such as Manfred Bischoff are up again for breakfast, immaculately dressed and freshly scrubbed, ready for a day's business. Guests, stumbling out of bed with large hangovers, tend to be amazed at the Germans' stamina.

If wine and parties are important lubricants, preparation should not be underestimated. This is Schrempp's third ingredient for success in business. He tends to assume that anyone who comes into contact with him is an absolute master of his or her brief.

On occasions, Schrempp likes to give the impression that he has not done his homework. He marches into a board meeting and with a rustle of papers feigns to be acquainting himself with the agenda for the first time. In fact, when it comes to anything important, he is always fantastically well prepared. 'He has a hunger to learn and to absorb the essential issues quickly,' comments a close colleague. 'He asks a lot of questions and does not mind admitting when he does not know something. A few minutes later he can present the issues as if he had known them all his life.'

His willingness to learn and improve himself explains his highly developed interest in courtroom drama. He owns a large collection of classic trial films such as *Twelve Angry Men* and *A Question of Honour*. He watches the videos over and over again, believing that he can learn to be a better negotiator by mastering the twists and turns of each case.

A great networker, he inhales information through his contacts within and outside the company. After a lifetime with Daimler, he knows exactly who to call inside the company. So far as outside experts are concerned, he is never more than a phone call or e-mail away from a leading figure in any field he may be considering. For example, if he wants to know about e-commerce he talks to Lou Gerstner, the chairman of IBM, then double-checks what he's heard by ringing his son Alexander, a designer of websites. In fact, when developing Daimler's internet strategy in 1999–2000 he listened to thirty-five separate presentations from a variety of experts ranging from Carly Fiorina, the president of Hewlett-Packard, to pony-tailed programmers from San Francisco.

For hard facts, he can access the company intranet through his Clara, a black IBM portable given to him by Gerstner, from which he is inseparable. He pushes the intranet hard within the company, saying that 95 per cent of the information available to him is shared by all the company's employees. 'The extra 5 per cent is why I get to be chairman,' he says. With his son's help, he has also learned how to use the internet, multiplying the sources of information he consults before taking a decision.

With Schrempp setting the pace, business can be entertaining, intellectually demanding – and hard on the liver.

In his early days as CEO, his sociable side got him into trouble. In the summer of 1995 he garnered unwelcome headlines as a result of an incident close to the Spanish Steps in Rome. After spending the morning in Munich he flew down to Rome for an afternoon meeting. After dinner, he and Hartmut Schick, his chief of staff, went out to toast his assistant Lydia Deininger's thirty-first birthday. It was 18 July 1995, a balmy summer's night. They returned to the Hotel Hassler Villa Medici and found it was too late to have another drink in the bar. So they bought a bottle of Chianti and went for a stroll from their hotel down the steps to the piazza below where a crowd was milling about for a fashion show. Halfway down, the Rome police stopped the party for a routine passport check.

'Show us your passport,' the police demanded. Schrempp bristled at the man's tone but volunteered to return to the hotel to collect the passports where they had been lodged – a requirement of Italian law. He returned to find that the dispute had intensified. Deininger and Schick were exchanging heated words with a group of carabinieri gathered around a police car. There was much mutual incomprehension as neither Lydia Deininger nor Hartmut Schick could say much more than *'stupido polizei'* in pidgin Italian, and the Italians couldn't speak a word of German or English. A fracas ensued, and Schrempp and his colleagues were detained by the carabinieri.

In the police station, the three refused to sign a police protocol which falsely alleged that one of the three had hurt a policewoman. They made a few calls on their mobile phones. A few hours later, they were released. By this time, however, the news of the arrest was circulating around the Mercedes-Benz Italian operation.

Within a few days the story leaked out in Germany too,

earning him a crop of censorious headlines in the tabloid press. Union officials complained that it was inappropriate for the CEO to be carousing in Rome when so many jobs were being cut at home in Germany. Colleagues criticised Schrempp for bringing Daimler's name further into disrepute. There was also a double-edged comment from Hilmar Kopper, chairman of the supervisory board. 'I would love to have joined you for this bottle of wine,' Kopper recalls saying to Schrempp when he called to tell him about the incident. 'But I also told him: don't do it again, you are CEO of Germany's largest company.'

'All I want to do is remain a human being,' Schrempp confided to Werner Breitschwerdt, a friend and former Daimler-Benz CEO, shortly after the incident.

'You have to restrain your humanity when you're in that job,' Breitschwerdt replied.

Looking back on the Rome incident, Schrempp says ruefully that he should have apologised profusely to the policemen and backed away from confrontation. This was an example of unconstructive conflict. 'It was fun,' says a chastened Schrempp. 'Disastrous fun.'

Schrempp is single-minded and uncompromisingly effective in fulfilling his objectives, combining feline stealth with careful preparation and swift action at the appropriate moment. 'He has an unusual mix of qualities,' observes one close colleague. 'He is part chess-player, part no-holds-barred street-fighter.'

'I always think three moves ahead,' Schrempp confided to a slightly shocked American executive shortly after the merger with Chrysler was announced. 'But I don't like to let anyone know more than the first move – if you give too much away too early your game-plan is ruined.'

He is willing to share his thinking on tactical issues, but only a handful of individuals are ever allowed to get a glimpse of his strategic game-plan. He not only thinks many moves ahead, he also creates feints and diversions, subtle deviations from the expected path which leave those watching the game either mystified about his true intentions or convinced that he has made a mistake. Then all of a sudden the pieces are aligned and mate is within his sights.

(When it comes to the board game, Schrempp is not always so formidable: it took Garry Kasparov just three minutes to get Schrempp into a position where he could not move any of his pieces without putting himself into check. 'He tortured me,' says Schrempp ruefully. In the boardroom, Schrempp never finds himself in this position.)

At the time of his appointment as Reuter's successor, the innermost core of his inner circle consisted of Lydia Deininger, Hartmut Schick and Manfred Bischoff. They spent weekend after weekend together brainstorming structure and strategy. Later, others would be admitted to this charmed circle, including Eckhard Cordes (soon to be appointed the board director in charge of strategy), Rüdiger Grube (number two to Cordes), Christoph Walther (Daimler's communications supremo) and Alexander Dibelius from Goldman Sachs.

A few others have his ear as well, including Klaus Mangold, the head of Daimler's services division and an old friend from Freiburg; Victor Halberstadt, a wily Dutch economics professor; Vernon Jordan, the Washington insider and confidant of President Clinton; Mike Taylor, a friend from South Africa who is the chairman of a London public relations agency; Bernard Attali, the former chairman of Air France and now head of Deutsche Bank in France; Anton Rupert, the South African luxury goods and tobacco tycoon; David K.P. Lee, the chairman and CEO of the South-East Asia Bank; and Karel Vuursten, CEO of Heineken.

Schrempp makes a distinction between outsiders such as Halberstadt or Dibelius, to whom he looks for comment on a variety of issues, and those involved in running the company, such as Cordes and Bischoff. He relishes long one-on-one discussions with other board members, inviting them to his home for a frank exchange of views ahead of more formal meetings.

Needless to say, there is great competition to be in the inner circle, and incessant speculation about who is on the way in or out. When they gather privately they engage in no-holds-barred brainstorms in which nothing is sacred. He is blunt and open with those few people who are equally direct with him. Schick may be softly spoken, but has no problems telling Schrempp that he is talking bullshit. Deininger is slight and feminine but has a fiery temper. 'Do you think I'm stupid just because I'm a woman,' she yelled on one occasion when Schrempp challenged her insight into an upcoming board meeting.

To those outside and inside the inner circle, Schrempp can display a quick temper. Those who have been around him for a long time learn how to read his reactions and learn not to take criticism too personally. They recognise that what angers him most is incompetence or a simple lack of preparation. 'He hates questions, loves recommendations,' is how one inner circle member describes this trait. Colleagues learn to think things through very carefully before they approach him.

They clearly fear getting on the wrong side of him. He will forgive an honest mistake or tolerate a well-argued viewpoint with which he does not agree. But if he gets the slightest sense that you are trying to double-cross him or go behind his back, you run the risk of being cast into outer darkness. His detractors credit him with an extraordinary sensitivity to disloyalty. 'He can smell a challenge to his authority from a distance of five miles,' says one victim of Schrempp's elbows. 'When it comes to a power game, he always wins.'

Schrempp does not willingly make compromises on personnel issues. His path to the top is strewn with former friends and allies who stood in his way. Chief among these is Edzard Reuter himself, Schrempp's former mentor. In this case, Reuter and Schrempp fell out long after Schrempp moved into the top job and reversed his predecessor's strategy – a strategy which Schrempp had helped develop and implement while at DASA. The final break came in 1996 when Reuter published his autobiography in which he fired off a series of broadsides against Schrempp and other former Daimler colleagues.

In another case, Schrempp was obliged to cut loose Gerhard Liener, again a mentor and friend. Liener wrote a long article excoriating Reuter's egotism and management mistakes. It found its way into *Manager* magazine, bringing Daimler's reputation into disrepute. Schrempp had no choice but to cancel Liener's consultancy contract with the company. In this case, the two men remained close friends until Liener tragically took his own life.

We will see what happened to Helmut Werner when he and Schrempp fought a battle over the structure of the company.

If this paints a picture of a brutal, insensitive teuton, this would be incorrect. He emphasises the importance of people and emotion in a business context in a way that red-blooded American capitalists may find soft-centred. He is proud that the Chrysler merger created jobs, not destroyed them. With the experience of Euclid at the back of his mind, he declares himself horrified at the thought of buying a company simply to cut the workforce and close factories. Cutting jobs may be necessary, but will never be an end in itself. After the botched introduction of the A-Class, not a single person was sacked.

'I have always maintained that people should be allowed to make mistakes,' Schrempp says. 'If I then fired people because of a mistake I would lose all credibility.'

At the level of individual employees, he has the common touch. On occasions, whatever the preoccupations of his day, he will walk the few hundred metres out of the Möhringen complex to a nearby *Trinkhalle* where he will order curried sausage along with the lowliest employee. The mass-circulation *Bild* newspaper admires him as a man who prefers *maultaschen* – a local Stuttgart delicacy – to caviar.

People are used to their superiors affecting to take an interest in the details of their job, but extremely surprised when the boss follows up when he says he is going to. Schrempp always follows up. Rüdiger Grube remembers the first time he met

Schrempp. Grube made a presentation to the board of DASA recommending improvements to an employee motivation programme. Schrempp was impressed and promised to get back to him within a fortnight with comments. On the fourteenth day, Schrempp's call came.

Once, a security guard at the Munich-based DASA head office refused to let Schrempp through without his pass. Schrempp, by then chairman of the DASA subsidiary, sent the lowly employee two bottles of wine to congratulate him for doing his duty.

In the months before Schrempp took over as chief executive of Daimler-Benz, he tried several times to fix up a meeting with Reuter to discuss the handover. It would have been pretty normal for the outgoing CEO to spend some time with his successor, Schrempp reasoned. It would be helpful to be shown the basics: which files were which, what was personal, what would be archived and what was kept in the safe. He had done the same when Manfred Bischoff took over as head of DASA. Any tips on how to pull the levers of power at Europe's biggest industrial company would have been welcome.

In fact, a handover meeting never took place. Calls from Schrempp's secretariat to Reuter's assistants went unreturned. Apart from a brief conversation on a flight back from China, he and Reuter had barely spoken about what the top job entailed in the year since he had been named Reuter's successor. So on Friday, 26 May, two days after the company's shareholders approved his appointment, he arrived on the CEO's floor with little idea of what he would find.

As he stepped into the large corner office, he was struck as usual by the room's cold furnishings. He had of course spent many hours with Reuter in the chief executive's office, and had never liked the décor. The whole room was decorated in grey: grey carpets, grey tiled walls, grey furniture. Today, he saw at a glance, the office was even more bare than usual. Every document, every file that had belonged to Reuter had gone.

The door of the safe was open, there was nothing inside. The office had been cleaned out.

One of his earliest decisions was to alter the layout of the eleventh floor. He got rid of the grey furniture and fittings inherited from Reuter. He had his office divided into two, introducing antique furniture and oak panelling into his half. The other half would be occupied by Lydia Deininger, head of the chairman's office, who would in due course adorn every nook and cranny of her room with a collection of outsized teddy bears gathered on the CEO's frequent trips around the world.

Reuter left behind an empty office – and a company poised unknowingly on the verge of the most radical shake-up in its history.

CHAPTER 5

Blood on the Piazza

From vision to value – how Schrempp
sorted out his inheritance

Shortly after he took over as CEO, Schrempp summoned the top two levels of head-office management to the Mercedes Forum, a white-tiled conference room which borders the central piazza in the Möhringen headquarters.

The meeting took place just before lunch on Friday, 14 June and a buffet and drinks were laid on. People arrived expecting to hear a jolly, motivational chat from their new boss. Instead, Schrempp marched to the podium and delivered a hard-edged speech peppered with the language of war.

'We are at the front and we are at the centre of the global economic battlefield,' he exclaimed. 'We have the best weapons to fight the struggle of life, so long as we do not deviate even one millimetre from our course . . . which is to become the most competitive company in the world.'

After setting the scene, he unsmilingly explained that his first step would be to cut the head-office staff from 1,200 to 300. The atmosphere was suddenly icy. Schrempp explained what he was going to do and what this would mean for the very cadre of bureaucrats gathered in front of him. 'If I have to restructure the company, I have to start here,' he barked. 'We have to clean the steps from the top.'

To make clear just how serious the situation was, he concluded his speech with a provocative reference to Winston Churchill. 'In another battle situation – namely 1940 – [he] warned his countrymen that they would face nothing other than blood, sweat and tears until they achieved their final success . . . and today I cannot promise you anything other than "many long months of struggle before us".'

Schrempp, still unsmiling, said he would not be taking any questions. He walked out, leaving the room in stunned silence. 'Are we dreaming?' people asked themselves, half expecting him to come back and say it was all a joke. There was genuine astonishment at the harshness of his style. After ten minutes, the room was empty, the food and wine untouched.

If this appearance unsettled his senior staff, the real earthquake would come a few weeks later. On 28 June Daimler issued a humiliating profit warning, a curt one-page statement which predicted severe losses for 1995. The warning, all the more chilling for being unspecific about the severity of the deficit, came like a thunderbolt from a clear sky. When the losses for the year were finally quantified, they came to a total of DM5.7 billion. This would turn out to be the biggest loss ever reported by a European company – that is, of a company that did not subsequently go bankrupt. It would be the first full-year loss chalked up by Daimler-Benz since the Second World War.

Surely, Daimler-Benz was out of the woods? After a couple of difficult years it was back on track? At least, this was the impression conveyed by Edzard Reuter's farewell speech a few weeks before.

On Wednesday, 24 May 1995 Edzard Reuter and Jürgen Schrempp, together with around 7,000 others, attend Daimler-Benz's annual shareholder meeting. This event is an important ritual in the German corporate calendar, the only time in the year when the titans of the management and supervisory boards come down to earth and go through the motions of making themselves accountable to the great mass of ordinary shareholders. Pensioners, employees, shareholders, journalists and plain cranks pack into the Hans-Martin-Schleyer Conference Centre close to the Untertürkheim car factory to participate in the elaborately choreographed event. Nourished by 14,000 pairs of sausages, 12,000 sandwiches, 3,000 pretzels, 12,000 cups of coffee and 16,000 glasses of cold alcohol-free beer and apple juice, they hear a series of set-piece speeches by the chief executive and the chairman, followed by a seemingly endless sequence of questions and answers on everything from company strategy and finances to its policy on arms export and the environment.

Part of the fun of the day is that its routines and rituals are predictable. Invariably, the management and supervisory board directors, gathered together on the podium like deities exposed to a credulous populace, grow bored and uncomfortable as the day wears on. Hilmar Kopper of the Deutsche Bank, who chairs the meeting in his capacity as chairman of the Daimler-Benz supervisory board, grows increasingly gruff and grumpy as he deals with intemperate shareholder activists. After several hours, he becomes visibly irate and limits the questions to no more than a minute apiece. When the questioners waffle on, he simply disconnects the microphone. On one occasion, he becomes so tired of the imprecations of Eckhard Wenger that he has this university professor – a man who has made a name as the architect of many a shareholder protest – picked up by bodyguards and physically removed from the podium.

Typically, the Daimler-Benz meeting lasts at least twelve hours, finishing late at night. When the voting finally comes, the result is a foregone conclusion: Deutsche Bank's big stake means that any sensitive issue has been decided long in advance. But the meetings are about spectacle, not shareholder democracy. A good time is had by all, such a good time that the numbers have climbed steadily since the appointment of Schrempp and a throng of nearly 20,000 people attended the first annual meeting after the merger of Daimler and Chrysler.

At the 1995 meeting, the focus was on Edzard Reuter. All were intrigued. This was Reuter's last speech as chief executive and Schrempp would formally take over the reins at the end of the meeting. What account would Reuter give of himself after nearly eight controversial years in the job?

Reuter's speech was statesmanlike, but also puzzling – a curious blend of the pessimistic and the positive, of the grandly general and the highly specific. At one moment, Reuter was quoting poetry (some lines from Sophocles' *Antigone*), the next he was talking in some detail about the business prospects for the individual business divisions. He ranged from macro-economic bugbears such as the evils of unfettered free-market capitalism to purely personal concerns. In words of unusual humility, he admitted that he had made some mistakes along the way, although he wasn't specific at this point. He explained that in his twenty-two years on the board of Daimler he had always done his utmost to shoulder the responsibilities of office. Not once did he refer explicitly to his vision of an 'integrated high-technology group', saying simply that he hoped that he had laid the foundations for Daimler to be a proud, competitive company in 2005 as well as in 1995. He concluded generously, wishing Schrempp the very best of luck for the future.

A draft of the speech, as with all important external policy statements, had done the rounds of Reuter's staff ahead of the event, and several of his aides had suggested that he tone down the more optimistic comments about the outlook for the business. But the final version contained a number of unambiguously positive pointers for the future. He proudly chronicled the success of the Mercedes-Benz division in introducing a completely new product range in five years. He said that AEG's fate as an integral part of the Daimler group had been secured. He was more cautious when it came to DASA, warning that the aerospace division's results for the year would be critically dependent on the DM/US dollar exchange rate and that as a result it was unlikely that this division would hit its targets. Signalling confidence rather than caution, Reuter revealed that the management board proposed increasing the 1994 dividend from DM8 to DM11.

As the outgoing CEO put it, this was a sign that the company had taken all the right steps to ensure good growth in 1995 and beyond. After some difficult years, the company was now stable, he insisted. 'Our confidence is not merely wishful thinking, but is based on data and facts that prove our measures are taking effect,' he said emphatically. 'Seeing how quickly and effectively we overcame the serious recession of 1992 and 1993, the bleakest years in your company's post-war history, we have even more cause for optimism.'

Schrempp's first priority was to get together with Manfred Gentz, the lawyer and former personnel chief who was promoted to chief financial officer on the same day that Schrempp took over as CEO. From a purely personal point of view, the two men have little in common. While Gentz is courtly and reserved, Schrempp is down-to-earth and outspoken. Gentz is a patrician from Berlin, while Schrempp comes from the south of the country and has a comparatively modest background. From a professional perspective, though, they have complementary skills. Gentz's punctilious attention to detail balances Schrempp's skills as a creative thinker and a ruthless deal-doer. Their first task was to get a grip on the finances.

They sat down and reviewed the basis on which Reuter made his optimistic comments. 'I looked at Manfred Gentz and Manfred looked at me,' Schrempp recalled later. 'We then both looked at the numbers.' They both had to take a deep breath.

As in previous years, the forecasts contained a classic 'hockey-stick' prognosis for the remainder of the year. After a difficult start, profits and revenues would rise steadily, culminating in a fourth quarter that would amply compensate for the problems of the earlier parts of the year. And underlying the figures was the assumption that if necessary one could raid the group's accumulated capital reserves. The group had made so much money for so many decades that it was standard practice to take full advantage of flexible German accounting rules in presenting profits to the outside world.

By making use of the many, perfectly legal loopholes in the domestic accounting code, management could smooth out the progression of profits as reported to the outside world. In 1993 and 1994, for example, the group had sold off land, disposed of a holding of shares in the Allianz insurance group and other assets. They had also released a variety of provisions, stores of wealth sheltered from the taxman and ready to be channelled back into the company at the appropriate time. All these one-offs were lumped in together with the losses from normal activities so that the group could report a small profit to shareholders.

Should we play the same game as before or should we put a stop to this once and for all? This was the key question for the new CEO and his finance director. Schrempp decided to call Reuter, with whom at that stage he was still on excellent terms, and ask him to explain the numbers in more detail.

'Edzard,' said Schrempp. 'Let's sit down and discuss the figures. Do me a favour, let's get together with Manfred Gentz and talk through the forecasts.'

According to Schrempp, Reuter replied, 'Jürgen, I haven't got time, and in any case, don't get nervous. This is only June and things always get better in the autumn, you know that. And you know there's plenty of substance in the company. There's nothing to worry about!'

They called each other a few more times and Reuter did eventually spend twenty minutes with Gentz. But he and Schrempp remained unconvinced about the outlook for the year. The more they delved into the picture, the worse it looked. AEG, a venerable name in the German electrical and electronics industry, was once again predicting a return to profitability, but it always did at this time of year and by now Schrempp had become totally cynical about the division's ability to meet its plans. AEG could be relied upon to make a loss for the full year, no matter what management was forecasting at this stage.

As for the aerospace business, he had just come from DASA so he understood this division's acute sensitivities to movements in exchange rates, particularly the relationship between the US dollar and the D-Mark. Virtually all DASA's customers, whether governments or airlines, paid for their products in dollars. And yet around 80 per cent of DASA's costs were denominated in D-Marks. The result was a terrible squeeze on the division's earnings, with every 10 Pfennig increase in the value of the D-Mark spelling a DM300 million decline in operating profits.

The story at Mercedes-Benz, as ever the engine of the Daimler group's cash flow, was better: having recovered to a respectable level of profitability in 1994 it was on course to hold its own once again in 1995. As had been the pattern for most of the past decade, Mercedes was expected to bail out the rest of the group.

For a day or two, Schrempp considered following Reuter's advice to sit it out and hope for something to turn up. But Schrempp decided against procrastination. 'Gentlemen,' Schrempp told his colleagues at the first board meeting after he took office, 'the chips are down.' With the backing of the board, Schrempp and Gentz decided to bite the bullet and do something that Daimler had never done before in its proud history. The profits warning did not quantify the scale of the deficit, except to say that the situation was so bad that the company would have to spend at least an extra DM1 billion on further restructuring measures. At this stage the internal estimate was that losses would amount to around DM2 billion. No one then really suspected just how bad they would turn out to be.

The official justification for the dramatic change in the outlook for the company was the unrelenting strengthening of the D-Mark. What had been seen as a temporary phenomenon at the time of the annual meeting less than five weeks before was now a permanent feature of the group's operating environment, the management board reasoned. So while Edzard Reuter's prognosis had been based on the most optimistic assumptions, Schrempp and Gentz took the opposite course, ordering the forecasts to be prepared on the basis of an exchange rate of DM1.45 to the US dollar rather than DM1.65. This new pessimism would mean many billions of unforeseen losses and provide the economic rationale for Schrempp's brutal restructuring of the company over the next eighteen months.

At the time of the announcement, little of this was explained. The impact came neither in the technicalities nor the convoluted language in which the Daimler board struggled to justify its volte-face. The real importance lay in the symbolism. For those who know Machiavelli's *The Prince*, it had the same impact on Daimler-Benz as the discovery of a dismembered body in the Italian writer's city state. In the Renaissance text, the body was cut in half and left in the square. It was a powerful statement and the populace realised that the prince meant business. 'The brutality of the spectacle kept the people of Romagna for a time appeased and stupefied,' commented the Italian writer in *The Prince*, the definitive management textbook for the Renaissance era.

Schrempp's profit warning was tough, abrupt, frightening, a clear break with what had gone before. Schrempp was asserting his authority. It was a challenge to the complacent and arrogant culture of the past. 'You post the highest loss in German history and your own people understand you have to do something,' is how Schrempp puts it now.

The announcement had a predictable effect on Daimler-Benz's share price. It dropped sharply as investors' worst fears were confirmed. The big international fund managers saw no reason to revise their view that Daimler was a basket-case. They remained profoundly unsure of what to make of the new arrival. Schrempp, after all, was the architect of the catastrophic Fokker acquisition and a protégé of Reuter. It was too early to hail the beginning of a new era.

At this stage, Schrempp was not desperately concerned about

the stock market reaction. Winning over the outside world would have to wait. His priority was to create an atmosphere conducive to change *within* the company.

The company he had taken over was like a severely injured hospital patient. The heart, namely the Mercedes-Benz automotive business, was still pumping away vigorously, but the body was wounded. It was time to stop the bleeding.

In the year before Schrempp took over the helm, he developed a private blueprint for his first few years of office. There were three things he wanted to achieve.

First, he had a mind to reorganise the group's convoluted legal and administrative structure. The structure he inherited from Reuter was cumbersome and got in the way of swift decision-making. Something would have to be done, Schrempp felt.

Second, he wanted to continue the restructuring of the aerospace business, fulfilling Alfred Herrhausen's wish that Daimler-Benz should lead a pan-European aerospace and defence industry.

Third, he wanted to make an acquisition to give the core automotive business greater scale and global reach. It was clear from the many Daimler-Benz board meetings Schrempp had attended that something had to be done to bolster the Mercedes-Benz business. Quite what was far from clear at this stage. But a deal was at the back of Schrempp's mind even in 1995.

These were broad aspirations and Schrempp had certainly not developed the ideas to any degree of detail. Nor had he shared these ideas, knowing that talking about these objectives in public would make it harder to put them into practice. He also recognised that it was pointless dwelling on long-term plans for Daimler-Benz when the company's short-term situation was so precarious. 'One more year like 1995 and the company would not have survived,' Schrempp recalls now. 'I had to park the strategy. If you die, you don't need a strategy.'

Schrempp and his team decided to take a dispassionate look

at Daimler's thirty-five business divisions. Starting as if with a clean sheet of paper, they went through one division after another and asked the question that had been taboo for most of the last decade: 'Should we be in this business at all?'

The moment of truth came in October 1995 when the results of the analysis were presented to the capital side of the supervisory board. The man who gave the presentation was Eckhard Cordes, a former financial controller of AEG whom Schrempp co-opted as his head of strategy. Cordes was not yet a board member and he felt that the occasion was a test of his fitness for further promotion.

Cordes' presentation was all the more compelling for the sober, almost scholarly way in which the bespectacled strategist outlined his conclusions. In his no-nonsense German style, he described the failure of the ten-year attempt to create an integrated technology company. With his words, the grandiose dream that had cost Daimler and its shareholders in the region of DM100 billion over the past decade came crashing to the ground.

'If we carry on like this, we will hit the buffers in two years' time,' Cordes warned. He told his audience that the group's true profit and loss position was far worse than expected. Daimler's product portfolio was too broad, distracting management attention from the businesses that really mattered, he said.

Daimler's directors listened in stony silence. It was as if their eyes were opening up to the true awfulness of the company's position after years of slumber.

His recommendation was that Daimler-Benz should dramatically reduce the scope of its businesses and concentrate on what it was good at.

His words marked a turning point in the group's fortunes, signalling the first step on the path to restructuring and recovery. The logic would lead inexorably to the decision to concentrate on the automotive industry and ultimately to the merger with Chrysler.

Schrempp picked up where Cordes left off. 'Gentlemen,' he said, 'we have reached the point of no return.'

Everybody in the room knew it would be a bloody road ahead.

There followed a massive divestment programme. Some businesses were axed because of lousy management; others because Schrempp and Cordes deemed that they would never develop the critical mass to turn them into world leaders. Over the course of eighteen months the number of divisions was reduced from thirty-five to twenty-three. By the end of 1997, 60,000 jobs had been shed – 15,000 people made redundant or offered early retirement and 45,000 transferred to new owners.

These bare facts understate the scale of the change forced through by Schrempp in these early years. It was a cultural revolution, starting at the top. Board meetings, which had previously been strictly regimented and had simply rubber-stamped Reuter's decisions, were suddenly thrown open to debate. Rather than finishing punctually in time for lunch, they went on all afternoon as the directors thrashed out their decisions.

Still reeling from the impact of the profits warning, a proud, introspective organisation was forced to acknowledge severe limitations and reinvent itself. Hierarchies were flattened in the name of flexibility, tradition jettisoned in favour of the new mantra of shareholder value. This radical cure was the necessary precursor to the merger with Chrysler, from whose freewheeling culture Daimler had a lot to learn.

It was deeply unsettling for many traditionalists, but for younger managers it was a thrilling time. Suddenly, nothing was sacred. Even better, the new generation was given licence to slaughter yesterday's sacred cows.

The first test case of the new culture was the dissolution of AEG. The Frankfurt-based AEG was a household name, a venerable institution older than Daimler-Benz itself which employed more than 50,000 people. Since it had been acquired by Reuter in the mid-1980s, it had chalked up losses of an estimated DM5 billion. It had been subjected to a seemingly endless succession of unsuccessful restructuring attempts. More than a dozen businesses had been sold since 1982, leaving a handful of core divisions ranging from micro-electronics to automatisation technology and transport systems. Despite endless waves of restructuring, AEG never generated the turn-around in profits which successive CEOs had promised. It had a weak position in virtually all its collection of businesses. Emotionally, it was part of the Daimler-Benz family from which the old guard found it difficult to part. The problem was compounded by the fact that AEG was a separate legal entity, with a substantial minority of shares quoted on the Frankfurt Stock Exchange.

Cordes devised an elegant solution for the AEG problem. He would simply merge the separate AEG company into the Daimler-Benz parent company and then sell off the subsidiaries they did not want to keep. No longer would there be a separate board of management, a separate supervisory board and a separate group of shareholders who had to be pacified every time a business was sold. Schrempp and his allies would take control.

It was a simple solution, but it met with massive resist-ance. When the AEG board was told what was planned, they responded by showing Cordes and Dibelius pictures of Berlin before and after the war – the plan was the economic equivalent of the bombing raids which flattened the German capital. The old guard took their own legal council and declared that the deal was 99.9 per cent impossible to do. Unions took to the streets, protesting at the closure of AEG's Frankfurt headquarters, carrying coffins and effigies of the 'grave-diggers' Schrempp and Cordes.

At one crucial meeting, one of AEG's lawyers raised an objection to the plan. Cordes interrupted him. 'Do you have a legal or an economic problem?' It was an economic issue, the lawyer replied. 'Do you know how much money is at stake here?' demanded Cordes, dropping the DM7 billion figure into the conversation. 'So please accept that I will only ask you legal questions and if it's anything to do with the economics I'm in charge. When I want your opinion I'll ask for it.'

The room fell silent. This had never happened before: a younger man addressing his elder in such a peremptory manner. A board member could have slapped down his inferior, but Cordes and the lawyer were peers. This kind of attitude marked a clear break with the past. It was, says Dibelius who witnessed the exchange, the beginning of a 'can-do' rather than a 'yes, but' culture at Daimler-Benz.

The AEG case was typical of the way in which Daimler-Benz was restructured. A hit-squad of senior managers, backed up by expert external advisors, developed an action plan under conditions of total secrecy. When the plan was finally unveiled, it was forced through quickly despite internal resistance. It was a kind of guerrilla warfare developed for Schrempp's revolution. There was more to come.

Shortly before Christmas 1995, Schrempp was standing on the terrace of a friend's villa in Cape Town. It was lunchtime, the sun was shining, and Schrempp was feeling relaxed. The phone rang and his good humour was abruptly punctured. On the line were Manfred Bischoff, head of DASA, and Manfred Gentz, the Daimler-Benz finance director. They wanted to talk about Fokker.

Earlier in the year Schrempp had spoken to Wim Kok, the Dutch Prime Minister, and offered him an unappetising deal. If the Dutch government injected a further Fl3 billion, Daimler-Benz would match that investment and Fokker would be saved. If not, Daimler would not renew the credits extended to its subsidiary company and Fokker would go into bank-ruptcy. 'If you don't do this, you don't believe in this company,' Schrempp said bluntly to the Prime Minister. 'So why should we?'

By the time Schrempp flew to South Africa for his Christmas holiday, he had had no response from the Dutch government.

Perhaps they thought he was bluffing. To some extent, he was, but not in the way the Dutch might have expected: Schrempp's secret fear was that Kok would accept the deal and Daimler would thus be obliged to dig deeper into its pockets to keep the seventy-seven-year-old company aloft. As Schrempp paced about on the terrace, the two Manfreds briefed him on the latest appalling figures from the Dutch aircraft manufacturer.

There was no let-up in the conditions which had blighted the company since it had been acquired nearly three years ago. Four restructurings in a row and the near halving of the company's workforce, from 20,000 to 11,000, had done nothing to safeguard its competitiveness. It was haemorrhaging cash – losses amounted to around DM250 million a month. The three men mulled over the options: did they really want to pull the plug? 'Just imagine what it means for our reputation,' said one of the Manfreds. 'Daimler-Benz has never walked away from an investment.'

'Gentlemen,' said Schrempp after half an hour, 'I will take the responsibility. Here is what we have to do.'

He took a double decision: to withdraw financial support for Fokker and to take responsibility for the consequences. A few weeks later he appeared before a full meeting of the supervisory board to explain what he planned to do. 'I don't need a formal vote of confidence,' he said to the board, 'but I want to emphasise that I take full responsibility for what is about to happen.'

At this point, Manfred Bischoff piped up and said; 'Don't forget me, I take responsibility as well.'

Hilmar Kopper, chairman of the supervisory board, asked the two men to leave. Five minutes later they were invited back into the room. The message was clear: we trust your leadership and we back the decision of the management board to withdraw financial support from Fokker, a move which ultimately led to its bankruptcy.

Schrempp left the room and made a call to Wim Kok. He was put straight through. 'Mr Prime Minister,' he said. 'We have just decided to stop funding Fokker.'

There was a pause.

'Yes?' said the Prime Minister.

'Well, you knew it was the board meeting today and I promised to ring you to tell you the outcome. We have no choice but to do what we said we were going to do.'

There was frostiness at the other end of the line, but little surprise.

The decision to close Fokker was difficult for political reasons. There was a risk that Daimler-Benz would inflame traditional Dutch hostility towards their German neighbours. But it was hard for personal reasons too.

Fokker was Schrempp's baby. In the same way that Reuter had staked his personal credibility on the purchase of AEG, Schrempp had done the same with Fokker. Throughout 1992 he mobilised the full force of his personality to persuade his colleagues that they should seize the opportunity to buy this venerable company, a business with a reputation almost as prestigious as Mercedes-Benz itself.

The case for buying Fokker was clear: it would dramatically strengthen DASA's position as Europe's leading aircraft manufacturer. Fokker made short-haul aircraft with up to 100 seats. It had a superb reputation for making sturdy, reliable planes – there were around 1,000 commuter aircraft in service at the time of the acquisition. The company would complement DASA's existing aircraft manufacturing capabilities. Schrempp and Bischoff argued the case with great conviction. Through Dornier, DASA already made smaller regional aircraft with thirty seats, and through its 37.5 per cent stake in the Airbus consortium it made long-distance passenger jets with up to 300 seats. So Fokker plugged the gap, completing the product portfolio. Schrempp and Bischoff had considered building a mid-range jet from scratch, but this would have cost at least DM3 billion and taken years to bring to market. Why not seize the opportunity provided by Fokker?

Schrempp and Bischoff developed a ten-year plan for the civil aviation business. They would exploit synergies between the three separate companies. Engines and technology for cockpits would be developed for the full range of aircraft. This assumed a background of steady growth in demand for regional aircraft.

It was a compelling case. Within a year, though, the company was in serious difficulties. It turned out that Schrempp and Bischoff had made the wrong assumptions about the aircraft market, about prices and about the exchange rate scenario. The market lurched into a cyclical trough, prices dropped by 30 per cent over two years, and the D-Mark strengthened against the US dollar making it impossible to sell a Fokker aircraft at anything like a profit.

'It was an unforeseen accumulation of risks,' explains Manfred Bischoff. 'We could have lived with one or two of the negative factors but not with all three of them. We simply couldn't cut our costs as fast as conditions in the market were deteriorating.'

For Schrempp, these were difficult times. He used to come to Daimler-Benz board meetings week after week with a stark message: there is no solution to Fokker's problems. 'Normally he is the kind of guy who relishes a problem,' recalls one participant in these meetings. 'He says a problem is an opportunity because he will find a way to solve it. In this case there was nothing he could do, cutting costs had no impact. So he found it very tough.'

Following Schrempp's decision to let Fokker fail, the immediate cost to Daimler-Benz was DM2.3 billion. The total cost of the engagement was nearer DM3.7 billion. Clearly, this was not the most glorious episode in Schrempp's career. However, Schrempp was not alone in deciding to make the acquisition. The DASA management and supervisory boards, as well as the management and supervisory boards of Daimler-Benz itself, all voted unanimously, even enthusiastically for the deal.

'No one blamed Schrempp when he came back and said, "It's my mistake,"' says Hilmar Kopper. 'It was refreshing that he told things the way they were. There were no false promises. And besides we all did the deal and so shared responsibility.'

Of all the many people behind the deal in the first place, there seemed to be only one left. That was Schrempp.

'I played it that way because I wanted to make a point: don't hide behind others when something goes wrong,' says Schrempp.

'There are two ways a manager can act if he makes a mistake. He leaves or he asks to be given the opportunity to put it right. I put it to the board this way and they gave me that opportunity.'

Schrempp's willingness to admit a mistake and face the consequences strengthened his position at Daimler-Benz. It also won him friends in an unexpected quarter: the Dutch Economics Minister and the head of the country's unions would both write to Schrempp, praising him for the way he handled the situation.

In the early 1990s no self-respecting German CEO talked about his company's share price. 'The reaction would have been, oh my God this is tedious nitty-gritty,' recalls Hilmar Kopper of the Deutsche Bank. 'You were expected to talk about big-picture items such as vision and strategy.' The great mass of Daimler's ordinary shareholders were ignored. 'They were regarded merely as the providers of funding for a far grander project,' comments Nick Snee of J.P. Morgan, 'in which attention to financial returns represented a despicable short-sightedness.'

One of the first things Schrempp did after taking over as CEO of Daimler was to call ten senior managers and ask them if they knew what the share price was. Eight didn't know and two were wrong. 'Nobody knew because they couldn't care less,' says Schrempp. Their remuneration, indeed their very *raison d'être* as managers, was totally divorced from the share price.

Schrempp became a passionate advocate of shareholder value, German-style. 'Profit! Profit! Profit' was his war cry. At a time when he was cutting tens of thousands of jobs and shedding venerable companies such as AEG or Dornier aerospace this made him very unpopular. His trenchant insistence on creating value for shareholders went against the grain of German corporate culture. He was pilloried in the domestic press for his obsession with profit at the expense of social values. Fellow German CEOs looked on, horrified at this challenge to the comfortable status quo. Walter Riester, deputy head of the IG Metall union, nicknamed Schrempp the Rambo of the Nation.

'I looked at the way Jack talked and acted when he arrived at GE [in the early 1980s],' recalls Schrempp. 'He was real tough, he cut tens of thousands of jobs, he said he had to get out of all businesses where GE couldn't be number one or two in the world.

'The guy understood that in order to change a major organisation you have to have a few messages only and they've got to be clear-cut and you've got to repeat them day after day and then you have to implement them. So whenever I walked around talking to people I said look at GE, look at Jack Welch . . . I needed him to push through what I wanted to push through. It really helped that people thought I was a tough Americanised capitalist.

'I have to repeat the shareholder value message like a broken record,' he said at the time. 'I hate it, but I have to do it.'

He developed the notion of the 'Schrempp curve', the recognition that things are going to get worse before they get better. He learned the hard way how difficult decisions bring profound unpopularity – in the short term. You need to have a finely calibrated sense of the corporate mood, but not be despondent when morale plummets.

'As you make the necessary changes, morale will deteriorate at first,' says Schrempp. 'If you are convinced you are doing the right thing, you must absolutely not change course. What you must do is listen, listen hard, for at these times people will tell you the unvarnished truth.

'If you've taken the right decision, morale will climb again.

At this point you can stop listening because people will only tell you good news. Later on, you may need to repeat the whole process.'

From an international perspective, the controversy stirred up by Schrempp's language is very curious. In the UK or North America it is taken for granted that the creation of wealth for shareholders is the principal, possibly the only reason why companies are in business. In the UK a manager such as Sir Brian Pitman, chairman of Lloyds TSB, doubled his bank's share price every eighteen months throughout the 1990s. By creating value, he argues, the rest of society benefits through job creation and investment. If all private-sector companies focus ruthlessly on creating higher, sustainable financial returns for shareholders, the result is a capitalist nirvana. The evidence for this, insist shareholder value enthusiasts, is the extraordinarily prolonged boom in the US. Profit-focused companies with access to the world's biggest and most efficient capital markets are behind an unprecedented nine years' growth in the US economy.

In Germany this line of argument is still contentious. Until the late 1990s the stock market was of marginal importance to the economy as a whole. There were only 665 publicly listed companies compared with over 2,000 in the UK, a much smaller economy. The market capitalisation of the total market was barely 25 per cent of Gross Domestic Product as a whole, compared with 75 per cent in the US or more than 100 per cent in the UK. Only 6 per cent of German households owned shares, compared with more than 20 per cent in the UK or the US.

Germany prospered in splendid isolation from the international capital markets, its companies obtaining their finance from friendly domestic banks rather than stock market investors. Private investors shunned the stock market, preferring to invest in government securities or dubious property schemes, while the pension funds and insurance companies – the so-called 'institutional' investors – which drive the markets in the US and the UK were thin on the ground.

The reason for this capital market self-sufficiency was that for decades Germany operated a healthy surplus on both its current and capital accounts. All this changed with the reunification of East and West Germany. This required massive transfers of capital from west to east. By the mid-nineties, Germany was a net importer of capital for the first time since the aftermath of the war. The source of capital at the margin came from international investors, hard-nosed New York and London fund managers who wanted to invest in profitable companies that spoke their language – the language of shareholder value.

When Schrempp started beating the shareholder value drum, the broader macro-economic perspective was not widely understood by his peers in German industry let alone by the average member of the IG Metall union. Germany operated a social-market economy, with strong emphasis on the social. The pressures of competition – in life as in the capital markets – were tempered by an all-embracing social services net and a love of consensus. Schrempp might as well have been speaking a foreign language, so alien did his phrases and formulations seem. He came across as a pure, undiluted capitalist.

Schrempp admits now that the emphasis on shareholder value was deliberately exaggerated, part of his shock therapy for Daimler's complacent management. His provocative, controversial language made the media, the unions and fellow industrialists sit up and take notice.

'I didn't personally like all that negative publicity,' says Schrempp, 'but it helped me get things done.'

The result was that when Schrempp said he was going to do something, no one doubted that it would be done.

'When I started out [in 1995] I asked myself, do I want to be popular at the beginning or at the end?

'Machiavelli said in *The Prince* that it's best to get the brutality out the way first. I decided for the end. If you have to do something unpopular, it's much better to do it at the beginning.'

He created Germany's first option scheme which linked managers' remuneration directly to Daimler's share price. To ram the message home, senior managers were ordered to carry pagers programmed to bleep at the close of the Frankfurt stock market, displaying Daimler's share price together with those of peers such as Volkswagen, BMW and the big three American auto manufacturers.

Schrempp abolished the planning cycle which had contributed to the destruction of capital under his predecessor. Manfred Gentz introduced a new budgeting process, under which Return on Capital Employed became the yardstick by which business performance was measured. A benchmark of 12 per cent was introduced: if a business did not meet or exceed this benchmark, it would be sold. It was a crude but effective system, making managers aware of the capital resources at their disposal. Like shareholder value, the 12 per cent got into people's heads; managers became hugely focused on achieving the target. By creating a league table of achievers and underperformers, it gave the management board a rational basis on which to make investment decisions. Gone were the days when Mercedes-Benz was expected to cross-subsidise other loss-making divisions.

'The CEO of TEMIC [an electrical components manufacturer] came and said losses would be so and so many tens of millions for the following perfectly legitimate business reasons,' Schrempp says. 'We turned round and said thank you very much but you have another four weeks to tell us how you propose returning to profit . . . Otherwise you're out, we'll sell the place.'

No one had ever talked like that before; in the past it was permissible for TEMIC to lose DM100 million a year because it supplied other parts of the group. From now on it would have to stand on its own two feet or it would be out – and in December 1997 parts of the company were duly sold.

Decision-making was simplified and accelerated: in 1997 it took four weeks to decide to buy Ford's heavy truck division. Under the old system it would have taken six to eight months.

Old-fashioned *Betriebsergebnis* was cast aside in favour of US Generally Accepted Accounting Principles (US GAAP), the language of the international investment community. US GAAP is less easy to manipulate than German accounting so the divisional barons lost the ability to obfuscate their numbers. For the first time there was a clear link between internal performance measures and the statutory accounts.

By late 1996, with the worst of the restructuring behind him, he softened his tone markedly. Addressing the Friedrich Ebert Stiftung, a left-leaning think-tank, he gave a speech in which he promised never again to use the incendiary English phrase. In future, he would refer to *'wertorientierte Unternehmensführung'*, a more anodyne expression which translates roughly as 'value-oriented management'.

'Shareholder value is nothing more frightening than to say that management must strive to increase the company's worth. The return on an investment must be higher than the cost of financing that investment over the long term. That's all there is to it!'

He explained that there was a magic triangle which managers of publicly traded companies had to heed. The three sides of the triangle were employees, customers and society, and shareholders. 'If the triangle has equal sides, I'm doing a good job,' he said. 'For many years we had shareholder written in small print and the others in large print. When I came on board it was time to correct the balance.

'The point was that I am not the puppet of shareholders, that I know that I have broader responsibilities. But if a company is on the verge of going down the drain I'd better do something about it.'

If Schrempp needed to defend his philosophy to a domestic audience, there was no need so far as international investors were concerned. The very philosophy that marked him out as a ruthless capitalist at home won Schrempp an enthusiastic following abroad.

Ever since the first expansion overseas in the 1950s, Daimler-Benz had been a highly international company, with operations all around the world. This created plenty of opportunities for high-fliers to spend a tour of duty in Asia or the US,

South America or South Africa, before returning to senior management jobs in Stuttgart. By any standards, Daimler had an internationally experienced cadre of senior management.

However, from the perspective of the international capital markets, Daimler-Benz was still a provincial company. For decades it generated so much cash that it had no need to raise capital outside Germany and it maintained an aloof distance from the fund managers of London and New York as a result. This attitude started to change only in 1993 when Daimler-Benz became the first German company to list its shares on the New York Stock Exchange, thus creating a bridge between Europe's biggest economy and the world's largest capital markets. There was a fanfare when the listing took place, but little systematic follow-up. The amount of fresh capital raised was negligible and Daimler maintained very little direct contact with international investors or analysts, especially at the level of senior management. Reuter, for example, did not provide personal briefings. Granted, at the time few other German CEOs did either, but Daimler had a reputation for being especially standoffish. This changed with the arrival of Schrempp.

His first presentation to international investors took place in late 1995. 'He handled us with disarming frankness,' remembered one of the participants. 'Here was an entrepreneur who displayed a real willingness to take risks, to take action where things were clearly going wrong. There was no bullshit. He made it clear that the company not only needed turning round, it needed rescuing from itself.

'Behind this in-your-face approach was a complex, multi-layered individual. He was not just turning the company round – a phrase we in the market use as if it's as simple as turning a tap of water on and off – it was the complete re-engineering of the mind-set of the company.

'My initial impressions were – one – here is a tough-minded SOB. Two, he has a very clear idea of where he wants the company to be.'

International investors were not initially enthusiastic. They watched Schrempp's progress with scepticism. There was amazement that he had the guts to pull out of Fokker. They appreciated the signal effect of the move to targets for Return on Capital Employed (RoCE). But there was no solid, reassuring good news out of Daimler-Benz until the late summer of 1996. Then, at last, Schrempp was able to report that Daimler-Benz had turned the corner. The group made a profit of more than DM700 million in the first half of the year, a turnaround of more than DM2 billion. In late December the company announced that operating profits for the full year totalled an impressive DM3.7 billion, while turnover rose to DM130 billion. And Daimler was at last creating rather than shedding jobs, taking on a net 10,000 people during the course of the year.

By 1997 Daimler's share price had doubled as investors gave Schrempp credit for turning the company around. By mid-1998, the price was three times higher than in 1995. Schrempp had made the crucial discovery that a strong share price is the most powerful weapon in a company's strategic armoury. It gave him the currency for doing a deal.

CHAPTER 6

Lutz's Right Brain

*Bob Lutz and the renaissance of the
Chrysler Corporation in the early 1990s*

Scene 1

Bob Lutz is sitting astride a colossal cream-coloured Brahma
bull.

The bull is loping towards a campsite in the middle
of the Arizona desert where forty of the world's top auto
journalists have gathered for an unconventional barbecue and
press conference. Gradually, Lutz comes into view. He is as
ever immaculately dressed in jacket and tie, chomping on a
large cigar.

Just as he arrives at the campsite, the bull stops in its tracks.
There is a moment of awkward anticipation. The bull proceeds
to relieve himself, loudly and copiously, right in front of the
assembled press corps.

Scene 2

Lutz is uncharacteristically late for a plane-load of journalists waiting to fly off from Detroit to a product launch in the west. Finally, he comes out of a nearby hangar looking rattled.

As he boards the plane, still wearing his jump suit, fellow passengers notice that his face is white. He explains that he has just landed his Czech fighter jet with the wheels up. A moment of inattention meant that it was too late for him to follow normal procedures and he had to land on the plane's undercarriage. A lot of metal had been scraped off the fuselage and Lutz is lucky to be alive.

Lutz, the architect of Chrysler's recovery in the 1990s, is the master of the dramatic arrival.

At the 1992 Detroit auto show he launched the new Jeep Grand Cherokee by driving it up a flight of steps and through a giant plate-glass window.

That time, at least, the drama was planned, but there is a sense in which all his entrances – scripted or otherwise – serve a deeper purpose. There was a conscious plan to reinvigorate the Chrysler brand, to endow it with charisma. In the minds of the press and public alike, Chrysler would become intimately associated with Lutz, a former fighter pilot with a colourful personality.

When Lutz left Ford to join Chrysler in 1986 he faced a dilemma.

It was a tradition in Detroit that senior auto executives would be given up to four company cars. Two of these they would own outright, the other two they could lease at a favourable rate. What cars would Lutz put in his garage? It was easy enough for Lutz to pick the mini-van, still a desirable vehicle. 'But it was very difficult to find numbers two, three and four in terms of vehicles you wouldn't mind being seen in, let alone drive,' Lutz said later.

By the late eighties, the company's product portfolio had

started to look tired and threadbare. The design was stodgy and unoriginal, the engineering old-fashioned and unreliable.

Iacocca, still hanging on to the top job, had lost his touch. The nadir came in 1989 when no fewer than four new cars flopped when they were launched. The Dodge Spirit and the Plymouth were compact cars based on five-year-old designs.

Iacocca's inattention to product design and engineering contrasted with his extravagance in other areas. The turnaround of the mid-eighties had left the company with a cash mountain which Iacocca was busy spending. After sacrificing his salary during the difficult years, it was easy to justify a vertiginous increase in his remuneration. In 1986 he earned nearly $24 million in shares, bonus and salary – a record for the Big Three – followed by $18 million in 1987. More altruistically, he implemented a $2 billion programme to buy back the company's own stock, a common way of redistributing surplus capital and jacking up earnings per share.

In a curious parallel with Edzard Reuter's doomed diversification strategy, Iacocca used what was left of the cash to finance an acquisition spree which took the company away from its core automotive business. In 1986, while Daimler was contemplating its first move into aerospace, Iacocca bought Gulfstream Aerospace Corporation, a manufacturer of private jets. As Daimler-Benz was establishing Debis, a services subsidiary, Chrysler acquired FinanceAmerica, E.F. Hutton Credit and four car rental businesses. Taking the parallel with Daimler one uncanny step further, Iacocca even set up a holding company structure, dividing the business into four divisions: automotive, aerospace, financial services and technologies. The car business suffered from lack of investment and management inattention.

In retrospect, Iacocca redeemed himself with his most significant acquisition: the $800 million purchase of American Motors Corporation, manufacturer of the Jeep and the fourth largest automotive company in the US. It was making substantial losses when Chrysler bought it in 1987 and for years Renault, its French owners, had struggled in vain to make something of the Jeep brand, the jewel in AMC's crown. Chrysler had to take over AMC's liabilities to get at Jeep, but the deal turned out to be a masterstroke. With AMC came some talented engineers and a hardscrabble business philosophy from which Chrysler's management had a lot to learn. And, almost by accident, it set Chrysler up for years of prosperous growth in the market for sports utility vehicles, the fast-growing segment of the US auto industry which Chrysler came to dominate in the 1990s.

At the time, none of this was obvious. The deal weakened the group's finances on the eve of another cyclical downturn for the industry. By 1989 Chrysler was once again in trouble. Its net earnings tumbled to $359 million and its share of the US auto market slumped to just over 10 per cent. A year later, as recession took hold, earnings dropped to a nugatory $68 million and market share fell to 9.3 per cent. In 1991 Chrysler lost nearly $800 million and market share went down as low as 8.4 per cent.

As the stock price plunged from its 1989 peak of $30 to the $10 mark, it looked disconcertingly like a rerun of the crisis of 1980. Bankers refused to roll over Chrysler's commercial paper and some of its debt was officially downgraded from investment quality to junk. Iacocca announced a $1 billion cost-reduction programme and agreed to get rid of Gulfstream (the company – not the corporate jet). Only a $350 million issue of new stock helped restore the company's precarious finances. With a market capitalisation of a meagre $3 billion, Chrysler was once again on the ropes.

By the middle of the nineties there would be no problem picking half a dozen Chrysler vehicles that Lutz or any other car enthusiast would gladly flaunt in front of his house or gun down the freeway. 'When I left [in 1998] you could have had nine company vehicles and you'd still want two or three more,' Lutz says.

Among these would be the Dodge Viper, an outrageously powerful, eye-searing roadster; the Plymouth Prowler, another fast and original sports car; the Jeep Grand Cherokee, one of the world's first luxury sports utility vehicles; the aggressively styled Dodge Ram pick-up truck; the Dodge Intrepid, the first of a new generation of roomy 'cab forward' sedans, and even the distinctive Neon, a small car built on the LH platform.

Chrysler introduced more all-new cars in the nineties than in the previous two decades. It won one award after another for the design and execution of its cars and trucks. 'We became acknowledged world leader in developing exciting vehicles, and doing it faster than anyone else,' is how Bob Eaton summed up the proliferation of popular, charismatic cars (Preface to *Guts*, by Bob Lutz).

The transformation in Chrysler's fortunes was not limited to product. By the mid-nineties, Chrysler was the most profitable auto company in the world. It had made more money in the 1990s than it had done in the previous six decades of its existence put together. And in 1996 the influential *Forbes* magazine voted Chrysler the Company of the Year, recognition that Chrysler was once more a robust and respectable company.

The beginnings of the recovery can be traced back to Lutz's arrival at Chrysler in June 1986. Lutz, a tall, trim man with a close crop of silver hair and a distinguished bearing, looks more like a European banker than a Detroit car executive. As well he might, for Lutz's father was a senior banker at Crédit Suisse and he was brought up in cosmopolitan, prosperous circles which instilled in him a taste for the good things in life: fine wines, enormous cigars and fast cars. Following his father's peregrinations, Lutz spent his childhood and youth criss-crossing the Atlantic, growing up as part American, part Swiss German. (He can speak and write fluent German and French as a result and holds dual US-Swiss citizenship.) The frequent moves disrupted his education and he did not complete high school until the age of twenty-two. Thereafter he joined the US Marine Corps where he spent five years on active service, learning to fly planes and helicopters.

After taking an MBA, he finally fulfilled his lifelong ambition to work in the auto industry. He had a stellar career, rising quickly to head up sales and marketing for General Motors in Europe before being poached first by BMW (where he worked for three years as marketing director) and then Ford. He was promoted to run Ford Europe, where he introduced the novel Ford Sierra and helped deliver handsome profits just when the company needed them, at the beginning of the 1980s when the US industry was deep in recession. Within eighteen months of crossing over to Chrysler, Lutz was appointed president and chief operating officer.

By now, Lutz was more than a seasoned international executive. He was a well-known maverick who rejoiced in unconventional behaviour and thinking. He once addressed a sales conference wearing nothing but a pair of (wet) swimming trunks. He rode around Europe on a motorbike in a skin-tight leather biker's outfit. He bought himself the ex-Czech fighter jet in which he would indulge his lust for speed. He was cocky, good-looking, flamboyant, beloved by the press as a source of stories and wonderful, off-the-record indiscretions.

In short, he was an archetypal, larger-than-life 'car guy', in the tradition of Walter P. Chrysler himself.

With Iacocca increasingly distant from the day-to-day running of the business, Lutz identified a small team of like-minded executives who made it their mission to restore Chrysler's fortunes. Lutz's cabal included François Castaing, a Frenchman who came to Chrysler via the acquisition of AMC; he was an automotive engineer of genius who designed Formula 2 racing engines when he was still an undergraduate at university and went on to develop numerous revolutionary engines for Renault's racing programme. There was Tom Gale, a Chrysler veteran and design guru who would be responsible for developing the new look for the company's products. Tom Stallkamp would become the procurement tsar, cutting billions from the group's costs. Dennis Pawley joined Chrysler in 1989 after a career with GM and Mazda, where he had been one of the first

American managers to introduce Japanese work practices into US manufacturing industry.

Drawn from a variety of backgrounds and disciplines, brought to Chrysler as much by accident as design, this was an eclectic bunch of certified car nuts who shared some common values: love of the product, impatience with hierarchy and bureaucracy, a willingness to take bold decisions rapidly. 'We were fast-moving anti-bureaucratic types who believed that it was better to make a less than perfect decision quickly, rather than a perfect decision which took ten months,' says Lutz. 'We were all doing it for the love of the game.'

There was a long hiatus between Lutz's arrival and the first fruits of his leadership – such is the nature of the auto industry, where there is a three- to five-year lead time between conceiving a new car and its appearance in the showrooms. The big year was 1992, when Lutz launched the Jeep Grand Cherokee at January's motor show. It wasn't the first luxury sports utility vehicle in the world, but even as it crashed through the plate-glass window in Detroit's Cobo Hall, it was an instant hit.

It looked good, it felt more like a car than a truck to drive, it was both comfortable and rugged. More than any other, this vehicle started the worldwide craze for off-road vehicles that are driven chiefly in towns and suburbs, but give the owner the vicarious thrill of the wild. It built on the historic strengths of the mini-van and helped Chrysler define and ultimately dominate North America's fast-growing light truck market. Chrysler's light truck sales rose from a modest 200,000 units at the beginning of the eighties to 1.6 million at the time of the merger with Daimler-Benz. Market share climbed to a whopping 23 per cent.

For financiers watching Chrysler's dwindling cash flow, the launch of the LH generation of sedan cars later in the year was more important. The new Jeep alone would not be enough to guarantee the company's recovery; it had to have products for the mass market. The successful launch of the Dodge Intrepid, the Chrysler Concorde and the Eagle Vision convinced bankers to back the ailing company and marked the beginning of Chrysler's comeback. (These were called 'cab-forward' because Chrysler's designers moved the windshield further forward than usual, creating more room inside the car as well as a visually distinctive exterior.)

The preparatory work, though, had been done in the previous five years. Lutz and his team had fostered a fighting spirit that helped the company not merely survive the difficult times. 'There was a real underdog mentality that turned us into relentless competitors,' recalled Jim Holden, then a fast-rising sales and marketing executive.

'We took a lot of chances because we knew we were going to go out of business if we didn't, and as a result we beat the other guys' brains in. We went from being third-class citizens to being the darlings of the town.'

In the dog days of 1988 and 1989, Chrysler executives were reduced to paying emergency visits to their dealers. 'Twice a month we went round showing pictures of products we knew were coming three or four years down the line,' said Holden. 'If we could only survive to execute the product plan, we knew we were going to make it.'

Lutz developed a plan which would carry Chrysler through the recession and guarantee the company's recovery thereafter. The plan had a number of elements. First and foremost, and certainly most visible to the customer, was a new approach to design. 'We wanted to be ahead of the curve in terms of design and not follow any established pattern,' says Lutz. 'Everything we did had a strong personality.'

This was a radical approach for Detroit. Car companies, like film studios, have to invest gigantic sums well in advance of knowing whether the customer will like the end product. They can carry out market research, they can analyse the market, but ultimately they know that many productions will fail dismally at the box-office. They rely on good fortune to produce the occasional blockbuster that will generate so much revenue that it covers for all the losers.

One approach to the uncertainty is to play safe: to launch cars or films that follow tried and tested formulae. That way, your revenues are likely to be predictable but your profits uninspiring. Alternatively, you can turn your back on market research and follow your gut. In other words, you can act like a traditional Hollywood studio. Or, you can aspire to be Steven Spielberg, whose *Schindler's List*, for example, does not conform to any standard criteria of what should make a movie successful.

'Spielberg eschews formula movies because he has a personal vision, he has his own personal conviction of what is going to make a great movie. He doesn't do what he does based on market research or an accountant's revenue forecast,' said Lutz.

And so Chrysler turned its back on conventional wisdom. Tom Gale, one of the architects of the strategy, explains: 'We had always been successful as a company where we were meaningfully differentiated from everybody else. We set out to create products that would be so remarkable that they would speak for themselves.'

'We had no problem doing vehicles which were under-researched or which in research showed a strong polarity,' Lutz says. 'For example, 25 per cent of the public loved [the Dodge Ram] so much they absolutely had to have it whereas the other 75 per cent said it's so ugly I wouldn't touch it. When you have 4 per cent of the market for full-sized pick-ups, and your research is telling you that 25 per cent of these people say they must have your product, then you are making the right decision.'

The Dodge Ram went on to be one of Chrysler's great commercial successes of the mid-1990s. It was 'in your face', bold and blatantly different from what everyone else was doing.

Lutz attributes Chrysler's comeback to 'right-brain' thinking in a 'left-brain' world. Right-brainers are creative, lateral thinkers, while left-brainers are linear, quantitative and controlling. He maintains that the auto industry has for too long been dominated by left-brainers – accountants and planners who regard car production as a purely scientific business. Not so, says Lutz, buying a car is an emotional decision, and a car manufacturer should follow its instincts.

'We did an awful lot by intuition, there was remarkably little staff work. We cut out all the crap normally associated with launching a new product . . . all of us had a strong, personalised sense of what would work.'

To some extent, Chrysler had no choice. Starved of cash, it didn't have the resources to invest in long-winded research and development processes. It had to take risks, otherwise it wouldn't have survived. It made a virtue of necessity by going as quickly as possible from idea to production. 'By going straight to the right car, we cut out all the waste,' says Lutz. Throughout the 1990s Chrysler's product development costs were less than half those of their two big US competitors. By the time of the merger with Daimler, they were just 2.8 per cent of revenues, compared to 6 per cent at Ford and 8 per cent at GM.

Cost-cutting went hand in hand with an entirely new approach to manufacturing. Lutz and his cohorts determined to learn all they could from the Japanese. In view of Iacocca's increasingly splenetic tirades against Japanese trade practices, this was a bold step internally, but the engineers knew that Chrysler – and American manufacturing industry in general – had fallen a long way behind their Japanese competitors. They took a hard look at Mitsubishi, Chrysler's long-term joint venture partner. They also conducted an exhaustive study of Honda, whose success in selling innovative, stylish cars to the American consumer had consistently wrong-footed Chrysler and its Detroit peers. Lutz and his adjutant Castaing came to the conclusion that Chrysler could steal a march on its competitors only if it took on board the best of Japanese manufacturing practices.

A key lesson from the Japanese: break down the barriers between the different processes that go into manufacturing a car. 'Our engineering department was very balkanised,' wrote Lutz in his autobiography. 'Body engineering, chassis engineering, power-train engineering, electrical engineering, and so on were all not-so-little chimneys unto themselves, complete with their own re-do loops. As a result no programme inside engineering could move any faster than the organisation's slowest-moving part. For instance, if the door locks, handles and mechanisms department got swamped with work at any given time, then the whole system got bogged down waiting for them to catch up.'

The solution was to create 'platform teams' where people were responsible for creating not isolated components, but an entire car. Design, engineering, sales and marketing, and procurement – traditionally located in their separate organisational 'silos' – were all forced to work together to deliver a car on time and on budget. A separate platform was created for each type of vehicle: large car, small car, mini-van, Jeep and truck. This lean, team-based approach to manufacturing was commonplace in Japan and would soon be popularised in the US with the publication of *The Machine that Changed the World*, the influential study on the future of the car carried out by the Massachusetts Institute of Technology. Chrysler was the first US automotive company to put it into practice.

Lesson number two from the Japanese: develop a new approach to procurement. Instead of encouraging many suppliers to fight each other for its business, Chrysler identified a smaller number of suppliers with whom it would develop stable, long-term relationships. Instead of demanding price reductions, Chrysler would give suppliers incentives to work with the manufacturer to identify efficiencies and common savings. It was consciously modelled on the Japanese *keiretsu* system, but it went further than that, Lutz insists. 'In terms of engaging our suppliers in genuine dialogue, we went beyond the Japanese, we weren't just imitating them,' he says. Tom Stallkamp's SCORE system – short for Supplier Cost-Reduction Effort – is reckoned to have saved Chrysler more than $5 billion between 1989 and 1998.

The new approach to manufacturing found powerful expression in the Dodge Viper, a thunderous two-seat sports car launched at the end of 1992. This was a right-brain project if ever there was one – the only market research took place in Bob Lutz's head. He had the idea of developing an inspirational 'kick-ass' 400 bhp sports car that would act as a showpiece for Chrysler's hidden potential. Despite some initial internal reluctance, Lutz secured the investment funds for this madcap project and a prototype of this voluptuous vehicle was unveiled at the Detroit auto show in January 1989. It was rapturously received. When it finally came into production, it had become 'a potent symbol of our new spirit, our unconventional thinking, our daring, and the speed with which we were regaining our strength' (Lutz, *Guts*).

At that point, of course, the Viper had a left-brain rationale: it was the first car to be produced by a platform team so its success validated the company's shift to this new form of production. Even if the Viper would never make any money on a stand-alone basis, the car cast a halo over the rest of Chrysler's cars and trucks. 'Gee, is that a Dodge,' people were heard to say. Bankers put their names on the waiting list to buy the new car even as they approved the company's refinancing package.

On the Tuesday before Easter 1995 Bob Eaton was in New York when he received an unwelcome telephone call. On the other end of the line was Kirk Kerkorian, the Las Vegas-based investor who was Chrysler's biggest shareholder. Kerkorian informed the Chrysler CEO that the next day he would be announcing a $23 billion bid for the company.

Eaton, busy putting the finishing touches to a speech he was planning to give at New York's auto show, cancelled all engagements and took the company's private jet back to Detroit. Gathering together a war council of his closest directors and advisors, he started work on a strategy to defend the company from the predator's unwelcome attentions. Kerkorian's offer for Chrysler was the second biggest bid in US corporate history since R.J.R. Nabisco was acquired for $25 billion in 1989. For the Chrysler management team it was intriguing and irritating in equal measure. Intriguing, because everything about Kerkorian and his motives was shrouded in mystery.

At the age of seventy-seven, Kerkorian was often likened to Howard Hughes: he lived in Las Vegas, he shunned the limelight, he loved to fly, and he was very rich. His 10 per cent stake in Chrysler, worth about $2 billion at the time of the offer, was part of a total portfolio including MGM Grand Hotel in Las Vegas, the world's largest hotel complex.

Like Iacocca, Kerkorian came from humble beginnings to become one of America's most prominent businessmen. He was born in Fresno, California, the son of an immigrant Armenian fruit farmer. He dropped out of high school at the age of sixteen, taking a variety of jobs before he found a vocation for flying: for a time he was a professional boxer, a floor-sweeper at a Hollywood movie studio, and a bingo hall manager. A cargo pilot during the war, he set up his first business with a $60,000 loan secured on his own two-seater plane. He used the cash to develop a charter service which ferried gamblers between California and Las Vegas. The business prospered and in 1968 he sold out to Transamerica Corp for $107 million. Thereafter he proved himself a shrewd, if controversial, investor. He made a lot of money out of his investment in the Metro-Goldwyn-Mayer film studios, but critics accused him of asset stripping. He bought much of his stake in Chrysler when the stock stood at between $10 and $13 a share. His investment had at least trebled by the time of the bid.

Kerkorian's investment company Tracinda – named after his two daughters Tracy and Linda – swore blind that the offer was not hostile to Chrysler's senior executives or employees. Eaton was however quick to declare that the company was not up for sale and that he would resist the bid.

Despite the huge fanfare surrounding the approach, it wasn't quite clear where Kerkorian and his cohorts would be getting the money from. The offer was not fully financed when it was announced.

The Kerkorian camp did say, however, that it would draw

on $5 billion of Chrysler's own cash reserves to help make the sums add up. In other words, it would adopt the tactics of 1980s corporate raiders, who ingeniously used the cash belonging to their targets to pay off the very debt that would finance the acquisition in the first place. For Chrysler this was especially exasperating, as the company had carefully husbanded its resources so that it now had more than $8 billion in cash and marketable securities on its balance sheet. Eaton and his colleagues were adamant that they needed at least $5.5 billion of this to weather the next recession and avoid the cock-ups of the past. Now, it seemed, predators could come along and use this cash as a weapon against the very team that had managed the business so prudently in the past few years.

The final insult was that Lee Iacocca had lent his name – even $50 million of his estimated $200 million fortune – to the bid. Iacocca had stepped down as chairman and CEO only at the end of 1992 and remained a director until late 1993. It had not been a graceful departure. Non-executive directors had had to exert their influence to ensure that he left when he did. To Eaton and his team, it smacked of rank disloyalty for Iacocca to support Kerkorian's approach.

In his last years at Chrysler, Iacocca had become a caricature of himself. He became heavily involved in a campaign to raise funds to restore the Statue of Liberty and flirted with the idea of running for the US presidency. He travelled to Europe to hold a series of lofty discussions with Gianni Agnelli, chairman of Agnelli, about merging the two companies. Nothing came of this.

Iacocca made his influence felt in the decision to appoint Bob Eaton as his successor, rather than the obvious choice of Bob Lutz. Lutz had crossed him too often on too many issues, and the phlegmatic Eaton, former head of GM's European operations, was brought on instead. He joined as vice-chairman and chief operating officer in March 1992.

Contrary to all expectations, Lutz had not departed in a fit of pique when he was passed over for the top job. A rational left-brain look at the situation persuaded him to stay and work with Eaton. Lutz continued to run the day-to-day operations, while Eaton represented the company to the outside world and developed Chrysler's strategy.

The strategy could be simply expressed. Chrysler determined to be the leading car company in the US by 1996, and the leading car company in the world by the year 2000. For a company that had tottered on the verge of collapse half a dozen times since the war, this was an extraordinarily bold objective. Astonishing, therefore, that by the time of Kerkorian's onslaught, Eaton and Lutz were well on the way to pulling it off.

They had identified numerous criteria by which Chrysler wanted to be judged the best: product distinctiveness, customer satisfaction, quality, cost leadership, financial strength. If there were still problems with engineering quality, the financial performance was outstanding. In 1996 return on sales would be more than 6 per cent, significantly more than Ford or GM, and return on capital would be 20 per cent, more than double for the industry median. Profits and sales per employee – the best measure of productivity – were the best in the industry. Chrysler was strongly cash generative, on track to spend $23 billion on new products and plant expansion in the next five years. Dividends were running at $1 billion a year. It had a fully funded pension plan for the first time in forty years. Stock buy-backs were on the horizon.

Unfortunately for Chrysler, the stock market had not honoured the revival in the company's fortunes. On the day that Kerkorian announced his $55 a share bid, the stock price was $39.25. The tried and tested way of looking at a company's valuation is to measure in terms of a multiple of earnings per share. At the pre-bid level, the shares were trading at just 4.4 times the company's earnings. This compared with an average of 15 times a typical industrial company's earnings at that time.

The reason for this insulting undervaluation? Simple: the likelihood of recession in the US and investors' fears that Chrysler's profits would crumple as they had always done in the past. And yet, Eaton was entitled to ask himself, was the company not girding itself for the next downturn? Surely, by hoarding cash he was pursuing precisely the right strategy to cushion shareholders from the worst of the coming recession? Ungrateful shareholders now wanted to strip the company of both its cash and its security.

Kerkorian saw it differently: the company belonged to its shareholders, and it was sitting on too much cash. The Las Vegas-based investor argued that Eaton was being too conservative. Chrysler was a lot stronger than it had been ahead of previous downturns, Kerkorian said, so it didn't need all the cash. It wasn't as vulnerable as Eaton maintained. Much better to give the cash, or some of it at least, back to shareholders.

On Thursday of that week, Helmut Werner of Mercedes-Benz read about Kerkorian's approach to Chrysler and had a brainwave. He was on a skiing holiday in Davos, Switzerland, and it occurred to him that Chrysler might be interested in getting together with Mercedes to fend off the unfriendly bid.

He rang Eaton on Good Friday and suggested in very general terms that they should meet – perhaps there would be something they could do together in the light of the unfriendly approach.

'I don't know,' said Eaton, hesitantly, 'perhaps it's a good idea.'

He rang back on Sunday to invite Werner over to the US. That evening, Werner took the Concorde to New York and the two men met the next day in a private apartment in Manhattan.

A few weeks later, Schrempp took a call from an advisor to Kirk Kerkorian. Kerkorian wanted to explore the possibility of linking up with Daimler-Benz to give his proposal the industrial logic that it patently lacked.

For a brief time, Daimler-Benz and Mercedes-Benz looked as though they would be on opposite sides of the same takeover.

CHAPTER 7

Reunification

The merger between Mercedes-Benz and its parent company

'It's like two trucks on a highway,' said Manfred Bischoff. His fellow board members fell silent as the aerospace chief pursued his analogy.

'I can see these two great big Freightliners approaching each other at high speed. At the moment they are a long way apart but they are moving very quickly towards each other. Before too long they are going to crash into each other, because the highway they are travelling on only has one lane. There is no way out!

'Gentlemen, one of these Freightliners is called Jürgen Schrempp. The other is Helmut Werner!'

Bischoff, a moustachioed former professor who bears more than a passing resemblance to the film star Omar Sharif, thus applied a spark to a boardroom conflict that had been smouldering for several months already. As early as March 1996 the press had reported Schrempp's plans to restructure the holding company to the detriment of Helmut Werner. In early September, when Bischoff made his remarks, the dispute flared into the open at last. It quickly developed into a naked power struggle that came to an end only with Werner's resignation in January 1997.

At the heart of the conflict was an apparently innocuous proposal: Schrempp wanted to tidy up the holding structure of the Daimler-Benz group. It was, he felt, an anomaly that Mercedes-Benz should be a separate *Aktiengesellschaft*, an independent but wholly owned subsidiary of Daimler-Benz. Edzard Reuter had turned Mercedes into an independent company in 1989 at a time when the automotive business was deemed peripheral to the group's main activities. Following Schrempp's divestments, the automotive business was once again the focus of the Daimler-Benz group. In 1996 it accounted for three-quarters of Daimler's DM106 billion turnover – and because other divisions were loss-making it made more money than the group as a whole.

According to Schrempp's logic, the structure was the last relic of the Reuter era and needed to be swept away. The bureaucracy needed to be replaced with a rational structure that reflected Mercedes' restored position as the crown jewels of the group and the centrepiece of its future strategy. In August, Schrempp got together with Eckhard Cordes and Rüdiger Grube in New York's Four Seasons Hotel to rehearse their objections to the status quo and to discuss alternatives for the future.

The problems were easy to identify. The current structure gave the board of Daimler-Benz limited control over the management of its largest subsidiary. The process of making decisions affecting the automotive business was cumbersome and time-consuming. The only representative of Mercedes on the Daimler board was Werner, while Schrempp was the chairman of the Mercedes supervisory board. Decisions had to be ratified by the Mercedes management and supervisory board before the Daimler board would discuss them. Sometimes, the Daimler board would be excluded from the decision-making altogether – as when Mercedes and Daimler struck up different negotiating positions with the unions during a recent wage-round. Eliminating a layer of management would help Daimler-Benz create shareholder value: this was the conclusion of a helpful review of fifty peer-group companies produced by the Goldman Sachs investment bank.

There was one other objection that the three men kept to themselves throughout the ensuing battle. They recognised that the convoluted structure would make it impossible for Daimler-Benz to take a proactive role in the coming consolidation of the automotive industry.

In other words, it would prevent Daimler doing any deals. They knew this from experience. The talks initiated by Helmut Werner in 1995 had come to nothing. One key factor behind the failure of the talks was that Mercedes was a subsidiary of a conglomerate. Mercedes had no separate stock market identity and as a result had no currency which it could use to structure a transaction with another company. Moreover, its management was under-represented on the board of the holding company. The discussions had foundered because the structure was so convoluted.

It was important to keep quiet about merger plans as the time was still not right.

'Daimler was out of the intensive care unit, but had still not left the hospital,' says Cordes.

Besides, the three knew, talking about plans for a deal would create the conditions for failure, because a leak would push up the share price of an intended bride. And as yet, they were a long way from identifying a potential target.

Grube, who was still working at DASA in Munich and would formally join Schrempp's team on 1 September, had helped Schrempp and Cordes prepare ten possible boardroom structures for the group. These ranged from a pure holding company in which a curtailed board would exercise minimal direct control over the affairs of the subsidiaries, to a series of models in which the core businesses were represented directly on the holding company board. The core team favoured Model 6,

117

which would allocate a mix of functional and divisional responsibilities to an enlarged management board. This, they decided, could be achieved very simply and at significant tax advantages to the group by doing what they did to AEG. Mercedes-Benz could simply be merged together with Daimler-Benz and then be dissolved.

Implementing the plan would be a great deal more difficult than developing the idea, the three men recognised. Meeting again in the atmospheric surroundings of Gottlieb Daimler's birthplace – a wood-timbered house in the centre of Schorndorf – they forged a kind of blood brotherhood, agreeing that they would all resign if they did not get their plans through. They forced what Schrempp calls a 'digital decision' – black or white, yes or no.

Over the next few years Schrempp would adopt a similar approach in the face of complex management challenges. Here's how it works.

First, a small group of trusted colleagues carefully analyses the options. Second, they decide on the most radical way forward where there are only two possible outcomes: total success or total failure. Finally, they execute the decision as swiftly as possible, with no half measures.

If the outcome is successful, Schrempp emerges strengthened and can bask in deserved praise for the boldness of his gambit. If it goes wrong, on the other hand, Schrempp takes full responsibility and is prepared to buy a one-way ticket to early retirement in South Africa.

For several months, Schrempp and his team lived on a knife-edge. It was by no means certain that their strategy would be effective. Looking back, Schrempp says that the merger with Mercedes was much more painful to prepare and execute than the eventual deal with Chrysler. Mercedes had been separated from the parent for less than seven years, but knocking them back together again was a corporate version of *Wiedervereinigung* – the traumatic reunification of East and West Germany in the early part of the decade.

It was painful because it was personal. The press and some of the parties involved saw it as a rerun of the campaign to succeed Edzard Reuter. In one corner was Schrempp, still, despite his growing popularity with international investors, an outsider by German standards. The group as a whole was not yet out of the woods. Schrempp had made his enemies at home, but not yet delivered the recovery in profits that would validate his harsh approach.

In the other corner was Werner, a man hailed in Untertürkheim as the saviour of the car business. He had been CEO of Mercedes-Benz since 1993 and deputy head since the early 1990s. He inspired almost fanatical loyalty in his subordinates. Colleagues remember the declaration of independence he made one night in the Untertürkheim canteen. This was late in 1996 and the conflict with Schrempp had intensified. Speaking to around 400 Mercedes managers, he insisted that the Mercedes brand and the Mercedes company should stay intact. Split them asunder and the integrity of the Mercedes marque would be violated, he proclaimed. It was powerful, emotional stuff and he was rewarded with a standing ovation.

Admiration for Werner extended beyond Stuttgart. *Business Week* magazine identified him as the only German among the top twenty-five global business leaders of 1996. The German media called him the personification of the Mercedes-Benz brand, quite an honour for a man who spent the best part of his career in the tyre industry before being called by Alfred Herrhausen to Daimler seven years before.

In the short period of time that he ran Mercedes-Benz, Helmut Werner introduced major changes and reversed the decline in the core car business that dated back to the mid-1980s. The number of cars sold by Mercedes peaked at 590,000 in 1986 and then stagnated at around 580,000 for five years.

For any car manufacturer, this is a perilous situation, as from year to year costs invariably rise just as the price at which you can sell your cars to customers will come under pressure. The result is a squeeze on margins and profitability. The post-reunification boom in the early 1990s simply delayed the day of reckoning for Mercedes. Eventually, in 1993, Mercedes made losses of DM1.3 billion, its first since the Second World War. These were losses according to German *Betriebsergebnis* – under US GAAP they would have been much higher.

Mercedes was a sleeping giant, secure in its past success but complacent in the face of current challenges. As Gary Lapidus, investment analyst with Goldman Sachs, put it, 'Its products were shrines to engineering capability without regard to cost.' Neither the customer's wishes, nor the production process's costs were given undue consideration. Eckhard Cordes recalls how the head of the engineering department used to say: 'We define what the market wants, the market does not tell us what we are going to make.' This was a relic of the proud Swabian culture of the past: the overriding philosophy was still *'Das Beste oder Nichts'*, – the best or nothing at all. But Gottlieb Daimler's mission statement was not well suited to the modern, highly competitive world of car manufacturing.

With the new S-Class – introduced at the Geneva motor show in 1991 – Mercedes-Benz consciously sought to set a new international standard for the luxury saloons. It was the first car to have double-glazing and self-closing doors. Seat, mirror and steering-column positions had a computer memory so they would adjust themselves automatically according to who was driving. It had a massive six-litre, twelve-cylinder engine. It was the first car in the world to have an activated charcoal filter with automatic climate control.

These innovations were the result of a five-year development programme costing more than DM3 billion, yet the resulting vehicle was an ugly, over-engineered monster that initially found little favour with customers.

'Under no circumstances would I ever have aspired to drive one of these,' recalls Bob Lutz, 'no matter how old I got.' At

5.10 metres long and 1.89 metres wide, competitors joked that it had those dimensions simply to be bigger than the rival 7 Series BMW (which was 20 centimetres shorter). Its size and weight (2.2 tonnes) ran counter to social and political pressure for smaller cars that did less damage to the environment. It became a national laughing stock when the press discovered that the car was so heavy that it could legally hold no more than three passengers and a briefcase.

'Overweight, overpriced and over-engineered,' was the verdict of Nick Snee at J.P. Morgan. The early problems with the S-Class were all the more galling in that this was the first new model to be launched by Mercedes since the E-Class introduced in 1985 – and it was the first replacement of the S-Class range in eleven years.

Meanwhile new, unexpected competitors were muscling into the Mercedes patch: in the late eighties and early nineties Toyota, Nissan and Honda all attacked the luxury segment of the market for the first time. The Stuttgart engineers were dismissive, but customers were more enthusiastic – especially in the US. Vernon Jordan recalls a meeting of Daimler-Benz advisors in New York early in the 1990s. Jordan mentioned the simple fact that the underground car park at his Washington law firm was now full of Toyota's Lexus cars and not Mercedes (nor, for that matter, were there any Chrysler cars to be found in the basement). It wasn't that the Japanese had suddenly found the secret of building better cars than the Germans, theirs were just better value for money.

Werner took over from Werner Niefer with a mission to wake the giant. This he did with a flurry of initiatives designed to restore morale at Mercedes-Benz while making the company more competitive on the world stage. There was a Product Offensive, a Productivity Offensive, a Learning Offensive and Globalisation Offensive. The headcount dropped from 95,962 in 1990 to 77,078 in 1995, and productivity improved dramatically as a result: sales per employee rose from DM377,000 to DM517,000. The number of management levels was chopped back from six to four. Costs were reduced by several billion a year.

The most tangible result of these initiatives for the outside world was a series of new cars and variations on old models. The first was the new C-Class, a small sedan designed to replace the old 190-Series, which acquired the nickname 'the rescue wagon'. ('We didn't like it,' says Jürgen Hubbert who helped develop the car and who would take over from Werner, 'but it wasn't far from the truth.')

Then came the new E-Class estate – the Mercedes with new eyes as the press called it. For the first time, Mercedes developed a car by reference to the price that it would ultimately command in the market-place. This so-called target pricing was a Japanese technique, the very antithesis of the philosophy that produced the over-engineered S-Class. 'Mercedes-Benz [was] now applying its world-renowned "German engineering" within a framework that considers value to the consumer, pricing and target costs, rather than one that focuses on quality at any cost,' said Lapidus at Goldman Sachs. 'The result [was] products that are more competitive in the market-place and more profitable to Mercedes-Benz.'

Later came two glamorous sports cars, the SLK and the CLK. These fast, elegant vehicles were the very opposite of the ponderous S-Class and captured the spirit of the revitalised Mercedes-Benz. Then there was the A-Class, a controversial, squat, four-door hatchback that was designed to be Mercedes' answer to the Opal Astra and the VW Golf. The M-Class was Mercedes' first move into the fast-growing luxury sports utility vehicle segment. Finally, there was a new V-class van and – long after Werner had left the company – the Smart car, a compact two-seater designed in partnership with SMH, the Swiss manufacturer of Swatch watches.

Werner's legacy is not uncontroversial. There is a question mark over his strategy to take Mercedes-Benz down into the small car segment of the market. The A-Class had a wobbly start in more ways than one when the car overturned during a test drive. The jury is still out on the futuristic Smart car. But Werner's impact on Mercedes can easily be summarised. When he took over in 1993 there were five main classes of car, with nine main variations. Five years later, there were ten classes and fourteen variations, not including Smart. Together with his then adjutant Jürgen Hubbert, Werner created the conditions for the surge of growth in the latter half of the 1990s which saw Mercedes' sales rising from 600,314 in 1995 to burst through the 1 million barrier in 1999 for the first time.

Werner's success stirred up complex emotions. The Mercedes-Benz subsidiary started to feel real pride in itself after a few difficult years, but the pride was compounded by deep-seated resentment at the contribution of the holding company. Since 1989 car executives had been made to feel like second-class citizens within an 'integrated high-technology company' whose priorities were explicitly outside the automotive heartland. And yet the diversification pursued by the centre had proved disastrous. 'We were the real heart of the group,' is how one board member recalls the situation in the early to mid-1990s, 'and yet some of what was going on around us was hardly contributing to the value of the company. To put it more bluntly, we felt that were having to pay for all the shit.'

Schrempp's 1996 initiative was designed to put the automotive business back on the pedestal from which it had been dislodged. Naturally enough, Werner's team saw it differently. The move to merge Mercedes with Daimler looked like a form of emasculation.

Schrempp paced around the boardroom on the first floor of the Hochhaus, the tall building at the heart of the Möhringen office complex which is now the nerve centre of DaimlerChrysler's operations. The *Klausursitzung* took place in conditions of unusual secrecy. Not even secretaries were allowed to remain in the room for this crucial meeting – only board directors witnessed the showdown.

Schrempp's fellow directors were sitting round a semicircular table.

'Who is for this plan,' he demanded, 'and who is against it?'

This was 16 October 1996, six weeks after Cordes and Grube had first presented the various options to the full board. Over the intervening period, the Freightliners had been racing towards each other. Attempts at compromise had failed; Werner had turned down a variety of positions which would have kept him on board under the new structure. Today was the moment of collision.

Schrempp knew the answer to the question. He had managed to win consensus among six out of his seven boardroom colleagues. The only opposition to Model 6 came from Werner. But the board had yet to take a formal vote. Starting with Manfred Gentz on the left of the table, Schrempp walked around asking each director in turn to provide a brief, reasoned summary of their position. One after another they voiced their support for Model 6. Werner was sitting in the middle of the table. When Schrempp got to him, Schrempp did not ask for his views, moving instead to the right-hand side of the table. One after another the remaining directors gave their vote until Schrempp had worked his way back to Werner. Werner's isolation was exposed as he laid out his by now familiar opposition to the plan – that the integrity of the Mercedes brand could only be preserved if it remained a separate legal entity.

'Well then, Helmut,' said Schrempp. 'We have a choice. It's either going through, in which case the two of us have a problem because there will only be one CEO. Or it's not going through, in which case you might be invited to take my place.'

Up until this point, Werner knew that even if he were a solitary voice on the Daimler-Benz board, he had the support of his boardroom colleagues at Mercedes-Benz. In the next forty-eight hours, his legs were cut from under him as three of the most important auto executives defected to the Schrempp camp.

It was reported in the *Stuttgarter Zeitung* of 17 October

that Jürgen Hubbert (responsible for passenger vehicles), Dieter Zetsche (marketing chief) and Kurt Lauk (commercial vehicles) had held one-on-one conversations with Schrempp during which they had signalled their willingness to join the expanded Daimler-Benz board.

'I appreciate your loyalty,' Schrempp said to each man. 'But could you imagine being on the board of Daimler-Benz?'

He didn't ask for an answer there and then, and before they had time to think things through the newspaper article appeared. Had the trio denied the reports, there would be no future for them at Daimler. Meanwhile the headline alone was enough to undermine Werner's position.

The next step was to take the impasse to the supervisory board. On 6 November Schrempp and Werner went to Frankfurt to explain their positions. The capital side of the supervisory board backed Schrempp's structure, but refused to accept that this meant Werner's departure. 'We support your plan,' Kopper told Schrempp, 'but we want the two of you to go away and come up with a proposal showing how you are going to work together . . . because we need both of you!'

'Helmut,' Schrempp said to Werner after hearing this judgement of Solomon. 'Let's go somewhere and have a chat. Do you have any ideas?'

'I haven't a clue,' said Werner, Schrempp's former boss. Even as the dispute intensified, the two men retained cordial relations, meeting up to discuss their respective positions just as they had done during the campaign to succeed Edzard Reuter.

Although Schrempp had the support of the capital side of the supervisory board, the unions were less pliant. Karl Feuerstein, deputy chairman of this organ and a tough leader of the IG Metall union, publicly condemned Schrempp for letting the conflict degenerate into a naked struggle for power. Schrempp told Feuerstein that he would quit if he did not get his plan through. He went further, saying he would stand aside and let

Werner take over as CEO of the new structure, so long as it was implemented.

'I am so firmly convinced that this is the right thing to do for the company, it absolutely has to get done,' he told the union leader. 'We'd sign the deal and I'd walk out. Of course I'd cry but at the same time I'd be very happy because I would have done the right thing for the company. I want this to happen so why should it stop without me?'

He said the same thing to Helmut Werner. 'If you want the top job instead of me, you can have it,' Schrempp insisted. 'I'm not going to let my personal interests stand in the way of what is best for the company.'

Werner turned it down, saying that he didn't want to have anything to do with the non-automotive parts of the business.

Schrempp tried the same tactic on Hilmar Kopper. 'If you say that again I'll throw you out!' Hilmar Kopper said, not entirely jokingly. The unions also told him this approach was not on – that they didn't want him to go.

If this looked like a gamble, Schrempp had carefully calculated the odds. He was in a formidably strong position, as subsequent events made clear.

Schrempp and Werner went to see Kopper in December in the vain hope of thrashing out a compromise. Werner said that he would accept the structure so long as he could become CFO of the group. Kopper told him that Manfred Gentz was doing a good job and would not be replaced.

In mid-January, the capital side of the supervisory board met at the Deutsche Bank in Frankfurt on the eve of the decisive meeting of the full supervisory board. Schrempp picked Eckhard Cordes to present a neutral assessment of the various options. By now, the board members were thoroughly sick of the technical arguments about holding-company structures. Cordes galloped through the slides, slapping them rapidly one after another on to the overhead projector.

Kopper asked Schrempp to comment on the basic structure.

Not surprisingly he said he was all in favour. The astonishing development came when the same question was put to Werner.

'That's a great structure,' he replied, 'that's just what the company needs.' At this point it dawned on those who were present that they really were going to have to make a choice between Werner and Schrempp.

The two men were sent out of the Deutsche Bank boardroom. Hour after hour went by without a result. Also waiting around outside were Hubbert and Zetsche, who were supposed to be called in to discuss their forthcoming appointment to the board. While Schrempp grew steadily more angry, Kopper and his colleagues were embroiled in an increasingly personal argument about Schrempp and Werner. There was no longer any issue about the structure, as all by now were in favour of Schrempp's plan. Two board members spoke out against Schrempp. The language was personal, they were friends of Werner who disliked Schrempp's combative style.

Kopper fought for Schrempp. Schrempp had proved his worth by sorting out AEG and Fokker and putting Daimler back on a growth track. He had delivered billions of value for the Deutsche Bank as Daimler's biggest shareholder. For him, the case was closed years ago and Werner's attempt to 'have another go' at getting the top job was a frivolous distraction. In the end, the board voted unanimously in favour of Schrempp and his structure.

By this time, Schrempp had flown back to Stuttgart, still seething and dreaming of early retirement in South Africa.

'Hilmar, that's not on,' he said the next morning when Kopper came to see him privately with news of the board's decision ahead of the full supervisory board meeting.

'Relax,' said the banker, 'that's life.'

On the morning of 16 January 1997 Christoph Walther was summoned to a conference room on the eleventh floor of the Hochhaus. Gathered there was the four-man praesidium of the supervisory board (Kopper, Professor Johannes Semmler,

Karl Feuerstein, Bernhard Wurl) together with Schrempp and Werner.

'Dr Walther, would you please sit down,' said Kopper.

Walther took a seat, noting that Werner was looking pale.

'We have agreed a press release. I'll read it to you.'

Kopper read out a brief statement announcing Werner's resignation from the company with effect from the end of the month.

'Please take care that it goes out this afternoon,' Kopper said.

In 2000 Werner is far from the rancorous, embittered man he could have been after losing the struggle with Schrempp. He is calm, tanned and charming. He declares himself fulfilled in his current occupation as chairman of the Hanover Expo Fair.

He refuses to be drawn on the rationale for his tactics during the 1996–7 power battle; the suspicion remains that he misread the degree of support he would garner from the supervisory board. He says he stood up to Schrempp because he was not convinced that his former deputy had the best interests of the automotive division at heart. 'In view of how things turned out,' Werner says magnanimously, 'I was wrong.'

CHAPTER 8

Swimming with Sharks

*Profitable growth – Schrempp's strategic
thinking ahead of the Chrysler deal*

E arly in 1997 Jürgen Schrempp bumped into Eckhard
Cordes in the corridor outside his eleventh-floor office
in Stuttgart Möhringen.

'Eckhard,' quipped Schrempp. 'You must be getting fed up
with selling all these companies. I think it's time to think about
buying something.'

The worst of the restructuring was behind them, the company
had come out of intensive care into a normal hospital ward.
As profits started to climb, full recovery was in sight. With
the holding company structure dealt with, it was indeed time
to start thinking about growth.

However, Daimler's strategy team was acutely sensitive to the
pitfalls of the past. If it were going to pursue growth, it would
not be growth for growth's sake, which they felt had been the
ruling philosophy in the decade to 1995. It would be profitable
growth.

In a presentation given to the board on 1 July 1997, Rüdiger
Grube outlined a new approach. This was part of the annual

129

Konzernstrategiebericht, the highly secret group annual strategic review when all Daimler's divisions put their heads together to assess the company's longer term strategy. Grube explained how Daimler-Benz had doubled its sales in the ten years to 1985 and then again in the following decade. The plan now would be to double again in the ten years to 2005. Such was the magic of compound interest, that translated into growth of 7 per cent a year for each of the next ten years.

In the decade to 1995, he reminded the board, sales had gone up but the value of the company had gone down, dropping from DM65 billion in 1985 to DM34 billion ten years later. To ensure that this would not happen again, the revenue target would be coupled with a commitment to grow both return on capital and the absolute amount of capital employed. This would guarantee financial strength as well as size.

Based on a study of fifty top-performing companies from many different industrial sectors, Grube assured his colleagues that this was the recipe for continuing outperformance of the share price. The point was that in every industry, no matter how unattractive the fundamentals, there were winners and losers. Some steel companies made a lot of money, despite the industry's chronic overcapacity. To take the opposite example, there were some telecoms groups which destroyed shareholder value despite the fantastic expansion of their industry. 'It's not what you do, it's how you do it,' was the message.

There was just one catch, Grube explained. Having cleaned up its industrial portfolio, Daimler-Benz was now predominantly an automotive company. Other activities, for example services and aerospace, were strictly secondary. The problem with being a pure automotive company was that Mercedes-Benz on its own could not generate enough growth to meet what all agreed were perfectly reasonable targets.

The analysis was set out in a secret dossier, copies of which were distributed to each board member at the meeting. Each document was individually numbered to ensure that no copies would be taken. The precaution was understandable as the information was deeply sensitive.

The bottom line was that Daimler-Benz would run out of growth in 2002. This was just five years away, a blink of an eye in the life of a gigantic industrial group like Daimler-Benz. The implications were clear to everyone in the room. Either Daimler-Benz would have to diversify, an unpalatable course of action given the group's recent history. Or it would have to take steps to strengthen its core automotive business.

The board charged Cordes and Grube with investigating the options. They agreed to meet later in the year to discuss the way forward. Meanwhile, two other teams embarked on a similar strategic review. Jürgen Hubbert and his colleagues in the passenger car division carried out their own analysis of Mercedes-Benz and its future within the rapidly evolving automotive industry. At the same time, the Goldman Sachs investment bank carried out a third study. Approaching the same problem from three different perspectives, they reached broadly similar conclusions.

The fundamental conclusion was that the process of consolidation in the auto industry would continue. The number of independent manufacturers in the world (excluding the Koreans) had dwindled from forty-two in 1960 to twenty-eight in 1980 and a mere eighteen by 1997. The next phase of consolidation, perhaps triggered by the inevitable cyclical downturn, would take the total down to a dozen or less. The background was unrelenting competition and massive overcapacity, with the industry able to produce one-quarter more cars than the world needed. Out of 685 car factories in the world, some eighty would have to be shut before production capacity and customer demand could come into equilibrium.

At the same time, competition would intensify and the process of change accelerate. The conclusion was that the auto industry would change as much in the next fifteen years as it had in the past fifty.

Against this background what kind of companies would

131

emerge as winners? The feeling was that three, perhaps four groups would create a global super-league. They would be able to dominate the industry through sheer size and international reach. General Motors, Ford and Toyota looked assured of a seat at the top table. The other place was open.

Daimler reached the conclusion that the successful global automotive company of the future needed to offer a full product range, from the tiniest passenger car to the freight truck. To avoid confusing the customer, the company would have to be multi-brand as one marque would not be able to straddle the entire market. It would have to have genuine global reach. It would have to have a culture of innovation. It would have to have a sustainable cost advantage over its rivals. Only then would such a company be able to maintain leadership during the turbulent years ahead.

By contrast to this ideal, Mercedes-Benz faced serious strategic challenges. This had been recognised as long ago as the early 1990s when Werner and his team concluded that the absolute limit to growth for the stand-alone Mercedes-Benz company would be in the region of 1–1.1million passenger cars. Beyond that level, there simply weren't enough prosperous, middle-class customers in the world. Growth would run out in 2001–2, they predicted.

Even getting to annual sales of 1 million units would be fraught with strategic and operational challenges. Traditionally, Mercedes-Benz competed in the premium segment which accounted for 10 per cent of the total world passenger car market of 40–50 million vehicles. Werner's product offensive was designed to increase volumes by taking Mercedes down-market so that it competed in 20 per cent of the total market. This meant a doubling of the market available to Mercedes, but at what cost to the Mercedes brand?

There was a risk that the brand would be stretched and devalued as the company introduced more and more models. The crunch duly materialised when the A-Class was launched in late 1997. This new model was intended to be Mercedes' answer to small cars such as the VW Golf and the Opel Astra. Mercedes' designers felt that the magic of the Mercedes brand would rub off on this new segment of the market. The initial reaction to the 'Baby Benz' was euphoric. 'No automobile in the world combines the interior space, parking ease, crashworthiness, fuel economy and general engineering brilliance,' commented the *Automotive Industry* journal. 'The most space-efficient passenger car since the 1959 Morris Mini, the new A-Class – the first front-wheel drive Mercedes – redefines automotive design for the twenty-first century ... From this point on, small cars will never be the same.'

By the middle of October Mercedes had taken orders for 100,000 cars, a sell-out which took care of production volumes until the middle of the following year. With most of the new customers never having owned a Mercedes before, it looked as though Mercedes had pulled it off, expanding down-market while preserving its reputation for safety and quality engineering. There were a few Cassandras. Bob Eaton, Chrysler chairman, told a conference that the moment Mercedes started producing compact cars the fabled brand would be damaged. 'No other manufacturer has stretched its brand so far,' he said, prophetically.

In mid-October a Swedish journalist succeeded in overturning the new A-Class during a test drive. He put the car through a particularly aggressive trial, swerving abruptly to avoid an imaginary elk. The car flipped, the photos were published around the world and a hurricane of negative publicity was unleashed.

The story broke for the first time in Germany on 22 October. Daimler directors, gathered in Japan for the Tokyo motor show, were initially inclined to pooh-pooh the story. They suspected sabotage at the hands of competitors and thought – correctly as it turned out – that many of their rivals' cars would also flip if subjected to the same test.

'This is a serious problem,' Schrempp said to his colleagues.

133

'But in every crisis there is an opportunity. I don't know where the opportunity is yet, but we'll find it.'

A crisis team carried out an investigation. The first reaction was similar to that of a man experiencing a heart attack: a stubborn refusal to accept that anything was wrong, despite obvious symptoms. Grudgingly, Mercedes concluded that there were engineering faults. It was indeed easier to overturn the A-Class than other models, although tests on rival cars did show that if you pushed them hard enough they too would end up on their roofs. Part of the problem was solved by introducing the so-called Electronic Stabilisation Programme (ESP), a piece of technology originally designed for the latest generation of S-Classes. Swerve to avoid a moose, and an ESP-equipped car will slow down rather than flipping. Even Nikki Lauda found it impossible to overturn the modified A-Class.

In time, the Mercedes team identified the technical problems and set in motion a programme to put them right. The cars were called in for modifications on a purely voluntary basis. However, the negative headlines continued. Mercedes became a laughing stock. A Thuringian newspaper performed an elk test on an antiquated Trabant. The car proved impossible to flip, suggesting improbably that a Trabi was safer than a Mercedes-Benz. Books of elk jokes were published and the crisis escalated. It had reached a point where the facts of the matter were far less relevant than perceptions of it, and the principal emotion governing the reaction of the German press and public was *Schadenfreude*, glee at the arrogant Mercedes' misfortunes. Recognising that desperate times require desperate remedies, Schrempp intervened directly.

Schrempp took counsel from a hastily assembled group of experts who gathered at his home on the evening of Sunday, 9 November 1997. Among this group were Eckhard Cordes; Manfred Bischoff; Mike Taylor, the chairman of the Bell Pottinger PR agency; Konstantin Jacoby of the Jacoby & Springer advertising agency; and Christoph Walther, the company's top in-house PR official. Over a salad of pepperoni and mozzarella cheese, they sat in his living room and discussed the options.

As Schrempp saw it, there were three choices.

First, you could continue to modify the cars and hope that customers would understand that this was enough to deal with the problem.

Second, stop production and order a formal recall – dramatic steps which would reinforce the message that Mercedes was taking the problem seriously, but would contradict its assertion to date that the cars were fundamentally safe.

Third, a compromise of the above: stop deliveries of new vehicles, maintain production (albeit at lower levels) and offer customers incentives to have the cars modified.

'We have to jump ahead of the competition,' Schrempp said, 'we have to do the unexpected. Even if the car is absolutely fine as it is, we have to take dramatic steps.'

The next day, Schrempp convened a second meeting. This time, all Daimler board members were there, together with a number of outside experts, including Matthias Mosler from Goldman Sachs; the deputy editor of a leading German news magazine; and the head of a Mercedes dealership.

There was a heated discussion in which the journalist and the investment banker spoke out in favour of a 'Big Bang' recall. The car guys were equally passionately opposed to a recall: 'Take the car off the market and it will be dead,' they argued. It had never been done before in the history of the auto industry.

It may be that we will be dead anyway, Schrempp thought.

'Thank you, gentlemen, that's very helpful,' Schrempp said, after letting the debate take its course.

The outsiders withdrew, leaving the board directors on their own.

'I've got to get the emotional buy-in of my colleagues,' Schrempp said to himself. 'If they don't buy in to whatever we decide, the risks increase.'

Without showing his hand, he went round the table asking each one of the directors to express an opinion. 'Having heard all the arguments this morning,' he asked, 'what would be the right thing to do?'

One by one, the directors came out in favour of Schrempp's preferred approach: a three-month ban on new deliveries while existing owners were given a replacement C-Class and their cars were brought in to be modified.

'Mercedes-Benz is committed by its heritage to building only the best,' said Schrempp, when it was clear that a consensus had emerged.

The tough decision cost the company DM600 million, but it rescued the reputation of the brand. Overnight, the public mood changed. Mercedes met its deadline to correct all problems within three months. It took out advertisements to apologise for its mistakes and its unaccustomed humility won broad sympathy.

Schrempp was able to turn the crisis into an opportunity. It was not simply a question of making public relations mileage. After the three months were up, all A-Classes were equipped with ESP as a standard feature. This put pressure on rivals such as VW to introduce this technology into this class of cars and for a while Mercedes-Benz enjoyed a significant competitive advantage.

However, the A-Class affair still served to highlight the perils of the move down-market. The lesson is that it is not that easy to enter a new segment of the auto market from scratch, even when you are Mercedes.

For that reason the Smart cars do not carry the Mercedes star. These stylish, diminutive vehicles look more like motorised golf carts than automobiles. Developed in conjunction with Nicholas Hayek, the Lebanese entrepreneur who invented Swatch watches, they may well represent the future of urban driving. But Mercedes is not taking any chances. It has learned its lesson from the A-Class affair and the brands are kept separate. Meanwhile the Smart car has cost its parent company many hundreds of millions in development costs.

* * *

The move down-market was driven by a hunger for volume.

Giant producers such as General Motors (nearly 8 million units produced in 1997), Toyota (more than 5 million), Ford (around 7 million), or Volkswagen (4 million plus) enjoy huge bargaining power with suppliers. They spend tens of billions a year on components and services that go into the making of cars. This translates into economies of scale and a lower cost per individual car produced. Ultimately, the result is higher profits and returns for shareholders.

It is a virtuous circle as larger companies are better able to preserve a technological advantage over their rivals. New technology is typically introduced at the top of a company's range and then 'cascaded' down through the full range of the company's products. So a new steering device or braking technology is introduced first in the S-Class, then in the E-Class, the C-Class and so on. At Ford, the new technology would be launched in Jaguar or Aston Martin and then rolled out across the full range of brands from Lincoln to Volvo and ultimately the little Ford Fiesta. The more cars, the cheaper the cost of developing the new technology on a per unit basis. Crudely, that means that a bigger company can spend a lot more money on research and development than a smaller one.

According to Professor Garel Rhys of Cardiff Business School, the comfort zone starts at around 2 million units. At this level, manufacturing and financial economies of scale start to take effect. Below this the components supplier is obliged on cost grounds to sell the technology to more than one customer. The low-volume company faces a crippling battle to stay competitive.

For Mercedes-Benz, traditionally the world's leader in automotive technology, the challenge was particularly acute. For most of the post-war era it had operated in an environment where innovations such as anti-lock brakes or airbags or electric windows gave it a long advantage over its rivals. After all, it was the dominant player at the top end of the market and

137

so enjoyed the benefits of a quasi-monopoly: it could charge a premium price for its products without curtailing demand. But by the early 1990s automotive technology was becoming increasingly generic. The premium end of the market was no longer hermetically sealed from the rest of the industry. New competitors such as Toyota's Lexus and VW's revamped Audi brand started to muscle into Mercedes' patch, while BMW's 3 Series went from strength to strength. One by one premium manufacturers such as Jaguar or Rolls-Royce were acquired by industry giants. The period of technological advantage was shrinking, and with it the opportunity to charge premium prices. Mercedes' entire business model was under threat.

It was a similar threat that drove BMW, Mercedes' long-standing domestic rival, to acquire Rover in 1994. The purchase of the British volume car manufacturer was designed to take BMW's production levels into the comfort zone. The implementation went disastrously wrong, with BMW obliged to throw billions of pounds at the ailing British subsidiary without any sign of a profit. Finally, in early 2000, it decided to pull out altogether. BMW sold Rover to a consortium of Midlands industrialists for a nominal £10 – the end of a disastrous engagement. Privately, Mercedes executives admit that BMW's deal influenced their own strategic thinking. By introducing the A-Class and Smart, Mercedes was trying to replicate internally what BMW was hoping to achieve by acquisition.

To little avail. The various studies conducted by Daimler and its advisors during 1997 exposed the stark outlines of Mercedes' dilemma. Even though it competed only in 20 per cent of the world market, the remaining 80 per cent of the market was in effect out of bounds. It was missing out on the strong growth of entirely new passenger vehicle segments, for example people carriers. Its presence in another fast-growing area, the sports utility vehicles segment, was limited to the M-Class. It also faced geographical constraints. For a non-US firm it had a relatively strong presence in the North American market, the biggest market for passenger cars in the world, but

Benz and Cie launches the world's first patented motor car in 1888.

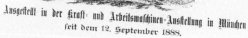

Wilhelm Maybach at the steering wheel of a Daimler motorised vehicle dating from 1889. The car had a top speed of 18 kmph.

Karl Benz driving one of the third generation of patented motor cars, 1890.

Emil Jellinek and his daughter Mercedes, whose name became one of the world's most famous brands.

Family outing in the first Mercedes of 1901. Adolf Daimler, son of the founder, is in the passenger seat.

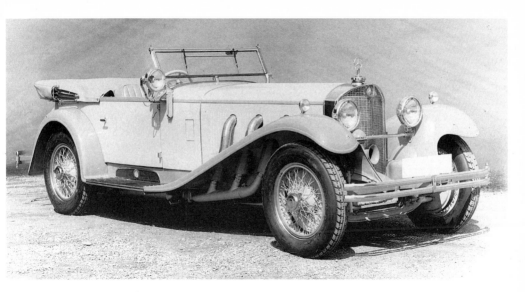

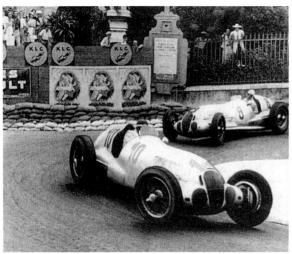

Above Speed and elegance – the hallmark of this 1928 sports car.

Left The legendary triple victory in the Monaco Grand Prix, 1930.

Below Juan Manuel Fangio wins the 1954 French Grand Prix in the W196 'Silver Arrow'.

Daimler's workshops in Stuttgart-Unterturkheim. The year is 1944 and they are in ruins, the victim of Allied bomb attacks.

The first model to be produced after the war, the 170V which appeared in 1947.

The 1950s: The Mercedes-Benz 300d Cabriolet.

The 1960s: The wing-doored Mercedes-Benz 300SL Coupé.

The 1970s: The Mercedes-Benz 450 SL.

Walter P Chrysler, the legendary founder of the company that bears his name, next to his first Chrysler model in 1924.

Robert Eaton with Walter P Chrysler's tool-box.

Walter P Chrysler and his 'three musketeers' – the innovative engineers Breer, Zeder and Skelton.

The futuristic Chrysler 'Airflow 8' won the Concours d'Elegance prize in 1934–1935.

The Chrysler Town and Country, one of the top models of it's era,
dating from 1946.

The model 300F, a typically stylish Chrysler car from 1960.

again Daimler had limited scope to grow beyond its up-market niche. In Asia, too, Daimler had a very profitable business, but a small share of the total market.

On the commercial vehicle side, Daimler was looking for opportunities to grow. Daimler-Benz was the largest manufacturer of commercial vehicles in the world and had to start thinking about acquisitions. In due course, the company would open discussions with Nissan Diesel, the commercial vehicle arm of the Japanese automotive group.

In the early autumn of 1997 Schrempp and his inner circle of trusted colleagues and advisors sat down to digest the implications of the analysis. Under one scenario, Daimler-Benz could have continued as an independent manufacturer of premium cars. But this would have been a recipe for stagnation. The reality in a world of open capital markets was that Daimler would not have the luxury to stagnate. 'We realised that we could only survive if we merged or had a partner,' Schrempp said later.

The question of survival was brought into sharp relief when the Daimler team heard a rumour a couple of months later that Ford had approached Goldman Sachs for advice on how to structure a hostile takeover bid for Daimler-Benz. Goldman, long-time advisors to Ford, turned down the mandate as in September they had been appointed by Daimler to advise on international acquisitions. This story confirmed the logic of Schrempp's thinking. Despite the dramatic rise in the share price since Schrempp had taken over, Daimler-Benz was vulnerable.

Paradoxically, the very actions that triggered the rise in the share price made the company more susceptible to an unfriendly takeover. For as long as AEG or Fokker were part of the Daimler portfolio, they acted as a poison-pill deterrent to potential predators. Now that Schrempp had disposed of the loss-makers, the company was all the more attractive to others. Capitalised at $30 billion, it was a relatively digestible morsel for a company as big as Toyota, GM or Ford. As Mannesmann would later find, you can be vulnerable even when you do all the right things – such are the laws of the international capital markets by which Schrempp had chosen to abide.

Deutsche Bank's large minority stake, 22 per cent by this time, was a worry rather than a consolation. 'If the bank decided to sell the stake we would go straight into someone else's portfolio,' recalls one Daimler executive. 'We didn't want to play along with that at all.'

Daimler had a choice: to take the initiative in the inevitable consolidation process, or wait passively for something to happen. If it did the latter, Daimler faced the prospect of ending up like Rolls-Royce, the eminent British manufacturer of luxury cars which in the following year would see its independence come to an end. Or like Jaguar, which is now a subsidiary of Ford. Or indeed like BMW, the fellow German company with a prestigious brand name but with no chance of evolving into one of the industry's handful of global leaders.

Given Schrempp's personality, it was clear which path would be taken. He decided to be proactive – to redefine the rules of the game.

The open questions were: with whom should Daimler do a deal? And how would such a deal be done?

Consolidation in the automotive industry is like an elaborate eighteenth-century dance in which everybody walks a few steps with everybody else. The participants all know that the dance is a ritual prelude to deeper commitment in the form of marriage. But only when the music stops does it become clear who will end up with whom.

Put more prosaically, the industry is a tangled thicket of joint ventures, co-operation agreements, participations, cross-holding and informal alliances. At various times in the past decade Mercedes-Benz has held talks with Mitsubishi, General Motors, Renault, Nissan, Fiat, Ford and Chrysler. Chrysler talked to Fiat, Nissan, Renault, Hyundai, BMW, Volvo and Mitsubishi. The same is true of other auto companies: they are a flirtatious, if not downright promiscuous bunch.

They all know that they are operating in a mature industry and association with others is one route to success. Like most human organisations, though, their behaviour is determined as much by emotional considerations as logic. Companies would prefer to remain independent for as long as possible and a joint venture which falls short of a full merger is one way of putting off the evil day. Typically, companies struggle along on their own until such time as they encounter recession or other unforeseen difficulties and are obliged to seek a partner from a position of weakness. For that reason, all the deals in the sector in the past decade have been takeovers of the weak by the strong. Then it is less a courtly dance than a feeding frenzy among sharks. All the players want to swim with the sharks. They do not want to end up as lumps of bloody meat.

The DaimlerChrysler merger would mean a profound break with convention. This time, it would be two icons coming together from a position of strength. In the event, the deal was arresting precisely because neither party felt under pressure to rush into the arms of the other at that particular time.

All the in-depth analysis showed that Chrysler was the obvious partner for Daimler-Benz. The fit with Mercedes-Benz was very snug. From a geographical perspective, Mercedes was strong where Chrysler was weak. Chrysler had a mere 1 per cent share of the European market. In the US it sold 2.9 million vehicles, compared to just 122,200 sold by Mercedes.

From the product point of view, the two companies were also highly complementary. Chrysler had a dominant position in the fast-growing mini-van and sport utility vehicles segment of the US market. The only area of direct overlap was between the Jeep Grand Cherokee and the M-Class, though even here the two off-road vehicles are sufficiently differentiated so as not to cannibalise each other's sales. The Jeep has a long off-road heritage while the M-Class is built for on-road cruising with off-road capability.

The growth would come from access to each other's markets. Products would be enhanced by complementary engineering

141

and production know-how. Chrysler was an acknowledged leader in developing innovative cars, bringing them quickly and profitably to the market. This was a useful counterbalance to Mercedes' own production-driven culture. It was also a skilful and effective purchaser of components and supplies. There would be significant potential synergies when the two companies pooled their $70 billion purchasing power.

'The combination is highly complementary,' commented the powerful Merrill Lynch investment bank when the deal was announced. 'It will allow each company to achieve its long-term objectives without the expensive and risky proposition of starting from scratch. DaimlerChrysler has leaped into contention for the prize of being one of the top three industry participants in an industry that may not have room for four.'

The merged company would come close to the ideal developed by Schrempp and his planners. It would have a balanced portfolio of vehicles in every major category and price class around the world. It would have a superior portfolio of brands. It would have world-class design and technical expertise. It would be financially strong and extremely profitable.

There was one strategic weakness: the combined company would have a sub-10 per cent share of the attractive market in Asia. This would be addressed in 2000 when Daimler-Benz took a controlling interest in Mitsubishi Motors.

Presented in this way, the merger of these two companies looks like a 'no-brainer'. This, ultimately, was the conclusion of both companies' shareholders, of the unions represented at both companies, of politicians on both sides of the Atlantic. It is surprising that all the experts inside and outside the industry had never speculated about this fit before it was announced in May 1998.

In practice, however, getting the two companies to the altar was far from straightforward. Daimler had a roving eye and was playing the field before alighting on a partner of choice.

Schrempp had taken a fancy to Honda, the most international of the Japanese auto groups. His admiration for the company dated back to his time in South Africa when he allowed Honda cars to be built in Mercedes' factories. Honda has a 7.5 per cent share of the US market and has successfully positioned itself as a premium manufacturer within the mass market. An alliance with Daimler would have addressed the German company's lack of penetration in Asia while adding to its market share in the US. The feeling in the Schrempp camp was that the cultural fit would be good, notwithstanding the fundamental difficulties of merging with a Japanese company. However, initial soundings among a few of the company's investors made it clear that Honda was not available.

'It takes two to tango and they didn't want to dance,' Schrempp said.

Other companies were considered, and ruled out. General Motors was deemed too big and bulky, and Daimler would end up being junior partner. Toyota was too expensive and too Japanese and therefore impractical. BMW and Volkswagen: a merger with either of the domestic companies would never get through on competition grounds, and even if it did the resulting job losses would be a political nightmare. Renault was a possibility, but with the French government owning nearly half the shares a deal with the heavily indebted company would be unattractive. Peugeot, Fiat, Volvo – none of these European champions would propel Daimler into the emerging super-league of global automotive giants. The Koreans – they were available, but the Korean market represented the greatest concentration of overcapacity in the world. Nissan was a possibility that would be explored very seriously at a later date, but the scale of its financial problems made the Japanese company unattractive.

That left Ford, the originator of the mass-produced motor car and a great emblem of Americana. Ford would later make a flirtatious approach to Daimler. The German company was by no means unreceptive and the two companies kept in contact with each other throughout the negotiations with Chrysler. But with the Ford family dominating the share register, it would be impossible to structure a deal that would leave Daimler-Benz in the driving seat.

Notwithstanding the other possibilities, Chrysler was the favourite. Together, Daimler and Chrysler would change the dynamics of the global automotive market. The combined group would leapfrog Toyota to become the world's third biggest automotive manufacturer after General Motors and Ford. It would be nearly twice as big as Volkswagen, its closest European rival. The merged company would enjoy what investment bankers term 'first mover advantage': having combined ahead of anyone else, DaimlerChrysler would approach the next phase of consolidation from a position of strength. DaimlerChrysler would be one of the largest and most profitable car companies in the world, with a leading position in many of the market segments in which it operates: the premium car market, in mini-vans, off-road and commercial vehicles. Manufacturing nearly 4 million cars a year, it would enjoy the benefits of volume while preserving its status as a specialist vehicle producer.

This is how it looked on paper.

However, there was a complication: last time the two companies had talked, it had been a disaster.

Chrysler had already inspected Mercedes-Benz as a potential bride, and the two companies had parted company without a result. This was two years before, back in 1995–6 when hundreds of people on both sides had gone through seven rounds of negotiations over a period of eight months with nothing to show for it.

It will be remembered that the trigger for the original talks was Kirk Kerkorian's bid for Chrysler. This led to discussions about the possibility of a cross-participation whereby Chrysler would have bought some shares in Daimler-Benz and Daimler would have bought a reciprocal holding in Chrysler. 'With Kerkorian complaining that we didn't have an international strategy,' recalls one of the Chrysler participants in these early discussions, 'it would have been very useful to turn round and say "Whaddya mean we don't have an international strategy?" Daimler has just bought 10 or 15 per cent of our shares.'

'It would have been a much better story to say they'd found a partner with tremendous growth opportunities,' said a member of the German negotiation team.

The stake would have been a useful counterweight to Kerkorian's holding and it would have signalled the beginnings of a useful co-operation between the two companies. Within weeks, however, Kerkorian's bid foundered, as the investor was not able to secure financing for his proposal. Although this meant that Chrysler no longer had an urgent need for a 'white knight' to rescue it from the unfriendly bid, the two companies carried on talking. 'We really admire you guys, you're doing everything right,' was Werner's message. 'We should explore the possibility of doing something together.'

The talks thus moved in a different direction. Mercedes and Chrysler compared notes about the evolution of the auto markets. They found that they shared a number of common assumptions, chiefly that growth potential in North America and Europe was limited. Much more exciting were the possibilities in the fast-growing economies of Asia, South America and Africa.

Mercedes had come to the conclusion that long-term growth would be in these developing economies, but that as a premium car manufacturer it was locked out from this opportunity. It did, however, have a distribution network through which Chrysler's products could be channelled. The plan had been to maintain the status quo in Europe and the North American markets, but to combine resources in the rest of the world. Thus emerged the possibility of setting up a jointly owned entity which would be responsible for manufacturing and marketing cars in the world excluding Europe and North America. Code-named Q-Star, the new company would be owned 50:50 by the two parties.

The two sides threw some of their top executives at the

project. Reporting to Eaton were Tom Gale and Jim Holden, while Helmut Werner worked with Jürgen Hubbert and Dieter Zetsche. They became tremendously enthusiastic about Q-Star. In their wilder moments they constructed growth forecasts which showed that within a few years the new construct would be so much bigger than its parent companies that it would be in a position to buy both of them out. Eaton offered Lutz the job of heading up the new entity, saying it would be an interesting challenge for Lutz in his retirement.

The trouble was that the structure was neither fish nor fowl: it fell a long way short of a full merger but it was much more ambitious than a joint venture. They went through round after round of negotiations and hundreds of people became involved. 'It was like a party convention in the old East Germany,' Eaton said a lot later. If they were going to make a success of it this time round, they would have to keep the negotiating teams a lot smaller.

It rankled with the Americans that the talks were never carried out at the highest level. 'Don't you think you should get your CEO involved?' Lutz recalled asking Helmut Werner. Werner was reluctant to involve Schrempp. The tenor of his response was that as he spoke for 80 per cent of the group's profits he could pretty much do what he liked. This, it would turn out, was a fatal misconception of his own power.

The two sides did not manage to clarify exactly how Q-Star would operate. On 9 October 1995 Bob Eaton and Helmut Werner visited Schrempp in his Stuttgart office to present their plans. Standing at his flip-chart, Schrempp asked a series of questions about the practicalities of such an agreement: who would manage the venture? Who would decide where investment was channelled? How would marketing be organised? How would they allocate costs and share profits? The killer question was: what would they do when the new company started exporting its products into Europe and North America? The subsidiary could end up competing with its parent company.

It was obvious to Schrempp that the structure would not work. The fate of the discussions was sealed.

On the American side, Jim Holden was given the job of visiting the various locations where the joint venture was supposed to take effect. He went to Latin America, where he was horrified at Mercedes' antiquated truck factories and its high cost structures. Not a fair trade, he thought. Chrysler would bring all the interesting product opportunities to this market, while Mercedes brought a loss-making truck operation in need of considerable investment. He went to India where Mercedes was proposing to sell C- and A-Classes. He rode around the rutted roads of Puna in search of the mooted middle-class customers. He visited Indonesia and Thailand before coming to the conclusion that there was no point in pursuing the deal.

'We're taking the worst of both worlds,' he told the Chrysler board in January 1996. 'We're going to partner up everywhere in the world where we are both weak. In any case, joint ventures don't work, we'll spend all our time arguing about who made the money and what we should charge each other ... and Mercedes is proposing to throw in their truck business which hasn't had any serious investment for twenty years. It's not a fair deal.'

His advice on India was even more succinct: 'Fly over the country in twenty years' time. If you see roads, land. At the moment, the market is simply not there.'

There were one or two places in the developing world where it would have made sense for the two to have combined. But the danger of entering into non-committal joint ventures in strategically insignificant places such as Thailand was that it could have poisoned the relationship between the two companies for the future. 'Either marry, get in bed all the way,' was his advice, 'or you'll end up hating each other.'

There was goodwill on both sides when the talks ended, but this was soon dissipated for the Germans. A few weeks later, they received a courtesy call from the Americans, informing them that Chrysler's affections had transferred elsewhere. The

Americans had gone straight from the talks with Mercedes-Benz into a joint venture with BMW – a project to build a new engine plant in Curitiba, Brazil. The new plant would provide Chrysler and Rover with small four-cylinder engines, but it was easy to jump to the conclusion that the arrangement would be a prelude to a closer relationship or merger. The cultural and industrial fit looked good and they were both independent, regional champions.

Through the first four months of 1998, the Chrysler–BMW link would prove useful camouflage for Daimler and Chrysler as they pursued their negotiations. The universal assumption was that Chrysler had pledged its hand to the Bavarians. Indeed, this is why Ford felt free to approach Daimler-Benz as it assumed the talks between Daimler and Chrysler would never be revived.

One of the reasons for the failure of the original talks was the convoluted corporate structure. Schrempp was sure that the abolition of Mercedes as a separate company would make things a lot easier this time round. But it meant that very early on in the negotiations he would have to demonstrate that Daimler was a very different company from the one that had held talks a couple of years earlier.

He took counsel from Jon Corzine of Goldman Sachs. The banker told Schrempp that geography, different legal systems and business cultures, personalities, accounting rules – all would present formidable obstacles to doing a deal. But, he went on to say, the deal could be done. There was no point in trying to do it against the will of Chrysler management, he advised; a hostile bid for a company that had been bailed out by the US taxpayer would be doomed to failure. It would have to be friendly, it would have to be a merger.

'So how should I go about it then?' Schrempp asked Corzine.

'Do it the way you always do these things,' replied the venerable senior partner of Goldman Sachs. 'Go and talk to him!'

Throughout the last quarter of 1997 nobody at Daimler-Benz outside Schrempp's inner circle had the faintest idea that the deliberations had reached this level of specificity. Indeed when Grube returned to the boardroom in November to give the follow-up to his August presentation, the board simply mandated Schrempp and the strategy team to develop ideas for expanding the Mercedes car and commercial vehicle business.

By that time, the first contact with Chrysler had been made.

CHAPTER 9

A Perfect Storm

Chrysler is open to offers

1 October 1997

Bob Eaton, chairman and CEO of Chrysler Corporation, is addressing the company's annual senior management meeting at Auburn Hills. As preparation for this get-together of the company's top auto executives, he distributes a copy of Sebastian Junger's *A Perfect Storm*, the bestselling account of a storm which converges on three fronts to sink a fishing boat off the coast of Massachusetts.

'I'm sure some of you have read this book,' Eaton says. 'For those who haven't, it's a true story about some fishermen who set out on a pleasant October afternoon five years ago for the Grand Banks off Newfoundland.

'But heading for the same area from the south was Hurricane Grace . . . and from the west, a cold front that had formed over the Great Lakes . . . and from the Arctic, a nor'easter. All three came together in the same spot on the ocean and formed the kind of perfect storm that might happen every hundred years or so.

'Read that book and you learn that when a seventy-two-foot boat tries to climb a hundred-foot wave and doesn't make it, it slides back down the face of the wave, out of control . . . plunges into the trough, stern-first . . . and then the wave breaks over it and buries it under tons of water.

'Sometimes the boat bobs back up. Sometimes it doesn't.'

A 'perfect storm' was brewing around the auto industry, Eaton elaborated. The first front was overcapacity; he predicted that in four years' time worldwide capacity would be 79 million units chasing demand of only 61 million.

The second front was the retail revolution. 'For the first time in the hundred years of this industry, there are some fundamental changes taking place in the way a car or a truck goes to the consumer. Let's face it, the factory and the dealer have controlled that process for a century. We've prospered with it. It's been good for the customer as well.

'But now along comes the internet . . . buy-by-phone organis- ations . . . superstore auto retailing . . . public companies buying up the old mom and pop stores . . . and who knows what's next?'

Eaton predicted that power would shift away from the auto manufacturers and the dealer networks to the consumer.

'For the first time, the customer is going to control the retail system,' Eaton said. 'Everything will be out in the open. The customer will have all the information about the vehicle and its price before she walks into the dealership. She's not going to be intimidated any more because of what she doesn't know. With a few strokes of a computer keyboard, she'll know everything that the salesman knows.'

The third storm, slower to build up but ultimately more forceful, would come about as a result of fundamental change in automotive technology. Chrysler, like all other car manu- facturers, was investing heavily in new propulsion systems. It would shortly unveil a diesel-electric hybrid and its research into fuel cell technology was also advanced. The pressure to develop environment-friendly cars was coming from governments and from society at large. It was irresistible.

Sooner or later, perhaps as soon as 2005, internal combustion engines would be obsolete. 'Never before has it been more difficult for companies to make investment decisions,' Eaton said. 'For example, we're building a new V-6 engine plant in Detroit to go into production in the year 2002. An engine plant today costs up to $1 billion. Traditionally, we would expect that engine to stay in production for fifteen to twenty years, and the plant itself to last about fifty years.'

If the internal combustion engine had been discarded by the middle of the next decade, it would mean gutting the new plant long before earning back the investment. Amid all these perils, what was the moral of the tale for the good ship Chrysler? Would she be tossed about in the storms and slip beneath the waves? Or would she negotiate a safe passage to calmer waters?

In the book, the lesson was that there's only one way to survive the 'perfect storm'. 'Don't go there!' expounded Eaton. 'Don't be at that place in the ocean where the three storms come together. Think ahead. Heed the warnings. Be somewhere else.'

The speech, which would be recycled to many different audiences in the months ahead, produced mixed reactions among senior Chrysler managers. Some ignored the content and were amazed at Eaton's largesse. 'Great speech, but Jesus you gave away all these books at $24.95 to 400 people!' exclaimed one colleague. Expenditure on this scale ran counter to Chrysler's scrupulously cost-conscious culture.

Others found the diagnosis compelling, but thought Eaton's tone was defeatist. At a time when Chrysler was experiencing record sales and profits, it seemed Cassandra-like to harp on about the problems ahead. 'My feeling was that there are always storm clouds,' recalled one fellow director. 'You just have to forge ahead and do the best job you can . . . and it's just as tough on your competitors as it is on you. Hopefully when you get there the storm clouds have receded.'

The triple storm message was the outward expression of a period of intense self-analysis for Chrysler. The company was enjoying unprecedented success, but where would it go from here? By the time of the speech, Eaton and his fellow directors were close to an answer. They were minded to merge, to abandon their cherished independence.

By 1997, Eaton had reached the conclusion that Chrysler could not possibly achieve the second of its two strategic objectives. The first, it will be remembered, was to become the premier car company in North America by 1996. This target had been met. The second was to become the premier auto company *in the world* by the year 2000. This was just not going to happen.

The weakness lay with Chrysler's international operations. No post-war CEO had managed to get to grips with the problem of how to expand outside the borders of North America. There was a historic reluctance to commit cash to build or buy foreign operations, out of fear that a domestic recession would coincide with a period of heavy investment overseas. The only high-quality foreign asset that remained at the beginning of the 1980s was the stake in Mitsubishi, and even this had to be sold under the terms of the Loan Guarantee Act. There had been a flirtation with Fiat in the dark days of 1990–91, but this would have been a pure takeover of the ailing American company at the nadir of its fortunes and Lutz and many other senior executives had fought to block the deal. Once Chrysler was back on its feet again in the early 1990s, its sole realistic option was to export Chrysler vehicles from the US to foreign markets – which it did with great success.

Between 1993 and 1996 revenues from overseas sales rose from $1.5 billion to more than $5 billion, and the number of vehicles sold climbed to 225,000. It was profitable business, but by 1997 sales had reached a plateau. 'We had to ask ourselves whether we could do everything organically, or whether we needed a larger vision,' recalled Tom Gale, who was responsible for international operations in the mid-1990s. 'We reached the conclusion that doing it on our own was just not possible, it

Edward Reuter, chairman of the Daimler-Benz Management Board from 1987–1995.

Alfred Herrhausen, from 1988 to his assassination in 1989 the 'speaker' of the Deutsche Bank Management Board and the chairman of the Daimler-Benz Supervisory Board.

Lee Iacocca, chairman and CEO of the Chrysler Corporation, 1979–1993.

Jürgen Schrempp, chairman and CEO of Daimler-Benz from 1995–1998. After the merger with Chrysler, co-chairman until 2000 when he took over as sole chairman and CEO.

Hilman Kopper, chairman of the Deutsche Bank Supervisory Board, chairman of Daimler-Benz Supervisory Board and one of the key players behind the deal.

Chrysler chairman Robert Eaton *(left)* and president Robert Lutz pose on the front of the Chrysler Prowler.

London, 7th May 1998, Jürgen Schrempp and Robert Eaton have one last look at the merger agreement . . .

. . . then sign the deal.

Getting to know each other, Schrempp and Eaton in Auburn Hills,
17th June 1998, in front of the new Chrysler 300M.

Detroit, 18th June 1998. The co-chairmen take a walk through the
Chrysler workshops.

New York, 17th November 1998. The new company's shares are about to be traded for the first time. *From left to right:* Jürgen Schrempp, Robert Eaton and Richard Grasso, chairman of the New York Stock Exchange.

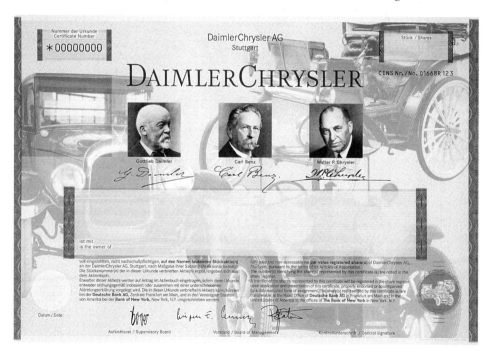

The DaimlerChrysler share certificate with the portraits of the firm's founders: Gottlieb Daimler, Karl Benz and Walter P Chrysler.

Winning Teams

From left to right: Eckhard Cordes, Rüdiger Grube, Lydia Deininger and
Jürgen Schrempp, May 1998 in New York.

From left to right: Karl-Heinz Zimmermann, Jürgen Schrempp, Lydia Deininger, David
Coulthard, Jürgen Hubbert and Norbert Haug at the Formula One race in Monte Carlo,
May 2000.

Schrempp with US President Bill Clinton, 18th May 1998.

Meeting of the International Advisors Board.
From left to right: Jürgen Schrempp, Katsuhiko Kawasoe, president of
Mitsubishi Motors and former US President George Bush, July 2000.

19th April 2000, Jürgen Schrempp addressing shareholders
at the Annual General Meeting in Berlin.

Jürgen Schrempp and German Chancellor Gerhard Schröder, 3rd June 2000.

takes for ever and the investment is much greater than if you do it in a co-operative fashion.'

There was one further consideration. Kirk Kerkorian's bid for the company had left its psychological scars. True, it had failed. Kerkorian and Eaton had eventually reached an accommodation under which the Las Vegas investor undertook not to increase his holding while Chrysler agreed to step up its share buy-back programme. A representative of Kerkorian's investment company had joined the Chrysler board. After the harsh words, Eaton and Kerkorian had learned to respect one another and had even become friends.

But the failed bid had raised questions for which there were still no answers. 'It was the wake-up call that told us we're vulnerable even when we're healthy,' said Jim Holden. 'It told us we're not big enough to be takeover-proof or recession-proof. It was proof that when we try to hoard cash as protection against the bad times, even that didn't work.

'We realised we were so much better at handling bad times than success, but then again that's not surprising as we have had so little practice at the latter.'

Kerkorian's presence on the share register was a constant reminder of the perils of going it alone. One slip-up, and the company would be 'in play' – vulnerable to an unwelcome takeover attempt. Very likely, if the shares slumped back down to where they had been, Kerkorian himself would engineer a break-up bid, with or without an industrial partner. With Kerkorian sitting on a 13.8 per cent stake, Chrysler was predisposed to finding a strategic partner.

Tom Gale sums up the thinking in late 1997: 'If you accept the fact that a certain amount of consolidation is inevitable over time, and if you accept the fact that it will be difficult to do things organically, then the choice is: who is the best partner? If the best one comes along, why not seize the opportunity? Or would you rather wait around and do it with someone infinitely less attractive?'

PART 3

Negotiations and Love Songs

CHAPTER 10

A Game of Poker

The first contact is made

Schrempp first suspected that Chrysler would be willing to play ball in September 1997. He found himself sitting next to Bob Lutz for dinner at the Frankfurt auto show. There was a particularly boring speech during which the guests on Schrempp's table formed little clusters and engaged in deep conversation to prevent themselves falling asleep. At one end of the table Wolfgang Reitzle of BMW was talking to Ferdinand Piech of Volkswagen. At the other end, Schrempp and Lutz started to kick around a few ideas.

'Look, what went wrong last time round?' Schrempp asked. Back in 1995 the plan had been to preserve Chrysler North America and Mercedes-Benz Europe as independent companies and create a new joint venture for international marketing. With hundreds of people involved in discussions that lasted for six months, the structure had proved unwieldy and unworkable.

'It was neither fish nor fowl,' said Lutz, voicing his constant complaint about the earlier talks. 'It was far too big and complex to be a joint venture and yet it would have fallen far short of a merger.'

He went on to explain that the Q-Star construct would have been enormous and would have consumed huge amounts of resource and investment. The two sides would have ended squabbling over who paid for what, not the case in a full-scale merger.

'Come on, that was not a very good concept, but in principle the two companies should work together in one way or another,' Schrempp said. 'If we are agreed that the joint venture doesn't work then maybe we should do a merger.'

'Whoah!' exclaimed Lutz, surprised at the turn the conversation had taken. 'You're right, though, that's where the logic takes you.'

'So why don't we get together and talk about this?'

'You can't talk to the Vice-Chairman about this sort of thing,' Lutz replied. 'You've got to talk to the CEO.'

'Well, you run the place, don't you,' said Schrempp, only half joking.

'On a day-to-day basis I do run the show but when it comes to an important thing like do we merge you've got to talk to Bob, the other Bob; he's the Jürgen Schrempp of Chrysler.'

Lutz said he should talk to Eaton. While Lutz went back to Detroit and reported the conversation to Eaton, the next day Schrempp asked his secretary to call Eaton's office to fix up an appointment. The earliest the two men could make was early January during the Detroit motor show.

Eaton didn't take the news from Lutz very seriously. In fact, it did not register with him that the Germans were seriously considering a merger. He thought that Schrempp was interested in reopening the wishy-washy discussions of 1995. 'We walked away from the first lot of talks and had no wish to get into those kind of discussions all over again,' Eaton recalled later.

By the time the January meeting came around, Eaton had forgotten about the reason for the appointment. 'The meeting just showed up in my calendar,' said Eaton later. 'You know I thought it would be a courtesy call. CEOs are always popping in for a chat during the motor show and this one didn't register as anything out of the ordinary.'

It was not to be a courtesy call. In the intervening months Eckhard Cordes, Rüdiger Grube and Alex Dibelius had fine-tuned the case for a merger. They had compiled a book of diagrams and charts which demonstrated the compelling logic of a deal.

Schrempp took this book with him when he went to see Bob Eaton for the short meeting on 12 January. It stayed in his briefcase as the German CEO, sitting in the corner of a big black sofa in Eaton's fifteenth-floor office, outlined the rationale for a deal. In a few succinct sentences, the German sketched out the intensifying competition in the auto industry.

'Here is where the industry was ten years ago,' he said. 'Here is where we think it will be in ten years' time. Here is why Mercedes-Benz needs a partner and here is why I think Chrysler needs a partner.

'I have lots of statistics and so forth and I have them with me and I can prove to you that Chrysler and Mercedes-Benz fit geographically first-class and they fit from a product point of view first-class.'

This had taken a total of three minutes. At this point he apologised for his rapid-fire delivery. 'I'm sorry I'm so impolite but I can't do it differently,' he said.

'You're not being impolite at all,' said Eaton, smiling and motioning Schrempp to continue. Although not expecting the conversation to take this turn, the American was far from shocked by what Schrempp had to say. He and Schrempp were obviously on the same wavelength.

'If you agree with what I said, which you can easily check out, then you must actually also agree that we should start talking about how to bring these companies together. However, if you disagree with that, we shouldn't waste our time. So, you know, what is your reaction?' Schrempp asked bluntly.

'We've started this as well, we've done our studies,' replied Eaton. 'Yes, I think you're right. I do not know when precisely we can start talking. I have to do a little bit of checking and I have to talk to a few people but I promise you I'll come back to you within a few weeks.'

Neither Eaton nor Schrempp mentioned how they might do the deal. 'Putting the two companies together' was as specific as they could be at this stage, as mentioning a takeover or a merger would have opened up a Pandora's box of complexity. Better to leave it vague at this point.

'Okay,' said Schrempp, 'there is nothing more to add; thanks very much for your time.'

Schrempp got up from his seat and Eaton offered him tea or coffee. Schrempp declined, fearing that small talk might dilute the impact of what he had said.

That was it. Subsequent accounts suggested that this meeting lasted seventeen minutes, but given that so little was said it is difficult to believe that it went on for much longer than ten.

Leaving behind his book of analysis, Schrempp got back in his chauffeur-driven S-Class Mercedes and was driven to the Fox & Hounds restaurant for his steak. Over lunch, he and Lydia Deininger agreed that the outcome was encouraging. Eaton's reaction suggested that he had been thinking along similar lines. 'I got the feeling there and then that the deal would happen,' says Deininger in retrospect. But there had to be a fallback position. It was to be developed at the next meeting, half an hour's journey south of Auburn Hills in the suburb of Dearborn, home to the Ford Motor Corporation.

Straight after lunch Schrempp paid a visit to Alex Trotman, then CEO of Ford. Trotman, together with Jac Nasser (soon to be his successor as CEO), was waiting for Schrempp in the nearby Westin Hotel. The meeting stemmed from an earlier conversation between Schrempp and Trotman. Several months previously Trotman had been in Stuttgart to sign a fuel cell joint venture. Trotman had asked Schrempp for a private chat and they had taken their champagne glasses up to Schrempp's private office. Trotman had explained how he thought the industry was poised for rapid consolidation and suggested that Daimler and Ford work closely together.

'Ford has to make a move,' Trotman said, very candidly. 'We can't survive as we are.'

The follow-up to this initial meeting was the invitation to get together in Detroit.

'Things are moving, there's a lot we could do together,' Trotman told Schrempp. 'We fit very well together, the consolidation in our industry is set to continue. We have to do something.'

'That's a great idea,' said Schrempp. 'What's your concept?'

'We haven't worked out a concept yet,' Trotman replied. 'But why don't we get a small group of guys together and talk it through?'

They agreed to appoint two teams to pursue matters further. And when Bob Eaton of Chrysler rang Schrempp's office ten days later, Schrempp had to tell him that the negotiations were not exclusive. In fact, the discussions with Ford were brought to a close only three weeks before the Chrysler deal was finally announced.

If Schrempp was vague about the nature of the planned alliance, it was for a good reason. Nothing quite like this had been done before. Cordes, together with Alexander Dibelius of Goldman Sachs, had studied fifty significant mergers of the recent past, and reached the conclusion that a transatlantic merger such as they planned would require serious 'out-of-the-box' thinking. They agreed that the best strategy was for the two sides to sit down together and work on a joint approach.

Schrempp gathered around him a war cabinet of his closest colleagues and advisors. Eckhard Cordes, the clean-cut board member responsible for strategy, was to lead the negotiations, often playing Mr Nasty to Schrempp's Mr Nice in a well-rehearsed 'good-guy bad-guy' routine.

Cordes is a man with an agile mind and a can-do mentality that marked him out for Schrempp in the years of restructuring.

Their personal styles could not be more different: Schrempp is gregarious while Cordes is calm and thoughtful. But the chemistry between them is exceptional and it is based on mutual respect and a shared sense of humour. Cordes is a genuine sparring partner for Schrempp. He has the confidence and intelligence to challenge his CEO aggressively and persistently on a broad variety of issues even when he knows that Schrempp has different views. He hates to repeat himself and tends to assume that everybody can keep up with the flow of his ideas. On occasions, he doesn't bother to finish his sentences, his words trailing off into an impatient 'blah blah blah' before he moves on to the next subject.

Rüdiger Grube quickly mastered the infinite structural and legal permutations presented by a transaction of this scale. Throughout the negotiations, and for long afterwards as he took responsibility for integrating the two companies, he would appear at meetings with a stack of slides. At every twist and turn of the debate he could produce a diagram to show that he had already thought the issue through and anticipated the range of outcomes under discussion. Mention a structural question that needed to be resolved, and a few hours later Grube would appear with a perfectly polished document showing exactly how all the variations would work.

He was known throughout the Daimler headquarters as a man of prodigious energy and a compelling communicator. An aeronautical engineer by training, he arrived in Stuttgart in the summer of 1996 bearing a colossal Apple colour printer. This machine, together with a modem, is one reason for his success as a manager. It provides a direct link to a lady in Munich whose professional life is dedicated to producing slides for Grube's famous presentations. On receipt of a draft from Grube, she can get to work at the drop of a hat, soldiering away overnight if necessary. A few hours later the slides will emerge out of the printer in glorious Technicolor.

The other ingredients of his success are a fanatical appetite for work and a limited need for sleep. He is in the office by

8 a.m. every morning and not home until after ten. He spends one hour with his wife before retiring to his study where he works on reports and correspondence until around 2 a.m. When he is home at weekends, he takes Saturday off. On Sunday he goes for a ten-kilometre jog before getting back to work. This is only when he is at home at weekends. During the course of 1999 he was away on business for forty-three out of fifty-two weekends. His desire to see more of his family was one of the reasons why he would eventually leave the company after the integration of the two companies was completed.

On top of all this, Grube is a nice guy. One Saturday morning during the post-merger phase he was obliged to hold a meeting at a colleague's house. He turned up with a bunch of flowers and chocolates for the wife and toys for the children. The wife was enchanted. 'Even in the niceness stakes, Grube beats me every time,' the colleague lamented.

The third member of the core team was another workaholic. Alexander Dibelius is the investment banker who was to be promoted to a coveted partnership at Goldman Sachs as a result of his work on the deal. He is a prodigiously intelligent and determined Bavarian who had two careers before he found his way into investment banking. In 1979 he graduated from high school with the highest marks in the state of Bavaria and qualified as a medical doctor at the age of twenty-three – approximately half a decade earlier than most of his contemporaries (German tertiary education takes a lot longer than in the US or UK). He quickly acquired a Ph.D. *summa cum laude*, specialising in transplant surgery. He spent two years as a surgeon in big South African hospitals, where he carried out a vast range of operations, from heart and lung transplants to surgery for burns and gunshot wounds.

He returned to Germany at the age of twenty-five with more surgical experience than most thirty-five-year-old German surgeons. He decided that a career in medicine would lack excitement and after military service he opted to move to McKinsey & Co. One Thursday he took out his last appendix;

165

the following Monday he started work at the consultancy firm.

Unlike many academically gifted individuals, Dibelius is very commercial – he ran a second-hand car business at university – and he quickly mastered the intricacies of finance. He also adapted rapidly to serving clients rather than curing patients. The joke is that he used to think so hard about his clients that he could not concentrate on the humdrum aspects of ordinary life. On one possibly apocryphal occasion he was thinking so hard about a client case study that he drove into the wall of the McKinsey garage. He was made a partner in four and a half years, one of the quickest times ever. Six months later he moved to Goldman Sachs, the first international investment bank to make inroads into the underdeveloped German market.

A slight, intense man with a fierce gaze and a mordant wit, he travels everywhere with a large briefcase. Like a snake-oil salesman, he pops it open to display his wares, although what he is selling is less tangible and more valuable than quack medicine. He carries around a thick book in which every page demonstrates a form of cross-border corporate structure. Here is a diagram showing a straightforward merger of equals, there the holding company is collapsed into a new subsidiary or spun off into a new entity. There are dozens of potential deal structures, easy enough to draw on paper but fantastically elaborate, time-consuming and expensive to put into practice. As he guides you through the book, you realise that he is an unusual investment banker in that he is extremely talkative. Most bankers are taciturn, as if waiting for their clients to give them a lead before they express a view. His thoughts pour forth in a torrent of words and ideas. Cordes is one of the few who can keep up with him and the two of them conduct their conversations at a ferocious pace.

The final member of the team was Lydia Deininger, the head of the chairman's office. She was responsible for choreographing Schrempp's complex schedule and for keeping the negotiations secret within Daimler as well as externally. In short, she was master of ceremonies.

For some years she had been Schrempp's assistant, coming up to Stuttgart with him from Munich when he took over as CEO-in-waiting. Much more recently she had become his long-term partner, moving in with Schrempp in 1998 after he split up with Renate, his wife of thirty-five years' standing.

Her powerful personality has given Lydia a position of considerable influence within the company. She gives good advice on how Schrempp will react to a given proposition. She is discreet enough to ensure that if you are proposing to say something totally stupid, it will not go any further. In the other direction, her words are listened to particularly carefully throughout the company as subordinates look for signs of how the boss is thinking. She takes infinite pains not to abuse her position, saying privately that she has to work especially hard to prove that she has her job by virtue of professional competence rather than because she lives with Schrempp. Close friends credit Lydia with giving Schrempp the emotional and professional stability that has enabled him to flourish in the highly pressurised role as Daimler CEO.

During the negotiations she provided a useful counterbalance to the testosterone-driven male egos locking horns on both sides of the deal. A dark, almost Sicilian beauty, her presence drew the sting out of several tricky situations throughout the merger. She can claim credit for saving the deal in the last hours as Eaton and Schrempp fell out with one another over the name of the new company.

These four kept the negotiations to themselves until late February when lawyers were brought on board for the first time. Only in March was the circle widened to include other executives and advisors. This was deliberate, a lesson learned from the 1995 negotiations with Chrysler and indeed the merger with Mercedes-Benz AG in 1996. In both earlier cases Schrempp had found his room for manoeuvre severely limited: lots of people were informed and as a result there were leaks and the press covered his every move. This time, by ensuring that virtually nobody knew what was going on, he kept total control over the process.

But let's go back to the days following that first meeting of the CEOs in January.

Bob Eaton was mulling over what Schrempp had said to him. The logic of a merger was compelling, it didn't take a rocket scientist to see that. He was convinced that the timing was right, too. His Triple Storm speech of the previous summer had signalled his readiness to do a deal. Far better to get together with the world's most prestigious auto company than to hang around waiting for others to take the initiative. It would, Eaton felt, be a merger of two strong companies getting together on their own terms.

Despite being favourably disposed to a deal, he was sceptical about whether it could actually be done. He spent a week or two discussing his options with his closest colleagues. 'Frankly, at that stage nobody thought it had a high probability of happening,' Eaton said later. He asked Gary Valade, Chrysler's chief financial officer, to conduct a quick review of the options. 'We looked at every company in the world,' he recalled, 'and Daimler-Benz came out as close to the best match we could make. The analysis confirmed that we had almost complete complementarity in terms of products and markets and strengths and weaknesses.'

Eaton did however identify a number of obstacles, questions of structure and governance and culture. He also cast his mind back to the previous conversations with Mercedes-Benz, back in 1995. Then, Daimler had been a messy, unfocused conglomerate. He knew that Schrempp had made an impact on the company in the intervening years, but he needed to know a lot more about the current state of the group. At least this time the negotiations would be at the right level – he would be negotiating with his direct counterpart at Daimler-Benz.

CHAPTER 11

Reefs and Shoals

The negotiations gather momentum

Geneva, 11 February 1998

A t the end of January, Eaton rang Schrempp to say that Chrysler wanted to proceed. They fixed a meeting for 11 February in Geneva. Eaton, together with Gary Valade, flew to Switzerland for the meeting with Schrempp and Cordes. All four men were tired as they sat together in a private room at the Hotel President Wilson on the shores of Lake Geneva. Schrempp and Cordes had been out for dinner the night before with his team, brainstorming until the small hours. They had only had four hours' sleep. Eaton and Valade had come direct from Detroit by private jet and had so little time when they arrived that Eaton had to take a shower in the pilot's hotel room before going directly into the meeting with the Germans. Apart from exhaustion, the feeling shared by all four men was curiosity. Just where was all this going to lead?

At this stage, the discussions were purely exploratory. The

purpose of the meeting was to decide whether to take the talks any further. 'Look,' said Eaton. 'We've looked into it and it's an interesting opportunity. But, you know, before we go much further, we need to know a lot more about your strategy.'

Schrempp and Cordes explained briefly that Daimler-Benz had been transformed since the last time Mercedes executives sat down with Chrysler executives, back in 1995. Valade and Eaton talked about the revitalised Chrysler in their turn. It was a free and frank discussion and they quickly reached the conclusion that the two companies should try to get together, leaving how they should do this deliberately vague. They agreed to move as fast as possible, convening a three-day meeting for the following week in New York. Eaton and Schrempp would not participate in this, delegating the next round of discussions to Valade and Cordes respectively. They would each bring along one other colleague and one investment banker. On the third day they would invite their corporate lawyers along as well.

And so, after a meeting lasting less than an hour, Project Gamma began in earnest. The code-name was mutually agreeable as it was neutral, unlike the working title used by the Germans and Goldman Sachs. They had called the original study Project Blitz, a word which had incendiary connotations when trying to promote a friendly merger between a German and an American company. From now on the companies would refer to each other as Cleveland (Chrysler) and Denver (Daimler-Benz).

That afternoon, as the Americans flew back across the Atlantic, Schrempp sat with Cordes and Dibelius. They were excited that they had got this far, but foresaw a number of complications. They identified a number of deal-breakers, each one of which had the potential to derail the transaction, no matter how sound the logic. If these were not dealt with in the correct way, in the right order with due respect to emotion as well as hard cash, the deal could fall apart.

The first was the question of temperament and leadership:

bluntly, if the two guys at the top did not get on, the deal would be stymied, no matter how strong the logic. And Eaton and Schrempp would not merely have to get on with each other, they would have to work out very precisely how they would share the top job.

The second issue was part emotional, part legal: where would the company be domiciled? Each side would of course attach enormous significance to the legal and physical headquarters of the merged entity. Would it be a German or an American company? Or would it be better to compromise on neutral territory such as the Netherlands, as indeed was contemplated at one point during the negotiations?

Wherever the company ended up being based, Schrempp and his team would have to negotiate the reefs and shoals of German labour law. Under so-called *Mitbestimmung*, translated as co-determination, German workers sit on Daimler's supervisory board. This did not give them enough power to block the deal, but gave them more than enough to add to the complications of the transaction if they were not on-side. So the workers had somehow to be won over even if they, like virtually everyone else at Daimler, were going to be kept in the dark until the very last moment.

Another legal problem: if the new company were to be a German *Aktiengesellschaft*, or limited company, rather than a US corporation, co-determination would have to be extended to the Chrysler workforce as well. How would Chrysler shareholders react to that?

There would be all sorts of other technical issues to be dealt with. For example, just how would the merger be structured? Would one company take over the other, or would it be a merger? If the latter, on what terms would the shares in Daimler-Benz AG be exchanged for those of Chrysler Corporation, or vice versa? And on which stock exchange in which currency would the resulting securities be traded?

Finally, there was one critical point around which issues of emotion, power, control and patriotic pride could easily

171

crystallise: the name of the new company. This would not be sorted out until the very eve of the announcement in early April.

The art of negotiation lies in timing: knowing when to bring an issue to the fore, and when to allow it to remain unfocused while something else is sorted out. In a masterful fashion, the Daimler side won every one of the important arguments, in the right order. The Americans got what they wanted, too, so it would be going too far to say they were outmanoeuvred. But they were certainly outclassed.

The German team dispersed. Schrempp went back to Stuttgart, Dibelius went to Frankfurt to prepare for the New York meetings, while Cordes flew to London. The next day Cordes was due to join Jürgen Hubbert and Dieter Zetsche for two days of talks with Ford. This was the follow-up to Schrempp's meeting with Alex Trotman in Detroit.

There was no formal agenda for this meeting. The Germans were expecting to have a general chat about the auto industry. Hubbert came with a piece of paper on which he had worked out his view of where the industry would end up. On the reckoning of the passenger car chief, the four most likely winners would be Toyota, General Motors, Ford and probably Volkswagen. Thereafter there were question marks against most of the rest. Daimler-Benz didn't make the cut, but Ford most definitely did. So the car men were curious about why Ford was so enthusiastic about holding the talks.

The first day passed without any answer to the question. The Ford team, led by head of engineering Richard Perry-Jones, took the Germans through their view of the industry. It was the standard consolidation story and the two sides found themselves agreeing with each other enthusiastically about what was likely to happen. It was on the second day that the talk became a lot more specific.

'It was very surprising as Ford presented to us their total rationale for why they wanted to move,' Dieter Zetsche recalled.

'They told us that they didn't consider themselves strong enough for the future battle.'

Dieter Zetsche recalled the conversation. 'What we are really lacking is a premium brand,' Perry-Jones said. 'This is where the music is going to be in the future.'

'Hang on a minute,' was the German reaction. 'What about Jaguar?'

'The problem is that Jaguar is in the luxury class, not a premium manufacturer,' the American team countered. 'So its growth prospects are limited. We need a partner and you're the ideal partner for us.'

Then they said something that almost had Cordes falling out of his chair.

'Well,' said Perry-Jones. 'We've done our analysis and while you're the best fit from our point of view, the best fit for you is Chrysler.'

Of course, he said, we know that you've spoken to Chrysler back in 1995 and the talks failed. So why don't we get together?

Cordes kept a straight face as the conversation moved on swiftly to structural questions.

'If you follow our logic corporate governance becomes impor-tant,' the Ford team continued. 'We don't like to see ourselves in the position of being acquired, and we can imagine that you don't want to be acquired by us.'

The logic argued for a merger of equals, but there was a catch. Ford family members hold a special class of share which gives the descendants of Henry Ford 40 per cent of the voting rights in the company. This would be a complication and the Ford team agreed to look into how it could be handled.

For Cordes, the meeting was a revelation. It confirmed the compelling strategic logic of the talks with Chrysler. Not sim-ply because Ford had independently said that Chrysler was Daimler's best partner, but because Ford itself was on the lookout for a partner. In all Daimler's planning scenarios, the assumption had been that the mighty Ford, the second biggest US car company, would be able to survive on its own.

'This was the ultimate confirmation that we needed to do something,' recalls Cordes.

Hubbert and Zetsche had a similar reaction, but so far as they knew all Daimler's eggs were in the Ford basket. Like the Ford executives, they had written off Chrysler as a potential partner for Daimler-Benz.

The meeting ended with Ford promising to get back with further proposals.

New York, 17–20 February 1998

Early the following week Cordes, together with Grube and Alex Dibelius, flew to New York for the next round of discussions with Chrysler.

The first stop for the Daimler team was a two-hour meeting with Jon S. Corzine, then senior partner of Goldman Sachs. He subsequently retired from investment banking with an estimated $200 million fortune and at the time of writing he is campaigning to be Senator for the state of New Jersey. Corzine is a soft-spoken man whose beard makes him look more like an avuncular college professor than the street-smart ex-bond trader who steered Goldman to a dominating position in the ferociously competitive global investment banking market. He had struck up a relationship with Schrempp soon after the latter took over as Daimler CEO.

In the dark days of 1995–6, when Schrempp was bereft of friends in Germany, Corzine was a welcome ally and sounding board. Then, he provided assurance that Schrempp was taking the right steps to restore Daimler to profitability and earn the respect of the international capital markets. Late in 1997, when Daimler's restructuring was virtually complete, Schrempp had asked the banker about the best way to approach Chrysler, and Corzine had explained that under no circumstances should Schrempp consider a hostile bid. Schrempp had toyed with the idea of a knockout bid for the US company but had been persuaded that an unfriendly takeover would alienate Chrysler's employees and customers, not to mention the politicians in Washington and Michigan who had organised the bail-out of Chrysler with taxpayers' money.

'This was good advice,' said Schrempp long after the deal was completed. 'I came to the conclusion that we should never be involved in a real hostile bid, not in the business that we're in. It has been difficult enough getting these two companies together, even in a merger of equals. Just imagine how hard it would have been if we were in a situation where they immensely disliked us as well.'

A deal could only be done with the support of management, Corzine counselled. With Eaton and his team on-side, the other constituencies – politicians at both the national and regional level as well as unions and individual customers – could be won over. Otherwise, Corzine said, there would be a ferocious backlash that would make it impossible to do a deal, no matter how sound the financial and strategic logic.

As the negotiations between the two companies began in earnest, Corzine reiterated this advice: don't push too hard, be as friendly as possible. It would be a guiding principle for the Daimler team that they would take all reasonable steps to win over Chrysler's management. It was in this first meeting that Dibelius came up with the term 'merger of equals' to describe the basis on which the two companies would get together. This proved a brilliant ruse when the deal was announced, but the phrase came back to haunt the two sides afterwards.

In the first meeting, which started at 11 a.m. in Goldman Sachs' downtown HQ, Cordes was conciliatory. He bent over backwards to be nice to the Americans. His job was to demonstrate that Daimler had changed its spots since the last time Chrysler executives had sat down with Mercedes-Benz. It still rankled with the Americans that they had spent so much time with the Germans back in 1995, with no concrete results. This time they would only go ahead if they thought there was a fair chance that a deal could be done on mutually agreeable terms.

'It will be cars plus trucks,' Cordes explained, running

through each of Daimler's business units and explaining in detail how Daimler's strategy and operating philosophy had evolved since 1995.

'I tried to get the message across that we had successfully refocused on the auto sector,' Cordes said later. 'I needed to convince them that we had reshaped the company, that we had simplified the group by abolishing Mercedes as a separate company. I wanted to show that we had a completely different management style.'

This was a critical presentation, as the Chrysler executives made it clear that if they weren't persuaded by what they heard they wouldn't stick around for the rest of the scheduled meetings.

Cordes did a good job and after lunch the two teams moved over to the office of CSFB (Crédit Suisse First Boston), Chrysler's investment banking advisers' headquarters, Daimler's chief negotiator was amused to see a picture of northern Germany on the wall of the conference room in which the meeting took place. He took pleasure in pointing out the town of Neumünster where he was born. They talked informally about how they would allocate boardroom responsibilities in a merged company, before adjourning for dinner in a nearby restaurant. They took a private room and fell silent every time the waiter came in to serve them. The number of people 'in the know' was still around a dozen.

They agreed to reconvene on the next day. True to form, Rüdiger Grube took the rough diagrams that came out of the meeting and stayed up late that night producing a series of immaculate slides showing the various organisational permutations. He distributed them at the next morning's meeting. This was the first time the Americans encountered Grube's diligence, and they were impressed.

At the end of day two, there was a clear consensus on both sides: it made sense to talk further. The fledgling deal was not merely the pipe dream of the strategy department, nor was it the whim of ambitious CEOs. There was, both sides soon agreed, marvellous compatibility between the two companies. They identified little overlap between the companies' products, and fundamentally a good fit in terms of the brands. ('Chrysler's brands are below ours but not too far below,' noted Cordes.) In terms of market presence, Chrysler was strong where Daimler-Benz was under-represented, and vice versa. Daimler acknowledged that it needed to expand in the US, while Chrysler admitted that it was weak in Europe and had no presence to speak of in the fast-growing markets of Asia. Put Chrysler's products together with Daimler's global distribution network, and the result would be a surge in sales which neither company could have managed on its own.

Both Daimler and Chrysler would learn from the way each other did business. Cordes and his team realised that Mercedes could usefully absorb Chrysler's skills as a low-cost producer. Moreover, the US firm was the world champion in terms of managing relationships with suppliers and bringing new products to market. This would complement Mercedes-Benz's unmatched engineering expertise.

From a strategic point of view, it was looking like the no-brainer that Daimler's planners had predicted. Infinitely less straightforward were the structural questions: how would the deal be put together? Where would the company be domiciled? What was the most appropriate accounting treatment for a combination of two companies from different sides of the Atlantic? What kind of security would emerge and on which stock exchanges would it be traded? Would Daimler have to throw in cash as well as shares to make the deal fly? How could it be organised so that nobody had to pay any tax when the deal was done?

'Doing a deal where nobody pays any tax is the most difficult kind of transaction under normal circumstances,' explained Mike Schell from Skadden, Arps. 'By normal, I mean without the complication of a cross-border dimension. Here we were dealing with two legal systems, two stock exchanges, two business cultures, two styles of corporate governance, two accounting systems. It is impossible to overestimate just how difficult and complicated it was to do this deal.'

On days three and four the circle of those in the know was widened to include lawyers who were invited to give the first, tentative answers to these questions. In the Daimler corner were Skadden, Arps, Slate, Meagher & Flom, together with Shearman & Sterling, while Chrysler was represented by Debevoise & Plimpton, and Cleary, Gottlieb, Steen & Hamilton.

Not surprisingly, the presence of lawyers served to complicate matters further. There was much mutual incomprehension as the Germans explained the principles of *Mitbestimmung* or co-determination, a concept wholly alien to the Americans. Privately, the Chrysler team thought that German law was convoluted and ill-suited for a cross-border deal, and they were sceptical when they heard Cordes and Grube outline the benefits of statutory worker representation in boardrooms. Conversely, the Germans thought that the Americans were absurdly parochial for assuming that everything would be done according to US principles.

Throughout the week, as they went up and down in the elevator between meetings, Cordes, Grube and Dibelius would give each other odds as to the chances of a deal being completed. After Tuesday's session, the best odds were 70 per cent in favour of it happening. After listening to the lawyers, the odds dropped to significantly lower than 50 per cent.

Lausanne, 2 March 1998

The timing of the next meeting was dictated by the Geneva motor show, which presented good cover for Eaton, Schrempp, Valade and Cordes to be in Switzerland. Lausanne was chosen precisely because it was an hour's drive from Geneva. It was very unlikely that rivals would rumble the negotiations by mistake, and for the first time the negotiating team met in public – in the near-empty dining room of the Hotel Beau Rivage overlooking Lake Geneva.

On the agenda for today were two key issues: location of the company, and leadership. Would the new company be based in Detroit or Stuttgart? Who was going to get the top job?

The latter question had been thrown into sharp relief by some recent news. Several days after the New York meetings, Dibelius had pointed out to Schrempp a story on the front page of the *Financial Times* describing how the planned merger of Glaxo Wellcome and SmithKline Beecham had fallen apart at the last minute. The reason was that the CEOs of the two pharmaceutical companies had not been able to agree on how to share responsibility for running the new group. So a deal with compelling industrial and financial logic had disintegrated after months of preparations because of personality issues. There was a lesson in this for the Daimler–Chrysler negotiations: better to sort out the leadership question sooner rather than later.

Schrempp originally planned to deal with the subject on his own with Eaton. But after an hour or two of discussions, the mood among the four men was relaxed and friendly. So Schrempp decided to raise the issue with Cordes and Valade at the table.

'Bob, now we have to talk about who is going to run the company,' Schrempp said.

'You know, I've been thinking about this,' came the reply from Eaton. 'I think I have possibly another three, four or five years in mind.'

There was a pause before Eaton spelled out his initial proposal: he would be chairman, and Schrempp his deputy.

'After a while, after a certain period of time, you take over,' Eaton explained. 'You know, I move out and you move in.'

'Bob,' said Schrempp. 'What I feel is, I'm so convinced of the deal that this is no issue for me. If you want to be the chairman, be the chairman, and I'll move out.'

It was a typical Schrempp negotiating tactic – offering to lay down his own career for the sake of something much larger than himself. He had done this on a couple of crucial occasions during his rise to the top of the corporation. There was no doubt in Cordes' mind that Schrempp meant every word: he would leave if that were the price of getting the deal through. However, Eaton responded as Schrempp expected, by making a similar gesture.

Of course, Eaton said, he would step down too if it were for the good of the deal.

'Okay,' said Schrempp, warming to the task at hand. 'Now we have come a step forward. Both of us would step down because we love the company and we love what we are doing. This is great!'

'Yes,' Eaton said, carried away by Schrempp's enthusiasm.

'That's fine,' Schrempp said. 'But there's something else. We need the support of both our boards. I guess if I move out we have a major problem, and if you move out we also have a problem. My proposal is, we do it together.'

Schrempp then asked Eaton how old he was. He was fifty-eight. At fifty-three, Schrempp was the younger of the two by far and would obviously be staying on longer than the American. So he refined his suggestion: 'We both know that over time it will never work, having two chairmen. So if we do it together we have to decide now how long for.'

Eaton nodded his agreement.

Schrempp continued. 'Bob, you know, your people don't know me. They might fear a German with my reputation, they would be up in arms. My people might like you because you are a gentleman, contrary to me, but they don't know you either. The bottom line is that both sides would like to have their leader staying on for a certain period of time.'

Schrempp came to the nub of his proposal: they would tell the world at the outset that they would be co-chairmen for a certain period of time. After this period, Eaton would resign.

'Okay,' said Eaton.

There still remained the sensitive question of just how long the period of time would be. Schrempp suggested two years. Eaton smiled broadly: 'Okay, Jürgen, we have a deal.'

At this point the four decided to go for lunch. Sitting by the windows overlooking the lake, they were all in a very good mood: the most sensitive issue of all had been addressed and dealt with. They were so relaxed that Eaton made a tactical error: he let it slip that he might well leave earlier than the appointed time if things were going well.

Several weeks later, Eaton came back to Schrempp and said that the Chrysler board had accepted the agreed three-year co-chairmanship. Schrempp was mildly surprised that Eaton's term of office would be three rather than two years as discussed. But he was not worried.

In Lausanne, Schrempp had realised that he would be in charge – whether he had a co-chairman or not.

Having resolved the leadership question to their mutual satisfaction, the four men identified five outstanding issues. These were:

First, the location of the company: would the merged group be based in Germany or the US, or a neutral third country such as the UK, Luxembourg or the Netherlands?

Second, a joint business plan which quantified substantial synergies arising from the merger.

Third, a financial structure which gave a fair deal to shareholders in both companies.

Fourth, the composition of the board: bluntly, who would get the top jobs.

Finally, they had to agree on a name.

Of these points, the joint assessment was that the first three were real show-stoppers. Without quick agreement on these, the deal would fail. The last two were deemed important but not so critical that they would endanger the deal.

'If we can't resolve these issues by the end of March, we should call it off,' said Eaton. Schrempp and Cordes agreed: the quicker everything was sorted out, the better.

They decided to leave the calculation of synergies as late as possible, as this would mean widening the circle of those who knew about the deal to include operational management. At this stage, the circle of those in the know was still limited to a handful of people in each company, plus the investment bankers and lawyers.

Both sides recognised that the greater the number of people involved, the greater the risks to the deal. One potential threat was a leak. If news of the negotiations found its way into the press, there would be no way of influencing the headlines and both companies would come under immense pressure. Without the benefit of a carefully co-ordinated communications campaign, the financial markets would most likely come to the negative conclusion that both Daimler-Benz and Chrysler had abandoned hope of surviving as independent companies. Hence the companies would be 'in play', susceptible to unfriendly approaches from other parties.

The risk of this was greater for Chrysler, as it was the smaller of the two in terms of market capitalisation and a more digestible morsel for another company. But Daimler, shorn of its loss-making AEG and Fokker and thus of built-in deterrents to takeover, could also be vulnerable.

There was another argument against widening the magic circle: the more people involved, the more they would fight for their own personal interests. A merger inevitably means a redistribution of power and responsibilities, with executives from both sides fighting it out among themselves for the prize positions. Involve too many people too early, and the jostling can disrupt and even kill off the negotiations.

Mindful of these considerations, the four deemed it too risky to bring the car guys into the loop. In any case, the back-of-the-envelope assumption on both sides was that there would be plenty of savings from bringing the two companies together. So the issue was parked until late April when Hubbert and Zetsche met their counterparts in London to hammer out the specifics. From now on, every individual who was told about the negotiations was obliged to sign a confidentiality agreement threatening dire consequences if any information leaked. The code of silence was rigorously adhered to, with wives and secretaries only finding out the details of what was afoot in the very last days of the negotiations.

The Lausanne meeting ended on an optimistic note. The four men agreed that the deal had a 50:50 chance of success. This was an improvement of the odds when compared with New York, but an awful lot had to be done in order to meet the self-imposed deadline of the end of March.

Schrempp had gone to Lausanne clear in his own mind that the merged company would have to be a German AG.

The bottom line was that Germany's largest company could not leave Germany, even if the financial logic argued for a move elsewhere. Daimler-Benz was too much part of the fabric of Germany to be turned into an American, Dutch or British company. The unions, politicians, the supervisory board, consumers, all would be against it. In short, the idea was a non-starter, he would never get it through.

However, Schrempp did not show his hand when he went to Switzerland. When Eaton asked him what he thought about the alternatives, Schrempp simply shrugged his shoulders and said: 'I just want a deal.' There was no point in bringing the issue to the fore before the lawyers had made their recommendations. In any case, he was reassured by what Eaton had to say at the same meeting.

'The AG itself is not the real issue, I'm sure that would be possible to live with,' the Chrysler CEO said. 'The problem is that German stock won't be very attractive to American and Asian shareholders.'

This remark gave the Germans a welcome insight into the Americans' negotiating position: delivering the best possible financial package for shareholders was probably their key priority. It also reflected both companies' concerns to ensure as broad and liquid a market for DaimlerChrysler shares as possible. This, they recognised, was the best guarantee for a full valuation of the combined company.

Eaton's concerns were justified, it turned out. After the deal was done, DaimlerChrysler's stock was excluded from the Standard & Poors index of 500 leading companies, precisely because it was a German company. The fact that more than half the new group's profits were earned in the US or that it accounted for 1 per cent of US Gross Domestic Product was deemed irrelevant by the index authorities.

The index is an important benchmark for North American professional investors, many of whom are legally obliged to invest only in companies that form part of official indices such as the S&P 500. As Eaton may have sensed, the result of the exclusion was that American institutions deserted the stock in droves. Within a year of completion, the proportion of DaimlerChrysler shares owned by US investors had dropped from 44 per cent at the time of the merger to 25 per cent, while the German share rose from 40 to 60 per cent.

Schrempp was ready to jump into the negotiations if they got sticky, but he did not have to. He kept in touch with Cordes to find out how the talks were progressing. By this stage, the teams of negotiators were flying back and forth across the Atlantic on an alarmingly regular basis, a punishing regimen for those involved.

One time, Grube arrived at the lobby of the Four Seasons Hotel at 9.45 a.m. after taking the Concorde over from London, only to be told by Cordes that they all had to go straight back to Germany. 'Hey Rüdiger, don't check in, we're going back,' Cordes told him. So he turned round, went to the airport and flew straight back to Europe.

In early March it became clear that the most sensible structure from a purely economic point of view was indeed to have a German company. The reason was tax: always a bugbear in complex M&A transactions, but a source of especially nightmarish complications in cross-border deals. An American company can merge with another entity across a border without crystallising a tax liability, provided certain conditions are met. In this case, the key criterion was that former stockholders in

Chrysler would end up owning less than 50 per cent of the new company. This, the investment bankers judged, would be reasonably easy to fulfil. On the other hand, if a German company is merged with a foreign company, its shareholders become liable for tax on the assets hidden away within the company.

Hidden assets were an eccentric feature of German balance sheets, mysterious because they were both big and undisclosed. There are less of them about these days as most big German companies have followed Daimler's lead and adopted American accounting. US rules encourage companies to disclose as much financial information as possible, the assumption being that this is what stock market investors want to see in order to make comparisons between companies and thus make informed investment decisions. Old-fashioned German accounting had different priorities, chiefly to protect creditors. Conservatism was the guiding principle, and companies were encouraged to accumulate retained profits rather than distribute them to shareholders. The scale of these retentions was not made public, with the result that published balance sheets understated the value of German companies' assets.

At the risk of gross over-simplification – remember that it took four firms of leading commercial lawyers the best part of a month to get their heads round this – a cross-border merger by a German company has the effect of realising any capital gains that may have accumulated within that company over decades. The gain, calculated as the difference between the value of the assets today and their value when they were first booked on the balance sheet, becomes subject to tax. In the case of Daimler-Benz in 1998, the rough and ready calculation among the advisors was that a cross-border merger would create a tax liability in the region of DM15 billion.

A tax bill on this scale was something to be avoided, both sides could easily agree. It would have destroyed the arithmetic of the deal. The Americans conceded the point at a meeting held in London on 18 and 19 March, with the caveat that a German

AG was the most sensible structure from a *pure economic standpoint* only. They would have preferred a Dutch NV: a neutral third country would have reinforced the impression that the deal was a merger. They even managed to develop a structure that would have allowed the company to relocate to the Netherlands, but it was hideously complicated. Notwithstanding the rhetoric about 'merger of equals', it was going to look as though an American company were simply being taken over by a German one.

Mindful of the negative PR repercussions, the Chrysler team introduced a new twist to their negotiation strategy. They insisted that they should be paid a higher price for their shares as a quid pro quo for moving to Germany. 'The size of the premium is influenced by whether the new company is an AG or a Dutch NV,' was the clear message. 'You pay more if it's an AG.'

From this moment on, the negotiations entered a new phase. There was growing acceptance that a deal could be done. The outstanding question was: at what price?

CHAPTER 12

Relative Values

*The discussions progress – the issue of
valuation comes to the fore*

The Dorchester Hotel, London, 9 April 1998

It was possibly the most nerve-wracking moment in Eckhard
Cordes' career.

Together with around fifteen other bankers and lawyers, he was sitting in a large conference room at London's
Dorchester Hotel. Bleary-eyed and exhausted, Cordes had not
had much sleep in the past month. People were dropping like
flies: one investment banker had worked non-stop for fifty
hours and staggered into a meeting with Cordes demanding to
be allowed to go to sleep. The Germans took pity on him, letting
him go to bed as he had been working without a break for two
days and two nights. Squadrons of advisors had worked round
the clock to reach basic agreement on the technicalities: the legal
structure for the merger and the so-called 'exchange ratio'.

Cordes was confident that this ratio – the rate at which

Chrysler shares would be swapped for shares in the new DaimlerChrysler – had now been settled to the satisfaction of both sides' negotiating teams. All that remained was the formality of a chairman-to-chairman eyeballing session. So Schrempp and Eaton had been shepherded into a small windowless room where, Cordes hoped, they would exchange a few pleasantries and agree on the formula that so many people had sweated over in the past few weeks.

Half an hour went by, then an hour, then another half an hour – everybody was getting worried. Worry turned to panic when the message came down from the room that they needed a calculator. Eaton and Schrempp were not supposed to get down to that level of detail; if they had started picking at the ratios, perhaps the deal was unravelling. Another concern was that Schrempp, though an inspirational leader, was not a finance guy: how would he understand the minutiae of the highly complex agreement?

'Jürgen, we have a problem,' said Eaton.

Inside the small room the atmosphere was fraught. Eaton spurned the offer of a glass of wine and was drinking water instead. He was insisting on a price of not less than $57.50 a share – equivalent to $37.1 billion for the whole company. The share price had emotional significance for him: taking into account share splits the Germans calculated that this was the value of the hostile bid made for the company by Kirk Kerkorian, the billionaire financier, who had been a thorn in Chrysler's side for years now. Eaton had fended off Kerkorian, but felt honour-bound to deliver at least the same price in any deal with Daimler.

Schrempp had been briefed by Cordes and Dibelius before he went into the one-on-one.

'I'm not interested in ratios, I want a deal,' Schrempp told them. 'All I want to know is how much leeway you can give me, how far up I can go and still have a good deal.'

They had handed him a small piece of paper in which the

parameters of the Daimler-Benz negotiating position were set
out. His stance was clear: Daimler could pay a 30 per cent
premium to the Chrysler price, but no more. So as an opening
shot he offered a 25 per cent premium.

'Are you insisting on that?' said Eaton.

'That's fair,' Schrempp said.

'I just can't sell it, I just can't get it past the board,' Eaton
replied. He got up and poured himself a glass of white wine.
'It's a great deal but I just can't do that.'

After a moment's pause, Eaton asked Schrempp for a pen. He
started doing calculations on a paper napkin. Schrempp looked
at the sums. 'Are you adding or subtracting or what the hell
are you doing?' Schrempp asked. 'Anyway those numbers are
wrong, you've added them up incorrectly.'

At this point they sent for a calculator.

Eaton and Schrempp sat there for a total of three hours. They
drank first a bottle of white wine then a bottle of red. The
advisors were frantically worried. Finally, Valade and Cordes
were called to the small room where Eaton and Schrempp
outlined what they had agreed. When Schrempp and Eaton
emerged back in the main conference room with broad grins on
their faces, more than a dozen bankers and lawyers breathed a
collective sigh of relief: the deal was still on.

Eaton told his camp that they had agreed the $57.50 a share
price, while Schrempp told Cordes and Dibelius that they had
agreed a 28 per cent premium. Cordes and Dibelius looked
at each other: they both knew that it was mathematically
impossible to agree a $57.50 offer price based on a 28 per
cent premium. Add 28 per cent to that day's closing share price
of $43.50 and you only got to $55.68, which wasn't acceptable
to the Americans. The chairmen had cocked it up after all!

Meanwhile Schrempp had gone with Lydia Deininger to the
Chinese restaurant at the Dorchester. 'Come on, why should
I do this deal?' he asked Lydia. He was in a good mood and
playfully rehearsed the arguments pro and con. He was looking
forward to informing the chairman of his supervisory board

about the deal in detail for the first time: perhaps he would visit him at the weekend. It was about time to tell the rest of the Daimler management board what was going on, too.

His good humour was disturbed when Dibelius and Cordes appeared at the dinner table. 'There's a problem, there's a problem,' they explained excitedly: the numbers didn't add up.

'You've misunderstood Eaton,' said Dibelius. 'We're going to go back and clear it up.'

Schrempp nearly lost his temper: 'I went into that meeting and did everything you told me to do and now you're telling me I should have said something different. I don't want to talk about it any more, I'm enjoying my Chinese.'

Downcast, Dibelius and Cordes retreated back to the war-room. Sitting down with their Chrysler counterparts, they too had a Chinese meal – but this was a take-away rather than the haute cuisine being enjoyed by Schrempp. After a few anxious moments they decided that the difference between the two sides was so small that they could risk a fudge in the hope of getting the deal done in such a way that both Eaton and Schrempp would be happy. They agreed to watch the share prices for a fortnight in the hope of finding one day when both Eaton's $57.50 and Schrempp's 28 per cent conditions were met. To everyone's enormous relief, the share prices moved into the appropriate conjunction with each other on 15 April, producing a share price of $58.72 and a 28 per cent premium. Daimler would be paying a final sum in stock equivalent to a cash value of $37.9 billion.

Dibelius and Cordes brought the news to Schrempp. They caught him as he was leaving the bar of the hotel to go to bed. 'You won't believe it, Jürgen,' Cordes exclaimed. 'We have a deal, we have a deal . . . let's have a drink.'

'You guys are mad,' Schrempp said. 'I don't mind having another drink, but why did you ever think we didn't have a deal?'

They all went back to the bar and Schrempp bought a round of whisky sours.

*   *   *

'Could you just explain to me what the premium is for?' a Chrysler advisor asked his counterpart at Goldman Sachs at around this time. He was relatively new to the deal and wanted some basic clarification about the rationale for the premium agreed between Schrempp and Eaton.

'It's there because we're taking you over, sonny,' came the unfriendly reply.

This was a rare breach of etiquette. Until well after the deal was signed and sealed, both sides stuck to the official line that the deal was a merger of equals rather than a takeover. During the negotiations, both sides worked together as equals to plot and prepare a mutually agreeable framework for their mould-breaking merger. Anyone looking carefully at the financial mechanics of the transaction could have seen easily enough that one party would be more equal than the other.

In an absolutely strict merger, there would be no premium to discuss. There would be a simple fusion of the two companies to reflect their relative values. So, to take a hypothetical example, if the market value of Daimler was 60 and that of Chrysler was 40, Chrysler shareholders would end up with 40 per cent of the merged company and Daimler shareholders with 60 per cent.

It wasn't as simple as that, of course. Daimler's shares were valued much more highly than those of Chrysler. When the deal was announced in May 1998 the shares of the German company were trading on a ratio of 26 times expected earnings for that year. The equivalent ratio for Chrysler was 8.2 times earnings. This led to an interesting anomaly. Even though Chrysler's profits were bigger than those of Daimler, its market capitalisation was about half that of the German company. Using the figures presented to Chrysler's board on 5 May, two days before the deal was announced, Chrysler was valued at $27 billion compared to Daimler's $53 billion. And yet Chrysler was expected to make $3.3 billion in after-tax profits in 1999, compared with just $2.9 billion at Daimler-Benz.

Why did the market value Daimler so much more highly

than Chrysler? One answer is that investors feared the impact of another downturn in the US market. They had seen what happened to Chrysler in the early 1990s and they were convinced that it would happen again. Chrysler's economics were peculiarly sensitive to a sharp drop in sales. Hence Chrysler's carefully husbanded cash mountain would be burned up. The company would be forced to keep on spending money at a time when it wasn't generating any income. According to the most pessimistic analysis, you could argue that the shares were actually expensive, rather than cheap, as the company's profits were likely to plunge before too long into heavy losses.

By contrast, Daimler was given a special, high rating. One factor behind this was Schrempp's success in revitalising the group's profitability. It was also a luxury car company, deserving a premium valuation as a result. Furthermore, history suggested that European car companies were much more effective in riding out the ups and downs of the business cycle than their US competitors. To put this in perspective, Ford and GM both had significantly lower ratings than the European auto companies, but they were valued more highly than Chrysler because they had international business which could offset the expected decline in the US market. Chrysler was a 'pure play' on the North American market and was thus deemed especially vulnerable.

Bob Eaton and his team did not see it this way at all. It irked the CEO of the world's most profitable auto company that Chrysler should have one of the lowest ratings in the sector. Like many CEOs, he was convinced that his stock was massively undervalued by ignorant and unappreciative analysts. At a time when technology stocks were being given ever more spectacular valuations despite the fact that many of them had never made any profits – and might never do so – one can well understand the frustrations of the CEO of this 'old economy' company. But the arguments deployed by the Chrysler team during the negotiations were disingenuous, none the less.

'They were overvalued and we were undervalued,' said Eaton,

reflecting later on the valuation anomaly. 'That was the reason why we sought a premium.'

Throughout March and early April the Chrysler team had pursued this line of argument. Daimler-Benz, they contended, should pay a premium price because Wall Street had failed to take proper account of Chrysler's profitability and its position as a specialist car and truck manufacturer. 'We are not Ford or GM,' they said. 'We are big in pick-up trucks and sports utility vehicles and we're not in the volume sector at all.'

The Germans agreed to pay a premium, but not because they agreed Chrysler was undervalued. It was the price to pay in order to end up in the driving seat.

By this time, the shape of the deal was clear.

There would be no cash paid by Daimler to Chrysler share-holders. In March, Daimler had signalled its willingness to pay up to half the value of the transaction in cash, but Chrysler had rejected the offer. It was to be an all-share transaction, structured so that it would maximise the profits of the amalgamated companies.

The hope was that the markets would be excited by the companies' joint growth prospects and scope for synergies. This would give the new entity a higher valuation than if you simply took the average of the independent Daimler and Chrysler.

Daimler's special valuation would be diluted as a result of combining with the lowly rated Chrysler, but they still expected it to be higher than the mid-way point between the two companies' ratings. The middle point would be less than 13 times earnings, and they were confident that the new company would trade on more than 14 times earnings.

To make the financial logic more compelling, both sides devoted considerable time and effort to ensuring that the transaction qualified for so-called pooling of interest. This is a mightily obscure topic which nevertheless had a big impact on the way the deal was structured. If the two companies could prove to the satisfaction of the Securities & Exchange Commission (SEC) in

Washington that theirs was a genuine merger, they could simply add up or pool the assets and liabilities in each other's balance sheets without creating any goodwill.

Goodwill has nothing to do with bonhomie or the milk of human kindness; rather it is a number used by accountants to plug the gap when one company buys another for more than the book value of the latter's assets. There is a lot of it about in today's business world, an environment where companies' assets are as much intangible (patents, know-how, processes, software, brands etc.) as rooted in the rock-solid world of plant and machinery. It tends to crystallise and give everybody a headache when companies merge or take each other over.

The problem with goodwill (under US accounting rules at least) is that it can't simply sit on a balance sheet and do the job of filling the gap between what was paid for the assets and what they were supposed to have been worth. It has to be written off against subsequent profits over an apparently arbitrary twenty or forty years. This means that profits are reduced by one-twentieth or one-fortieth of the total amount of crystallised goodwill every year for twenty or forty years.

Arguably, perhaps, goodwill could be ignored as little more than a technical adjustment. Probe the accountants, lawyers, managers and bankers working to stitch Daimler together with Chrysler, and more than a few would probably agree that the whole issue is chimerical, has no bearing on the substance of a company's performance and could really be ignored. Fundamentally, however, managers do not trust stock market investors to make the necessary adjustments, to give them credit for the fact that this is book-keeping not business. They fear that their shares will be at an unfair disadvantage when compared with rivals without goodwill mountains that need to be written off.

The practical reality was that the combined Daimler and Chrysler risked creating a massive $27 billion of goodwill on their new balance sheet. Without pooling of interest, this would have meant a $1.4 billion charge against profits every year for

194

the next twenty years. This would have cut earnings per share by up to $2 a share compared with a projected $7 a share for 1999. The feeling was that the share price would suffer as a result. If at all possible, goodwill was something very definitely to be avoided.

The path to avoidance was intricate. It drove the final legal structure of the deal. By now, the lawyers and bankers had worked out that if they wanted pooling, they could not simply do a classic 'triangular merger'. This is when you set up a new company and merge the other two companies into it: shareholders in the old companies end up owning shares in the new vehicle.

This classic triangular structure would not work because of a fundamental difference between German and US corporate law. If, under the procedure outlined above, the new company had acquired more than 50 per cent of Chrysler, that would be fine and dandy: this would give the new company the right to buy out the minority shareholders in an operation called a 'squeeze out'. This sounds painful but has the happy outcome that there are no disaffected minority shareholders lurking around threatening to sue you or generally make life difficult by holding on to shares in the old company.

Under German law, things are not that easy. It is an irony that a country with an underdeveloped equity culture should have a draconian set of rules to protect the interests of any minority shareholders left clinging on to their shares after the completion of a takeover. Basically, there are no squeeze-outs allowed in German law. Every disenchanted minority shareholder has the right to challenge the terms agreed by management in a process called a *Spruchstellenverfahren*. Though there is no way of translating this term into English, the impact is quite clear: months if not years after a deal is done, a German court can order a change to the financial terms of the transaction. It can require companies to pay compensation to the aggrieved minority shareholder. This means a potentially massive and

195

unpredictable ex post facto adjustment to the carefully nego-
tiated original terms.

Here lay the nub of the problem: the SEC would only
allow pooling of interest to take place if the two companies
got together in a merger where all shareholders were treated
equally. The *Spruchstellenverfahren*, which had the US lawyers
spluttering with indignation as they got their tongues around
its unfamiliar concepts and syllables, amounted to a severe
risk that some shareholders would one day be paid more than
others. This would mean unequal treatment. In which case, the
deal would be classified as a takeover rather than a merger.
Inexorably, therefore, there would be no pooling of interest,
which would mean a $1.4 billion goodwill penalty on earnings
each and every year for the next twenty years.

There was one way round it, as the negotiating teams saw
it towards the end of March: get 75 per cent of Daimler's
shareholders to vote in favour of the new deal. This would
eliminate the risk of a *Spruchstellenverfahren*, but would be
awkward and challenging to achieve.

Assuming all the pieces of the jigsaw came together, the result
would be one company with one type of share, a so-called
global share. This would be traded principally on the Frankfurt and New York stock exchanges, but also on a further
seventeen exchanges around the world. This would be a real
novelty, the first time that a German company's shares could
be interchangeably traded on the home market and in New
York, home to the biggest capital market in the world. The
individual certificates would end up being bilingual in German
and English, carrying pictures of Gottlieb Daimler, Karl Benz
and Walter P. Chrysler.

The whole of the structure broke new ground. Nothing like
it had been done before. The two sides would continue to
refine the details through April and early May, but it was
fundamentally this package that Schrempp and Eaton would
recommend to their respective boards and shareholders.

* * *

Meanwhile Hubbert, Zetsche and Cordes had waited in vain for a follow-up to the January meeting with Ford. Ford had been so enthusiastic back then, yet they had heard nothing since.

In early April Trotman called up Schrempp and asked for an urgent meeting. On 20 April he visited the German executive in Stuttgart with some not altogether surprising news. There was no way the two companies could merge, he explained. The Ford family wanted to retain 40 per cent of the votes in the company. They would lose control of the family enterprise if they backed a merger.

Schrempp was not interested in the alternative: allowing Daimler to be taken over by Ford. So the conversation turned to what each company would do next.

Trotman pulled out a couple of presentations. The first one dwelled on a list of ideal merger partners for Ford, topped by Daimler-Benz – and had Chrysler in second position.

'There is no way the competition authorities would let us go for Chrysler,' Trotman said ruefully.

He turned to the second presentation. This one dealt with the world from Daimler's perspective. Top of the list of merger partners was Chrysler. This of course validated Daimler's own strategic thinking. It was tempting to blurt something out.

'So what would you do if we made a move for Chrysler?' Schrempp asked playfully.

'Publicly, I'd welcome it,' said Trotman. 'Behind the scenes I'd go to Washington and cause such a stink . . . I'd stir up the kind of headlines you haven't read about Germany since the Second World War.'

Schrempp considered himself a good friend of Trotman. He knew, however, that if he disclosed what he was really up to, the deal would be off. So he bit his tongue. 'I felt such a rat,' he admitted later.

The next time Schrempp spoke to Trotman, it was the morning of 6 May. The deal would not be announced formally until the next day but the story had already broken across the front page of the *Wall Street Journal.* It was a very short, frosty telephone conversation. It took some time before Trotman and Schrempp were back on even vaguely friendly terms.

CHAPTER 13

Getting Everybody On-Side

Building consensus in the last weeks

Frankfurt, Saturday, 18 April 1998

Hilmar Kopper, the chairman of Daimler's supervisory board, has a great deal in common with Schrempp. Like Schrempp, he is what the Germans call a *Leistungsverfechter*, a man who has got to the very top entirely on his own merits. He started life as an apprentice at the Deutsche Bank, rising to become first chief executive and subsequently chairman.

When Schrempp proposed paying a visit to Kopper to give him details of the merger, he knew that this would be no ordinary encounter. He had spoken to Kopper about it informally earlier in the year, and had kept him posted throughout the negotiations, so the banker was at least in the picture as far as the transaction was concerned. But he had yet to have a good look at the proposed structure. Today, one way or another, history would be made. Either Kopper would raise objections, causing huge complications for the deal, or he would give it his blessing, bringing the merger one step further towards completion.

Both men's diaries were crowded so they arranged to meet at 4 p.m. on Saturday in Kopper's villa in the elegant Frankfurt suburb of Kronberg. Schrempp and Cordes were ferried past the armed guards to Kopper's private sanctuary.

As they sat down in Kopper's sitting-room, Schrempp outlined the deal and its strategic rationale. Typically, he spoke for only a few minutes.

'Hilmar,' he said. 'I think we are making some serious progress with this; it's time for you to know exactly what we are doing. It would be great to understand whether you support it.' Schrempp briefly ran through the industrial logic and then passed the baton to Cordes.

Cordes and Kopper soon immersed themselves in the details of the deal, fellow technicians discussing the exchange ratio and the legal structure. Schrempp helped himself to coffee and cake.

Kopper asked one difficult question after another. Schrempp and Cordes could tell that he was sceptical: they sensed that Kopper liked the idea, but didn't believe that it could be done in practice. One by one, Cordes dealt with the outstanding issues. The banker grew gradually more excited as he understood the implications of the deal. Finally, Kopper declared that the deal was 'absolutely marvellous' and went to his wine cellar to fetch his three best bottles of wine. He pulled the corks out from the 1975 Château Lafite, leaving the bottles on the sideboard to breathe with their labels facing tantalisingly towards the wall. After a decent interval, the three men drank the vintage claret.

'Hilmar,' Schrempp said as the afternoon drew to a close. 'Please remember that we've been talking to you in your capacity as chairman of Daimler-Benz, not wearing your Deutsche Bank hat.'

At that stage, Kopper was still chief executive of the bank.

'Well,' said Kopper, 'I'm going to have to involve some of my colleagues. You won't mind if I have one of your presentation folders to show to my people what you're planning.'

'No,' said Schrempp bluntly. 'If I did that they'd be circulating around the Deutsche Bank in a matter of minutes. I can't let you have them.'

The banker was disappointed, but Schrempp was insistent. He wanted to make the point that there was – or should have been – a Chinese wall within the person of Hilmar Kopper.

It was all very well giving him a briefing as a friend and as chairman of Daimler's supervisory board, but that wasn't the same as talking to him in his capacity as representative of Daimler's biggest shareholder.

Kopper conceded the point and Schrempp and Cordes were driven down the hill to Frankfurt.

Schrempp and Cordes joined Dibelius and Grube in the Gallo Nero restaurant in Frankfurt's West End. They reported that Kopper was on-side. So now, the essentials of the deal were in place. It was time for them at last to inform the Daimler management board.

Stuttgart, Sunday, 19 April 1998

A special board meeting had been convened for the next day. In the Möhringen boardroom, Schrempp and Cordes did their usual double act. Schrempp kept to the big picture, while Cordes ran through the details, skipping through the slides at his customary pace. The news came as a surprise to virtually all the board members. Hubbert and Zetsche, the two car chieftains, had been told in March that Schrempp had opened talks with Chrysler, but they did not know how far the conversation had gone. They, like everyone else, were astonished that the deal was so close to completion.

'This is great, this is fantastic, this is just what we need,' exclaimed Hubbert at the end of the presentation. For the passenger car boss, the news came as an answer to his prayers. For years, he and Zetsche had been urging Schrempp to do something to secure the long-term future of Mercedes, and Schrempp looked set to deliver at last.

Elsewhere in the room, the reaction was curiously muted. 'It's an interesting idea,' said Manfred Gentz, the finance director. Gentz was immediately sceptical that the complex structure outlined by Schrempp and Cordes could be made to work. He persuaded the board that they should take further legal advice before signing off on the deal.

Later, Gentz told Schrempp privately that he thought there was no way the transaction could be done. He said the deal looked too complicated and that there was not enough time to get the necessary clearance from all the parties involved. To minimise the risk of failure, he suggested delaying the timetable. Schrempp refused.

New York and Washington, Monday, 20 April and Tuesday, 21 April 1998

The next day, Schrempp and Cordes flew to New York. Cordes went on to Washington, where he and Gary Valade had an important meeting with the SEC, while Schrempp met Eaton for dinner.

For the first time, they discussed how they were going to share out boardroom responsibilities between the two companies. Eaton's opening position was that the jobs should be divided half and half, with eight board members from either side. Schrempp wasn't too happy with that. Rather than hammer out the details there and then, they decided to reconvene the next morning in Schrempp's suite at the Four Seasons Hotel.

Before Schrempp went to bed he spoke to Rüdiger Grube, filling him in on the latest conversation with Eaton. Grube knew what was needed and immediately got to work on the charts. By the next morning, Schrempp was equipped with a full set of slides showing how the company might be organised.

Schrempp was prepared in other ways. He brought along his

invaluable flip-chart, and he had his Clara – the IBM portable from which Schrempp is inseparable. The slim computer carried all Daimler-Benz's strategic and financial plans as well as organisational charts. It also gave him access via the internet to Daimler's 'war-room', a centralised database of information on every aspect of the company and its markets.

Eaton showed Schrempp a sketch of the board as he saw it.

'Mmm, interesting,' the German said, privately horrified at Eaton's plan to split the jobs 50:50.

He switched on his Clara and showed Eaton how he envisaged the structure.

Eaton didn't agree with this either, so it was time to go back to fundamentals.

At this point, Schrempp started to sketch out the organisation on the flip-chart. At the top, he filled in a box with his and Eaton's initials, signifying the two co-chairmen. That much was uncontroversial. Underneath, he drew row after row of small boxes, all empty.

'I need to keep my people who have nothing to do with cars, that much you must agree,' said Schrempp. It was obvious to him that Daimler's aerospace activities and its Debis service subsidiary needed boardroom representation.

Eaton saw the logic and nodded his agreement. Schrempp inked in the names of Klaus Mangold and Manfred Bischoff, head of debis and DASA respectively.

'And you can hardly disagree that my car and truck guys need to be there as well,' said Schrempp, inking in Jürgen Hubbert (Mercedes-Benz cars), Dieter Zetsche (passenger vehicle sales and marketing) and Kurt Lauk (commercial vehicles).

'Now we come to research and development.' Schrempp was on firm ground here. He knew that Daimler's R&D budget dwarfed that of Chrysler, which was well known for developing new products with a much smaller outlay than its competitors.

'Here are my R&D figures,' said Schrempp, punching on the keyboard of his Clara to call up a comparison between the two companies. 'Show me yours if you like.'

Eaton didn't have the figures with him.

Schrempp continued. 'Do you agree that basically you don't have any R&D?'

'Well, we have a little bit, but it's by no means what you have,' Eaton conceded.

Schrempp inked in the name of Klaus-Dieter Vöhringer.

So far, the count was seven Germans to one American. Time to add some Chrysler executives. Schrempp and Eaton got down on their hands and knees, Schrempp's diagram spread out in front of them on the floor. They each wielded a marker pen as they added and subtracted names from the chart.

In came Chrysler's head of production, out went a Daimler engineer . . . and so on until they had a list of fifteen or sixteen board directors. The posts that they hadn't filled were two of the most important of all; chief financial officer and head of global purchasing. And the two companies' CFOs, Manfred Gentz of Daimler-Benz and Gary Valade of Chrysler, were yet to be allocated a job.

'You know, the CFO is a pretty important guy,' said Schrempp. 'But possibly equally or even more important is the guy who spends the big money, the purchasing guy who spends $70 billion a year.'

'Are we going to have a centralised purchasing function or a decentralised one?' asked Eaton, wondering just how much power would be concentrated in the hands of the purchasing chief.

'That will be a centralised function,' said Schrempp. 'And I think that should be an American, because you guys are absolutely excellent at that job. So don't you think that your man Gary Valade should be the man in charge of $70 billion, while our man Manfred Gentz is the chief financial officer.'

'Jürgen, let me think about that,' said Eaton. He had assumed that Valade would be CFO of the new company; it was natural for an American to take on a role which would be as much about communicating with investors as holding the financial purse-strings.

'Bob, we haven't got time to think about it, we've got to decide now,' said Schrempp. 'I tell you what, let's take a break, you go and ask Gary if he's happy with this idea.'

Eaton went downstairs to the hotel lobby, spoke to Valade, and returned twenty minutes later. 'Okay, it's on,' he said.

There was just one issue left to resolve: what honorific to give to Tom Stallkamp, currently president of Chrysler Corporation. The title of president signified Stallkamp's special standing at Chrysler: he was Eaton's designated successor. Under the new structure, Stallkamp would be co-head of passenger cars along with Jürgen Hubbert. He would also be given overall responsibility for integrating the two companies. Beyond these responsibilities, Stallkamp wanted to keep the title of president. Schrempp explained that German companies didn't recognise this title, so it would be meaningless to make him president of the new entity. In the end he and Eaton decided Stallkamp could be president of the US subsidiary of the merged company – the future DaimlerChrysler Corporation – a subtle distinction from being president of the entire group. This would put him on a par with Jürgen Hubbert, the head of the Mercedes-Benz brand portfolio. Although not obvious at the time, it was the first sign that Stallkamp's star was on the wane.

By the end of the meeting, they had agreed who was going to do what. The outcome was a top-heavy board with a total of seventeen members. The only director from either Daimler or Chrysler not to keep his position was Dennis Pawley who was planning to retire at the end of 1999 in any case. (At the last minute Pawley was reinstated as the quid pro quo for Chrysler accepting the DaimlerChrysler name.) In essence everybody got to keep their jobs. It was obviously an unwieldy structure, the product of a compromise. The bloodletting would come later.

In the meantime, the result of the meeting was that Germans would dominate the board. Former Daimler executives would outnumber ex-Chrysler directors ten to seven.

There was one final piece of business: they had to fix a date for the announcement. They decided that things were going so well that they could shoot for a date in mid-May. They settled on 15 May.

The day after Schrempp and Eaton discussed the board, Cordes and Valade went to see the SEC in Washington. The purpose of the visit was to present the deal and to obtain the regulator's approval for the 'pooling of interest' which would make such a difference to the merged companies' financial results.

The argument turned on the effect of the dreaded German *Spruchstellenverfahren*. If a significant number of German shareholders won an extra payout as a result of a court challenge to the deal, the SEC would rule that it was a takeover not a merger. And if it were a takeover, then pooling would not be allowed. Cordes and Valade argued the case. The SEC promised to get back in touch within a week.

Stuttgart, Saturday, 26 April

'Mr Kopper, of course I'm in favour of the deal, but the timetable is very important. I'm not sure we can make it.'

Manfred Gentz was sitting next to Hilmar Kopper at a dinner held after a meeting of Daimler's international advisory board. Kopper was there as a guest in his capacity as chairman of the supervisory board.

'What are you talking about?' said Kopper, who had the utmost respect for the Daimler finance director but was in no doubt now that Gentz's conservative instincts had to be overruled.

'Look, we have less than three weeks to go. Do we have to do it in so short a period of time?'

'You know,' said Kopper, 'I tell you what, that's precisely what we are going to do.'

Kopper voiced his opinion: in a situation like this one, it is essential to put everybody under considerable time pressure. 'Because if it leaks out, the deal is off,' he said.

Later, Schrempp and Kopper agreed that the deadline should be brought forward: from 15 May to 6 May.

London, Monday, 27 April and Tuesday, 28 April 1998

The car guys from both companies had still not met to discuss the deal. The negotiations had been handled entirely by the CEOs and their finance and strategy executives, assisted by growing numbers of accountants, lawyers and bankers. Finally, ten days before the deal was announced, the engineers got together in London to work on a joint business plan.

The two-day meeting was critical. Up until now both negotiating teams had taken a lot for granted. They assumed, correctly as it turned out, that the engineers would back the deal in principle. But they also took a leap of faith when it came to concrete cost-savings and technical synergies. The financial case for the deal depended on the engineers being able to shave billions from their shared cost base.

'We did dozens of valuations,' recalled Cordes, 'and for all of them we just plugged in this or that number for synergies. We said to ourselves, we'll rely on the number for the time being and at the right time we'll get it confirmed by operations. Basically, if the engineers had said it's no use, no we can't deliver that, then the deal would have been off – it would have been unworkable from a financial standpoint.'

Each side sent a team of seven people. The German delegation included Cordes, Zetsche and Hubbert. Among the Americans were Tom Stallkamp, Tom Gale (head of design) and Thomas Sidlik (procurement and supply).

Fortunately for the transaction, the meeting proved tremendously productive. The two teams came up with dozens of ideas to cut costs and pool their resources. The biggest saving by far would come from combining their purchases of raw materials and components. Chrysler spent $30 billion a year on direct materials – everything from steel to electronic components, while Daimler's expenditure fell just short of $13 billion. If you put these two together and cut costs by a modest 1 per cent, the combined companies would be able to save $430 million in the first year alone.

That was just the start. They would save $150–80 million by starting to produce Mercedes' popular M-Class in a Chrysler factory. They would sell 20,000 Chrysler trucks through the Daimler distribution network in Latin America and other parts of the developing world, saving $55 million. Tens of millions could be trimmed from production costs by putting Daimler's diesel engines into Chrysler's off-road vehicles, the same again by combining their fuel cell and electric vehicle development programmes . . . and so on.

The engineers came up with savings of $1.4 billion in total short-term savings. After 1999, the first full year of the merger, the savings would get a lot bigger. Longer term, they calculated, the two companies would be able to shave $3 billion a year from their combined costs. The numbers were more than enough to satisfy Cordes. Plug them into the financial models, and the logic of the deal was as strong as ever.

Washington and Detroit, Frankfurt and Stuttgart, Wednesday, 29 April and Thursday, 30 April 1998

Bad news from Washington.

As promised, the SEC came back within a week of the deputation from Cordes and Valade. Despite their vehement arguments, the SEC rejected the Denver–Cleveland logic. The only way they would allow pooling would be if 90 per cent or more of the German shareholders tendered their shares in favour of the transaction.

This was an extraordinarily high threshold, especially considering that German shares are bearer shares whose owners are hard to track down. The news prompted a fretful conference call. Schrempp and Eaton, together with Cordes and Valade, discussed the implications of the SEC's ruling. Did it scupper the deal? Would they have to go back to the drawing board?

The Americans were in less of a flap than the Germans, for whom the planned tender offer was an extreme novelty. Daimler's conservative legal and finance executives still found it difficult to believe that the transaction could be carried out as planned. 'You'll make it,' said Eaton, a welcome voice of calm.

The negotiating teams decided to stick with the existing structure, although there was an unofficial Daimler-Benz board meeting scheduled for the next day in Frankfurt. The purpose of the meeting was to discuss 'legal problems'. A number of outside legal experts were due to pass judgement on the proposed transaction structure. This had the potential to develop into a serious stumbling block.

The SEC's ruling made the next day's meeting even more tense. It took place at the Kempinski Hotel near Frankfurt airport. Most of the Daimler management board members attended, as did more than a dozen lawyers from Daimler, from Deutsche Bank, as well as from the spiralling number of advisors. A special guest was Michael Hoffman-Becking, a man regarded by many as the doyen of German corporate lawyers.

Schrempp stayed away. He also instructed Goldman Sachs not to attend, as he did not want to be seen to be controlling or manipulating the result. In characteristic fashion he had little patience for the technicalities that were being debated so furiously. 'He had especially little patience to the extent that any of the legal problems were being put forward as obstacles to the larger objective,' observed one close colleague.

Cordes did go along, taking a low profile. He was exasperated to see the meeting degenerate into a bun-fight between his own side's lawyers. The can-do attitude that had characterised the negotiations so far was in danger of being overwhelmed by Teutonic pedantry. 'It was bloody,' recalled Cordes. 'Never again!'

The lawyers dispersed without reaching a definite conclusion.

'There are so many complications, we haven't had time to consider all the options,' Gentz told Schrempp after the meeting.

'It doesn't surprise me that the deal is complicated,' said Schrempp in response.

'Let's take the time to address all the issues in a special board meeting on Sunday. Don't get nervous – tell your guys to go and do some more homework!'

CHAPTER 14

What's in a Name?

*How the deal nearly fell apart at the last minute
over a legal misunderstanding and an argument
over the name*

Sunday, 2 May 1998

It is one of the drawbacks of the job: you have to travel around the world attending functions when there are many more important things to do back at base. On the first weekend of May 1998 the entire Daimler-Benz management board was obliged to attend a concert in Stockholm, where Daimler was sponsoring a performance given by the Berlin Philharmonic Orchestra.

Schrempp has a special loathing for such formal gatherings. There is nothing he likes less than being stuffed into a penguin suit and obliged to make polite conversation with businessmen and bankers. This time, his frustration was even greater than usual. He alone had to stay behind on Saturday night, while all his colleagues flew back straight after the concert. There was important business at hand, and Schrempp was keen to be at the centre of the action.

The next morning, Schrempp flew back to Stuttgart in time to join a special meeting of the Daimler-Benz management board. The directors were gathered together with their legal advisors, tidying up loose ends.

Although there were only a few days to go before the announcement, family and close colleagues still did not know what was afoot. There were no secretaries present on that Sunday and the board members found themselves having to perform menial tasks that they had not done themselves for many a decade. One director managed to break the photocopier, another narrowly escaped getting his fingers stuck in the shredding machine. Another still had problems detaching himself from overhead transparencies which became charged with static and remained obstinately stuck to his clothes.

All but two of the directors were casually dressed, but for all the informality it was a critical meeting. It took place in the formal boardroom on the first floor of the Hochhaus, the deliberations of the *Vorstand* watched over by Andy Warhol's giant tableau of multiple Mercedes 300SLs. Schrempp was concerned to win the board's approval for the complex legal structure underlying the proposed deal with Chrysler.

'Tell me, if we delay the process by one month or two months, will you be any the wiser? Will you be able to add any more to your assessment today?'

Schrempp was sitting calmly at the head of the boardroom table. His question was addressed to Michael Hoffman-Becking of Hengeler, Mueller & Weitzel-Wirtz and Georg Thoma from Shearman, Sterling, two external experts who had been invited along to this decisive board meeting.

'No,' each of the lawyers answered in their turn.

'What would you do if you were sitting in my place, would you take the risk or would you not take the risk? Give me an answer, yes or no.'

It was all untested ground. Eckhard Cordes kept quiet,

Manfred Bischoff voiced his support, Kurt Lauk took notes, Manfred Gentz looked sceptical.

'Just explain the risks to me,' Schrempp continued. 'I want a clear answer!'

There were basically two choices. First, a straightforward merger of Daimler with Chrysler. The second, which Schrempp supported, involved the creation of a new company which would make an offer to buy up all the Daimler shares. When the new company had taken ownership of the old Daimler shares, it would itself be merged with Chrysler.

The latter route was likely to minimise the risks of *Spruchstellenverfahren* – the legal challenge which could lead to a payout to disaffected shareholders.

'Not so fast,' Schrempp said at one point, interrupting one of the lawyer's elegant disquisitions on the pros and cons of various structures. 'Tell us what the risk is and whether there is a way to avoid it.'

'Is this a legal or an economic question?' he said a moment later. 'If it's legal, I want you to deal with it, if it's economic it's my decision.'

It was quite a performance. 'He managed to slice through some incredibly complicated issues,' recalls Christoph Walther. 'He boiled everything down to a series of yes or no questions and answers.'

Shortly after midday, the Daimler-Benz company secretary recorded that the board had formally approved the proposed merger. Schrempp left the meeting before it had finished, flying from Stuttgart to London where he caught the Concorde to New York.

As Schrempp was on the way to the plane, a number of other legal issues were discussed. There were two fundamentally important points. The first was the nature of the merger contract: so far, the two parties had agreed that the contract would be drawn up under Delaware law. Would it not be more appropriate for it to be constructed under German law? The second issue was board approval. The management board had signed off on the deal, but the supervisory board was not scheduled to meet until the Wednesday of the following week.

Not unnaturally, the Americans wanted assurances that the supervisory board would approve the deal. The management board was not in a position to speak for the supervisory board. Technically, therefore, there was no promise of board approval – a problem for the Chrysler directors. Eaton had made it clear that Chrysler's directors could not approve the deal until Daimler's had done the same.

Thus began a sequence of events that would lead to a misunderstanding which almost killed the deal.

After the board meeting finished, Siegfried Schwung, one of Daimler's legal team, was charged with passing on the gist of what had been agreed to the Chrysler side. The lawyer drew up a six-point memo to Bill O'Brien, Chrysler's general counsel. Schwung conveyed the message to O'Brien but O'Brien took it to mean he wanted to reopen the structure of the deal as Daimler refused to adopt the share option plan that the Chrysler team wanted. The message reached the US while Schrempp was on the Concorde.

The phone call had an explosive effect on the Americans. O'Brien and Eaton were horrified at both the substance of the message and the peremptory language in which it was framed. It looked as though the Germans did not want to do the deal after all.

'Each one of these points is a deal-breaker. We aren't going along with any of them,' was the response from the American side.

'Can it wait until Monday?' asked one German member of the Daimler legal team after hearing Chrysler's reaction.

'If Mr Schrempp doesn't give Mr Eaton a call when he arrives in New York, Mr Eaton will not be in town tomorrow.'

In other words, the deal would be off, just as Eaton and Schrempp were supposed to be getting together in Manhattan for a final wrap-up meeting.

* * *

Later that day Schrempp arrived at the St Regis Hotel in Manhattan to find an invitation for dinner with Jon Corzine, then senior partner of Goldman Sachs. As Schrempp arrived outside the Primavera restaurant on West 48th Street, a car pulled up behind them. Inside were Eckhard Cordes and Alex Dibelius. Schrempp was amazed when he saw the two men jump out of the car and run up to him. Shouting and waving, they were obviously panic-stricken. 'The deal is off, the deal is off,' they cried. They told Schrempp to call Bob Eaton as a matter of great urgency.

The various points relayed by one of Daimler's legal team had gone down badly with Chrysler. It was clear from what Cordes and Dibelius said that Eaton was enraged.

Schrempp insisted on sitting down for his Italian dinner before returning Eaton's call. It took forty-five minutes for him to eat his *spaghetti pomodore*, during which time everyone else at the table grew steadily more exasperated.

There was strategy behind the insouciance: Schrempp wanted to give Eaton plenty of time to calm down before he returned his call. Finally, he asked Lydia to see if there was a private room from where he could call Eaton. He and Lydia went off to the manager's cubicle. It was chaotic, with papers everywhere, and Schrempp had to sit on the manager's desk as there was only one chair where Lydia sat and took notes.

'Hi, Bob, how are you?' opened Schrempp.

'I'm not very well, actually,' said Eaton sourly.

'What's the problem?'

'If this is the way to tell me the deal is off why don't you at least tell me straight,' answered Eaton.

'What the hell are you talking about?' said Schrempp. 'I mean, do me a favour. I've had a long day, I've flown all the way here, I've had a marvellous *spaghetti al dente*, the red wine was fantastic as well, I'm looking forward to seeing you tomorrow.'

Eaton mellowed.

'Why don't we go through the points?' said Schrempp. And so they went through them one by one, with Lydia sitting taking notes.

'We don't have any problems,' Eaton said at the end of ten minutes, sounding somewhat amazed. They had easily settled the four relatively minor issues and Schrempp had conceded that the contract should be under Delaware not German law. They had agreed to talk about the question of boardroom approval at their meeting the next morning.

'Those crazy lawyer,' said Eaton reflectively.

'All lawyers are crazy,' agreed Schrempp.

There were three working days to go before the deal was to be announced, and some big unresolved issues needed to be cleared up. The most emotive was the name.

'What about the name?' said Schrempp when he met Eaton the following day.

It was a loaded question as Schrempp knew that the Americans wanted to call the company Chrysler–Daimler. He found this out only because one of Chrysler's advisors had dropped a draft presentation on to the floor. A sharp-eyed colleague had spotted the Chrysler-Daimler name in the document and relayed the information to Schrempp.

'Well, we've agreed the name haven't we,' replied Eaton. 'The company is going to be called Chrysler-Daimler-Benz.'

'No, no,' spluttered Schrempp.

'That was always the understanding.'

'No, I can't do that. Let's call it Daimler-Benz-Chrysler.'

'That's impossible for me, you know that. I've given enough already, there is no chance,' Eaton exclaimed.

'You know my board won't let me accept anything starting with Chrysler,' said Schrempp. 'What about Daimler-Chrysler-Benz.'

Eaton demurred; this was not what they had agreed.

'Okay, fine,' Schrempp said. 'I will give up something that hurts me most. You know we have two founding fathers of this company. There was Gottlieb Daimler from Stuttgart in Swabia and Karl Benz from Mannheim in Baden. That's where I come from. I offer you Daimler-Chrysler.'

'No, I'm sorry, it has to be Chrysler-Daimler-Benz.'

'That's not acceptable, it has to be Daimler-Chrysler. Have a think about it.'

'Consider Chrysler-Daimler-Benz,' said Eaton.

'Okay, I think we might have a problem here,' said Schrempp. 'I can't talk about it any more, I have to go to the airport.'

There was little point in prolonging the debate, Schrempp said to himself. The two men would simply dig themselves into increasingly entrenched positions if they carried on talking. It would become harder and harder to find a compromise without one or other losing face. The issue was left unresolved.

There was one more issue: Chrysler was worried about signing off on the deal without formal approval from the Daimler-Benz board.

'This is a major concern,' Bob Eaton had said earlier in the meeting. 'It means we can't have an announcement on the seventh because my board of directors can't approve the deal when it's still subject to your approval.'

'I tell you, Bob, just give me your hand,' Schrempp pleaded, taking Eaton's hand. 'Just trust me, trust me.'

Schrempp was confident that he could deliver the necessary approval. The problem was that under German law you had to provide a full week's notice of your intention to hold a formal supervisory board meeting.

Not only do you have to provide notice to all twenty members of the supervisory board, you need to provide a detailed agenda.

This presented a double problem. There was no way Schrempp could get the board together by the 7th as planned. And simply distributing the agenda would have meant endangering the deal, as one of the twenty directors would inevitably leak the news to the press long before the meeting convened.

'Jürgen,' said Eaton. 'I mean, I really trust you, but I can't take your word for it, the legal guys insist.'

Schrempp recognised that he wasn't going to be able to cut a deal. For a moment he was flummoxed, he couldn't see a way forward. Then it occurred to him to give Hilmar Kopper a call in Frankfurt.

'Hilmar, there's a problem,' said Schrempp, explaining the issue to him.

Kopper thought for a moment, then had a brain-wave.

He said he would call a special meeting of the Daimler supervisory board for the coming Wednesday, the eve of the announcement. He would issue the invitations there and then; there would be no need to explain what it was about, people would come out of simple curiosity. Technically, however, it would be a meeting for the purposes of disseminating information and no decisions could formally be ratified.

To get round this, Kopper said that he would be able to speak for at least ten votes at the end of that meeting. He would secure written pledges from all the shareholder representatives on the supervisory board. He would get them to say that they would definitely vote in favour of the deal at the formal decision-making board meeting. This would take place after the statutory two weeks had elapsed.

On top of the ten votes from the capital side of the board, there was also his casting vote as chairman. He was pretty certain he and Schrempp would be able to convince at least one of the labour representatives – Manfred Göbels, who represented middle managers on the supervisory board and could usually be relied upon to side with shareholders' representatives.

If Kopper were prepared to put all this in writing to Chrysler's lawyers, would they not have a deal?

Eaton took advice from his legal team and the answer came back that Kopper's solution would be acceptable.

Tuesday, 5 May 1998

Schrempp took the night Concorde back to London and went on to Germany.

Until now the negotiations had been conducted in the plush surroundings of five-star hotels and investment bank head-quarters. Today, Schrempp was to be reminded of his roots as he travelled to Baden, the western half of the state of Baden-Württemberg in southern Germany. More poignantly, he was to meet a colleague and sparring partner whose terminal illness served to put the deal into its proper perspective.

He was driven from Stuttgart to Mannheim to visit Karl Feuerstein. As the birthplace of Karl Benz, Mannheim has special significance in the Daimler-Benz culture. To this day, workers at the Mannheim factories see themselves as working primarily for Benz rather than a larger group.

Feuerstein, long a combative representative of the workforce on Daimler's supervisory board, was in hospital being treated for cancer. Schrempp apologised to the union leader's wife, before launching into a necessarily brief summary of the deal.

Schrempp needed to address the anxieties of the unions and explained to Feuerstein that the merger would mean more jobs rather than job cuts. The merged company would be a German *Aktiengesellschaft*, and worker representation would be rolled out to American employees as well. It was, Schrempp explained, a victory for the values Feuerstein had been fighting for all his life.

Feuerstein gave his approval and agreed to vote for the deal at the forthcoming supervisory board meeting.

Schrempp was in reflective mood as he was driven on from Mannheim to Frankfurt. He was certainly not ready for further negotiations about the Daimler name. He had, he felt, done enough by offering to discard the emotionally charged Benz name.

He and Lydia went for dinner at the Japanese restaurant at the Hotel Arabella in downtown Frankfurt. His mobile phone went – it was Eaton. The Chrysler CEO told him that he and the rest of his board refused to countenance the Daimler-Chrysler name.

For the first time in the entire negotiations, Schrempp played hardball.

'Okay, if you can't agree then let's go to Hawaii and have a party,' he said. 'The deal is off.'

'What?' said Eaton, somewhat stunned.

'Yes, the deal is off,' said Schrempp. 'It's a show-stopper, I'm not agreeing with that.'

'You can't say that!'

'Yes, believe me, it's a show-stopper,' said the German. 'But we are good friends, let's go to Hawaii.'

'Okay, fine,' said Eaton. 'The deal is off, I cannot get this past my board.'

That was the end of the conversation. Schrempp's tapanyaki were being cooked in front of him on a hotplate. He was just starting his meal a few minutes later when his phone rang again. It was Cordes.

Cordes said he had been talking to Gary Valade, Bob Eaton's chief financial officer. 'I think we have a deal,' he explained. 'If we give them an eighth board member, they will be prepared to let us have the Daimler-Chrysler name.' Up until then the plan was to have ten board members from Daimler-Benz and seven from Chrysler.

'Let me just ask you again, let me ask again,' Schrempp replied, getting angry. 'Do they insist that we give them an extra board member, or are they asking nicely?'

'Jürgen, what does it matter?' said an increasingly agitated Cordes. 'I mean if we give them the board member and you accept that we have the name and we have a deal.'

Schrempp and Cordes are close friends. From time to time, this means that they do not observe the normal civilities in the way they talk to each other.

'You can go back to them and tell them over my dead body,' shouted Schrempp.

Cordes lost his temper. '*Ich mach' jetzt nichts mehr*, I've had enough,' he shouted back. 'Do your own deals from now on!' He threw his mobile phone to the floor. The line went dead.

'What did he say?' asked Lydia.

'He wasn't very nice to me!' replied Schrempp.

'I won't let myself be blackmailed,' Schrempp explained. 'It's apples and pears, the name has got nothing to do with the board. I don't see why I should trade one for the other.'

'So what do we do next?' she asked.

'We're going to have some beef, and some wine and enjoy the meal.' Schrempp ordered some more saki.

Shortly afterwards Lydia left the restaurant on the pretext of visiting the bathroom. She called Rüdiger Grube.

'Guys,' she said, 'you know how Schrempp is, this isn't the way to approach him. Why not suggest to the other side that they ask for an extra board position. Don't link it to the name thing, just get them to ask tomorrow and I'm sure there won't be any problems. Just don't insist on it, you know what Jürgen is like.'

Grube passed the message on to Valade.

Later that night, Schrempp got a message from Christoph Walther. The cat is out of the bag,' he said. 'It looks as though the story is going to be in tomorrow's *Wall Street Journal*.'

CHAPTER 15

The Deal is Announced

The last two days

New York, Stuttgart, Detroit

While Jürgen Schrempp travelled to Mannheim to visit Karl Feuerstein in hospital, Steve Lipin was putting the finishing touches to an article which – when it appeared on the front page of the *Wall Street Journal* the next day – would be one of the great business exclusives of the decade.

Lipin, the thirty-five-year-old editor of the *WSJ*'s Heard on the Street column, was at last convinced that the story 'had legs'. He had been chasing rumours of a big industrial merger since the middle of the previous week. Before the weekend, he found out the names of the two companies and what they were planning to do. He was, he later acknowledged, 'absolutely stunned' by the magnitude of the story he had discovered. Yet, given his knowledge of the auto industry and of Daimler-Benz as the most Americanised of European companies, he also found it totally believable.

He could have run the piece there and then, but his antennae picked up news of last-minute disagreements. He held back – much better to run a story about a deal that does eventually happen than to report on talks that are ultimately abandoned. To use journalists' jargon, he spent Monday 'standing up' the piece by talking to trusted contacts. By Tuesday, his sources were telling him that the deal was imminent.

How imminent, Lipin did not know. 'The negotiations have foundered at least once, and there's no certainty that a deal will yet be reached,' he wrote. 'Still, the two companies have made significant progress in their talks, and the flash-point for the decision appears to be coming soon.'

With hindsight, the story was fantastically well-informed and brilliantly timed. It came out the day before the deal was announced, it got the numbers right, it explained the industrial rationale in detail, it asked all the right questions. Would it be a takeover rather than a merger? How would the companies grapple with different corporate cultures?

In short, it was the piece that everyone in the world with the vaguest interest in the transaction had to read on the morrow. It was the article that set the tone for the coverage produced on Wednesday by thousands of harassed and comparatively ill-informed journalists all around the world.

One question remains unanswered to this day: who talked to Lipin? Could it have been Gershon Kekst, the legendary New York PR guru who was working for Chrysler at the time? Was it Steve Koch from CSFB? Or Alex Dibelius from Goldman Sachs, or Christoph Walther, head of Daimler's communications department? Or did it originate from Kirk Kerkorian? Neither Lipin nor anyone else involved in the transaction is saying.

Was the story planted? A reporter like Lipin bristles at the suggestion that he may have been manipulated. Journalists of integrity look on their profession as the noble art of extracting information from a variety of sources and transmuting this raw material into truthful articles. On the other hand, PR people, investment bankers, corporate lawyers and CEOs see the press as an instrument of corporate policy. Journalists are there to be used, albeit in the nicest way possible. Ultimately the press is a medium for distributing information in such a way that it advances your corporate objectives.

Lipin's article appeared the day before the deal was announced – by no means perfect timing from the perspective of Daimler or Chrysler (although it did ensure a huge level of interest in the story when it was confirmed the next day). There was a void of twenty-four hours between the appearance of the *WSJ* on Wednesday and the press announcement planned for first thing on Thursday. During this time the companies could do nothing to influence the press other than issue a pre-prepared holding statement confirming that the companies were in talks.

In Stuttgart and Auburn Hills, the PR teams got wind of the coming story and girded themselves to issue the fall-back release.

Frankfurt and London, Wednesday, 6 May 1998

Bob Eaton arrived at Frankfurt airport. He had flown over from Detroit and was scheduled to visit Frankfurt before going on to London for the signing ceremony.

He took a quick shower in his hotel room and then went to Deutsche Bank's frosty-blue twin-towered headquarters. Eaton was ushered into the special entrance for guests of the board members before taking the elevator to Hilmar Kopper's office on the 29th floor. Awaiting him were Schrempp and Kopper.

Before sitting down for a German breakfast of sausage and scrambled eggs, Eaton and Schrempp walked over to the window. Looking out over the Taunus hills in the distance and Frankfurt's business district in the foreground, Eaton asked Schrempp for an extra board member 'as a favour'.

'Jürgen, can I talk to you for a moment,' said Eaton.

'Have you bought the cigars already?' Schrempp replied, smiling.

'Can you do me a favour? It'll help us resolve the problem.'

'I don't know what you're talking about,' said Schrempp, disingenuously.

'I think we need another board director there,' said Eaton. 'I mean, just for a short time while we sort a few things out.'

Schrempp pulled out the new company logo. He passed it to Eaton. It said 'DaimlerChrysler Aktiengesellschaft'. The letters were in blue and the background was grey – Daimler-Benz's corporate colours. It was produced overnight by Rüdiger Grube and Christoph Walther and it looked immaculate.

'Doesn't that look beautiful?' Schrempp said.

'That really looks good,' agreed Eaton.

All three men were in a buoyant mood; they were on the verge of making business history. There were just two remaining technicalities. Kopper had to deliver at least ten votes from the supervisory board. Wearing his other hat, he also had to deliver Deutsche Bank's formal approval of the deal. Only with the bank's 24.4 per cent stake lodged in favour of the transaction could the deal go through.

Kopper assured Eaton that both conditions could be met. Schrempp agreed to bring the formal letters – one from the Deutsche Bank, the other from Kopper – with him when he came over to London for the signing ceremony that night.

Reassured, Eaton took a plane to London. Kopper and Schrempp took a private jet to Stuttgart where the extraordinary supervisory board meeting was due to get started at 5 p.m. This left very little time to round up the stragglers.

As Kopper had predicted, the mysterious invitation to a surprise board meeting had proved a draw. Most board members had said they would attend. However, there were still four people from the capital side of the board who could not be there. Kopper was relying on these votes in order to give the necessary assurances to Chrysler.

The whole deal depended on tracking down the four absent supervisory board members. Deininger fixed up two private rooms from which to make their emergency calls. 'Okay, here's how we'll do it,' said Kopper. 'I'll introduce the topic and then you sell.' Lydia's job was to get the four men on the line and to say, 'Good afternoon, I have Mr Kopper and Mr Schrempp on the line, they need to explain something to you.'

One by one, they found the missing directors.

'It's unfortunate you can't come this afternoon,' Kopper said. 'There is something important we are going to be discussing and I need your help.'

Only one of the four had read Lipin's article or heard the news. Schrempp took ten minutes to explain to each of them what was going on.

'It sounds great, absolutely fantastic,' said one, agreeing to sign the pieces of paper Kopper's office was sending out (a commitment to vote in favour of the transaction at the next official supervisory board meeting, in both German and English).

'You know what, Jürgen,' said another. 'I don't in the slightest bit understand what it is you are trying to do, but I trust you, I'll sign anything you want me to.'

After tracking the four down and securing their votes, Schrempp called Manfred Göbels to his room. Within the peculiar world of German corporate governance, Göbels occupies a powerful position. As representative of middle managers on the Daimler-Benz supervisory board, he belongs formally to the ten directors who represent the company's labour force. But as a manager, he normally sides with the shareholders. His vote was needed today if Kopper were not going to have to use his own casting vote.

'My dear friend, please sit down,' Schrempp said. 'In precisely five minutes you are going to see Rüdiger Grube and he will tell you all about what we are doing. Right after that I'll need your signature to these letters in English and German saying you will vote in favour of what I'm about to tell you.'

'Okay,' Göbels said, taken aback by Schrempp's obvious agitation.

'Fine, we are merging with Chrysler.'

Göbels, amazed, started to ask questions.

'I have no time to answer your questions, you can ask Rüdiger

Grube all the questions you like afterwards,' Schrempp cut in. 'Do you trust me?'

'Of course I do.'

'Have I ever lied to you?'

'No.'

After Grube explained the transaction in detail, It didn't take long for Göbels to see the logic of the deal and he signed on the dotted line.

Schrempp took the papers to Kopper, who then signed a letter saying he had eleven members of the supervisory board who would vote in favour of the deal at the formal meeting in a week's time.

Schrempp put this letter in his pocket and went to the airport. Together with Lydia, he flew to Luton airport, arriving at 9 p.m. They were picked up and driven to the Dorchester Hotel where Schrempp joined Eaton and a roomful of colleagues and advisors. Waiting until the New York stock market had closed, they signed the formal combination agreement shortly before midnight.

The two teams went down to the bar for a drink afterwards. They were all jubilant, but there was little intermingling. The Germans stayed at one end of the bar, the Americans at the other.

London, Thursday, 7 May 1998

At 7.30 a.m. the two companies informed the relevant stock markets and regulatory authorities about their plans to merge. The official press release was distributed half an hour later.

Shortly after breakfast, Eaton and Schrempp called a dozen politicians and industrialists. They then called a similar number of journalists, starting with the news agencies such as Reuters and Bloomberg before moving on to those newspapers that would set the tone internationally and in the key national markets of Germany and the US. First to receive calls were the *Financial Times* (where Schrempp talked to the automotive correspondent as well as to a reporter from the influential Lex Column), the *Wall Street Journal*, the *Bild* newspaper, the *Frankfurter Allgemeine Zeitung*, the *Handelsblatt* and the

Stuttgarter Zeitung. Der Spiegel, the influential German news magazine, was not on the list as a reporter had already been given a telephone interview with Schrempp.

A lot of hard work had gone into making the story as succinct as possible. Working from a series of bullet points prepared by Christoph Walther, they hammered away five key messages. The script said:

This is a great deal – because the transaction will

- Merge two of the world's most profitable automotive companies
- Be a perfect fit of two leaders in their respective markets
- Bring DaimlerChrysler into a leading position in the automotive industry
- Position DaimlerChrysler uniquely to exploit new opportunities
- Not lead to job cuts

The merger makes excellent commercial sense – because

- It is a deal of two strong companies, a deal for growth not for rationalisation
- It creates the best portfolio of world-class brands in the industry
- It combines the technological, marketing and financial strength of both companies
- It offers benefits through sharing of engineering, manufacturing, purchasing and technology know-how

DaimlerChrysler: it will work – because

- It brings together an outstanding management team with an impressive track record
- The partners share a common culture of creating value through innovation, quality and customer satisfaction and a clear commitment to bottom-line performance

It will create real value through

- Innovation
- Global growth
- Job creation and stimulation
- Social responsibility

DaimlerChrysler – the creation of a leading global automotive company serving

- Shareholders – it enhances corporate value
- Customers – premier brands with excellent potential
- Employees – new growth opportunities through sales in global markets

The messages were simple, even simplistic. Paradoxically, this was precisely because the communications challenge was so complex. It was imperative to win over the workforces and unions on both sides – hence the emphasis on jobs and growth. At the same time, the financial markets had to be on-side. So talk of job creation had to be balanced with an appropriate emphasis on the long-term opportunities for shareholder value.

Furthermore, the deal had to be wrapped in a cloak of consensus. Any talk of winners and losers, of a takeover rather than a merger, could stir up a powerful, emotional backlash – particularly in the US where the company had so famously been bailed out with taxpayers' money. Hence the insistence that they were doing a 'merger of equals'.

The messages were drilled home at the London press conference which took place at 2 p.m. And then again when Schrempp and Eaton did a series of interviews for US TV stations. And yet again that afternoon when they held a conference call for American journalists. The press release was sent out to thousands of separate newspapers, news organisations and radio and TV stations around the world.

The key messages were also packaged up into a letter that was sent out later that day to 2,000 influential academics, consultants and analysts. A letter signed by Eaton and Schrempp was sent to all 440,000 employees. The facts of the deal were put up on the companies' intranet and internet sites. Staff could also watch pre-recorded TV interviews with Schrempp and Eaton. These had been put together on Monday afternoon in New York at the Four Seasons Hotel, with subtly different variations to ensure that Eaton spoke for longer on the US tape while Schrempp got more air-time in the German video.

The communications machine was working at full throttle. The aim was to create a virtuous circle of positive news. The press would be encouraged to write friendly articles about the merger. The resulting headlines would then influence unions, employees, customers, shareholders, regulators, the financial community at large. They would later be used in Daimler's advertising campaign to add third-party credibility to the merger. When journalists wrote their follow-up stories on Friday and over the weekend, they would turn to precisely these constituencies for comment and analysis. They would feed back the company's own soundbites, thereby reinforcing the initially positive reaction to the deal.

The deal was announced on a Thursday with the aim of making the communications process easier. It would give reporters relatively little time to contact potential sceptical third parties such as financial analysts and academics. On Thursday, they would be too busy reporting the facts, leaving Friday as the only full working day of the week in which to put together a balanced assessment of the deal. In the meantime, DaimlerChrysler would itself be contacting opinion-formers. The hope was that they would be singing from the official hymn-sheet by the time reporters caught up with them over the weekend or on Monday of the following week.

'We were trying to move faster than the press,' explains Christoph Walther in retrospect.

It did not go entirely according to plan. A receptionist at Daimler-Benz was asked by a journalist from the *Frankfurter Allgemeine* newspaper what she thought about the new American partner. She replied that she had had a Chrysler once but that it had rusted to pieces within a year. Chrysler employees in Auburn Hills appeared chiefly interested in the size of the discount they would get on Mercedes cars. On balance, though, critical articles were very much the exception.

'Initial press coverage of the deal matched the enthusiasm with which the companies announced and presented the transaction,' said a study of the first four days' media (prepared by Kekst & Co). 'All constituencies endorsed the concept, parroting, for the most part, the benefits and rationale presented by the company in press releases, press conferences and interviews.

'Many of the themes and soundbites presented by the companies repeatedly and consistently surfaced in the press: perfect fit, world-class products and brands, well positioned for global growth, substantial cost savings, no layoffs or plant closures, significant shareholder value, largest industrial merger.'

There was a distinction between news coverage, which tended to be positive, and editorials and opinion pieces which were more sceptical. Presciently, leader-writers identified cultural differences as a potential obstacle to the success of the deal, with many articles highlighting the differences between American and German management styles. There was little analysis of the complex financial mechanics of the transaction, and equally little anti-German sentiment.

'Chrysler produced tanks for General Patton and Mercedes was producing war armaments for Adolf Hitler. How do you explain this deal to your assembly worker,' a reporter from CNBC asked Bob Eaton on Friday, 'given the emotional remnants that may very well still exist?'

Eaton responded by saying that the world had become much more global and 'that issue' was behind the country and the companies. Barring one or two historical articles, that was about the limit of anti-German sentiment.

A few months after the announcement, Schrempp was talking to Rolf Breuer of the Deutsche Bank.

'You know, Jürgen, I have an advantage over you,' said Breuer.

'Go on,' said Schrempp, intrigued.

Breuer drew out the contrast between the way the press and public had reacted to Deutsche Bank's takeover of Bankers Trust, a venerable US investment bank, and Daimler's merger with Chrysler.

'The thing is, very few people think I've done a good deal,' Breuer continued. 'So if I come out of this even reasonably well, then I'll look as though I've done exceptionally well.

'On the other hand, if you do a fantastically good job with your merger, you'll still disappoint everybody ... because everybody is convinced that you have done the most brilliant transaction.'

Breuer was right. The publicity offensive on the day of the announcement created extraordinarily high expectations. Both sides were setting themselves up for disappointment later down the road. There was, however, a strong practical reason for the hype.

The deal required the approval of both sides' shareholders. Not merely the approval of a majority of shareholders, but 90 per cent (of Daimler shareholders at least) had to cast a positive vote if the deal were to go through as planned. With 800,000 individual Daimler shareholders, this was by no means a foregone conclusion, and stock market rules made it even harder to achieve.

Once the initial announcement had been made, neither company was allowed to put out any further information about the financial or industrial rationale for the deal until the process of tendering for the shares had begun. That was not scheduled to take place until September. As a result, the initial publicity had to create a tide of favourable coverage that would carry the deal through a period of several months. Better, under the circumstances, to over-egg the pudding than to sound a cautionary note. That could have tilted sentiment against the transaction.

Concerns about the tender process proved unjustified. Daimler, together with Deutsche Bank, embarked on a logistical exercise designed to flush out each and every one of the shareholders. The bank set up special units in twenty-one Daimler workplaces so that employees could tender their shares. There was a big advertising campaign, extolling the virtues of the merger, and of a special dividend entitlement for German shareholders should the 90 per cent threshold be crossed. Manfred Gentz and Eckhard Cordes appeared on television, mystifying viewers with their explanation of the convoluted rationale for the deal structure. Tender offers and goodwill accounting are hardly the stuff of prime-time television, but the public got the message.

At a marathon shareholders' meeting held on 18 September, Hilmar Kopper reported that 99.89 per cent of Daimler stockholders had voted in favour of the transaction. Some 13,300 of them attended the meeting at the Hans-Martin-Schleyer Halle in Stuttgart. It finally ended at 11.10 p.m. after Kopper, Schrempp and the entire twenty-strong board had been obliged to listen to thirteen and a half hours of speeches and questions. One source of complaint from the floor was that the official language of the new company would be English. This was blatantly discriminatory and would lead to a gradual erosion of German culture, the critics charged. Meanwhile, the ample supply of free sausages, apple juice, cake and non-alcoholic beer suggested that certain aspects of German culture were alive and well, notwithstanding the language question.

The equivalent meeting of Chrysler shareholders was a very different affair. At the Du Pont Hotel in Wilmington, Delaware, a mere 140 shareholders showed up to witness the end of Chrysler's life as an independent entity, and the assembly lasted no more than two hours. The outcome was equally satisfactory, though, with Bob Eaton reporting that 97.5 per cent of Chrysler's shareholders had voted in favour of the deal.

'You'll unquestionably end up with the strongest automotive and transportation company in the entire world,' Eaton told his shareholders, 'with a balance sheet and product portfolio that's unparalleled.'

'Today we have the opportunity to write a new chapter in industrial history,' Schrempp told the German meeting, 'from a position of strength, on our own initiative and with a partner of our choice.'

The tender process was still under way at the time of the shareholders' meetings. By 26 October 97 per cent of shareholders had exchanged their shares for new DaimlerChrysler stock. The deal was home and dry.

On 17 November, just 200 working days after Schrempp raised the idea of a merger with Bob Eaton, the two companies finally became one. Schrempp and Eaton flew over in separate private planes, while a posse of European journalists flew over to New York from Frankfurt in a specially piloted Boeing 777: Nikki Lauda was at the controls. Wall Street was congested with the new company's hospitality tents and products – a helicopter, a fleet of sports cars, Jeeps and a heavy truck. At 9 a.m. that morning, in a ritual steeped in tradition, Eaton and Schrempp stood on the balcony overlooking the floor of the New York Stock Exchange and sounded the bell to signal the opening of trading of the new stock (designated abbreviation: DCX) on seventeen exchanges around the world. They sat on the floor of the exchange in mocked-up vehicle front ends (a Jeep Grand Cherokee and an E-Class Mercedes) honking horns.

235

All around the world, in 800 separate locations, the 428,000 employees of the new DaimlerChrysler were celebrating too. When they arrived at work each one of them received a letter of congratulation from the two chairmen, a poster showing all the new company's products – and a Swatch watch. Daimler ordered 460,000 of these watches, making sure that contractors as well as full-time staff got one too. New DaimlerChrysler business cards were ready that morning and in an amazing logistical feat the two companies managed to change over all the signage at hundreds of locations around the world to show the new name.

Employees could watch the New York ceremony on the newly installed DaimlerChrysler TV channel. Cheerleaders gathered on Berlin's Potsdamer Platz, an American country band played for the workers of Untertürkheim. Canteens from Detroit to Tuscaloosa in the US served up *Wiener schnitzel* and *späetzle*, together with merger-blend cups of coffee, while in Sindelfinden and Untertürkheim doughnuts, cookies and muffins were on the menu for the first time.

By the end of the night the new company was well and truly christened – and a total of $45 million had been spent on the party.

Among the many letters of congratulation that flooded into Schrempp's office, one stands out. 'An extraordinary business attainment and the beginning of a vitally important global adventure,' is how Arthur Levitt, chairman of the Securities & Exchange Commission, gave his verdict on the deal.

The adventure was just beginning.

PART 4

Getting to Know Each Other

CHAPTER 16

Kultur Clash

The first steps towards integrating the two companies .

Summer 1998

In early July 1998 Bob Eaton invited the entire Daimler board to Auburn Hills, the suburb of Detroit where Chrysler operates out of an immense and futuristic office complex.

This was the first of a series of events designed to bring together senior managers from both sides. They would not formally be able to get to work on the integration of the two companies until November. But if they could thrash out as many issues as possible beforehand, they would have a head start when the deal was finally done. And they would get to know each other better.

After a formal presentation on the fifteenth floor, the Germans were taken out to the Proving Ground, a nearby racetrack, and given the opportunity to test-drive the full range of Chrysler cars. The party finished careering around the tarmac and went back to the plush Townsend Hotel in Birmingham, a wealthy Detroit suburb, for dinner. They sat down at 6.30 p.m. for what turned out to be a jolly, five-course affair. It augurs well for the merger, the Germans were thinking, when Eaton got up to make a speech. He spoke for three minutes, thanking his new German colleagues for travelling so far.

Then, without further ado, he and the rest of the Chrysler team left the room and went home to their families. It was only 8.15 p.m. The Germans were crestfallen – the night was yet young, and they had been deserted by the Americans. Schrempp asked Manfred Bischoff, head of the DASA aerospace subsidiary, to go to the wine cellar to find something to drink. Well known as a wine connoisseur, Bischoff discovered that the hotel had only one bottle of each vintage displayed on the wine list. So he decided to turn the evening into an informal wine-tasting. Schrempp invited the party back to the Presidential suite and they sat up drinking the individual bottles until midnight, with Bischoff delivering a running commentary.

There and then Schrempp determined to change the character of the return visit to Stuttgart. Scheduled for two weeks later, this had been envisaged as a formal, businesslike affair, but on Schrempp's intervention it became more emotional. 'We have to prove to them that we are not bureaucrats,' he said later.

So later that month the Americans were taken to the Untertürkheim racetrack and given the opportunity to test-drive Mercedes cars and lorries. Gentz drove a bus, racing Eaton who was in a Freightliner HGV. Eaton was also given a spin in the F200 concept car, a racing version of the CLK.

The original plan had been to ferry the executives to dinner in a fleet of the newest S-Class Mercedes. Hubbert came up with the idea of putting everyone on a bus. This was no ordinary journey. Instead of taking the turning off the track, the bus accelerated towards a ninety-degree bend. It reached a top speed of 137 kmph as it went into the bend. The driver took his hands off the wheel as the bus skidded round the corner. Hubbert was roaring with laughter as he hadn't told any of the other terrified passengers what was about to happen; Eaton and his team could not help but be impressed.

The destination for dinner was the classic car workshop at the Mercedes Museum on the outskirts of Stuttgart. This is a building steeped in mystique for car-lovers such as Eaton and Schrempp. On arrival, Eaton got into an old Mercedes SLR from the 1950s. He was driven around the collection of vintage cars. Eaton and Schrempp posed for photographs in the original three-wheeler coach invented by Karl Benz. The eighteen board members plus a dozen senior officials had dinner surrounded by these icons of automobile history.

'There have been three times in history when Chrysler and Daimler came close to one another,' Schrempp said in his address that evening. He revealed a number of historical curiosities such as the fact that there had been contact between Walter P. Chrysler and Daimler-Benz in the late twenties: in 1927, Hermann Josef Abs, the future chairman of both Deutsche Bank and Daimler-Benz, bought his first car – a Chrysler Cabrio. There had been further informal contact in the 1950s and again in 1969, when the two companies had discussed a range of possible joint ventures. There were of course the failed Q-Star discussions in 1995–6. 'Now, at last,' said Schrempp, 'we've finally found the moment to conquer the world together.'

Prompted by thoughts of their common heritage, both sides were relaxed. Gary Valade recounted the story of Chrysler's engagement in Gulfstream and the company's subsequent restructuring. The Germans found they could identify with elements of the story, noting ruefully that Chrysler had managed to sell Gulfstream at a profit whereas they had not been able to get out of Fokker so lightly. Dieter Zetsche talked about his time running the Freightliner truck operation in the US and Andreas Renschler recounted his experiences in Tuscaloosa, Alabama where he had established a factory for the production of M-Class Mercedes. Eaton described life in Switzerland and Germany in the early 1990s when he had run General Motors' European operations. There was plenty of good-humoured banter, but there were no

Americans left when, some time after midnight, the security guards brought in McDonald's hamburgers, fries and milk shakes.

The next day they visited the Bad Cannstatt engine factory and the Sindelfingen plant, rounding off the trip with a visit to Bierhaus West, a typical Swabian pub. Americans and Germans sat tightly bunched together on long benches as they ate local delicacies such as *Maultaschen* (a Swabian dumpling) and drank beer and wine. Eaton and Stallkamp, who had to leave early, were delighted with their farewell presents, a pair of remote-controlled model cars. They played with the SLK roadsters on the floor of the pub. At the end of the evening the two management teams were on their feet, watching the soccer World Cup on television. The ice had began to thaw.

The third of the set-piece events took place at the opulent Greenbrier country hotel in West Virginia. This is a vast colonial-style mansion surrounded by deep woodland, golf courses, riding trails and mountains. It was for many years the site of the secret bunker for the US Congress and Senate in the case of nuclear attack, so the Daimler and Chrysler teams had fun exploring the tunnels underneath the hotel. They also visited the hotel's landing strip – a sizeable runway built for the hasty arrival of Congressmen, Senators and their staff – where Manfred Bischoff had arranged for a display of four private jets (two different types of Gulfstreams, a Lear Jet and a Challenger). They reviewed the two Gulfstreams before making their choice of executive jets for the new company.

Here, over three days in late August, the work began in earnest. On the agenda were sensitive questions: how were they going to parcel out various departmental responsibilities between board members? How were they going to tackle the process of integration? What sort of cultural complications were they going to face? What did they have to do to ensure that this merger would be a success?

They were all under strict orders to wear casual clothes. ('T-shirts and sleeveless shirts are not permissible at afternoon tea,' the joining instructions said, sternly. 'No T-shirts, tank tops, jeans, and cut offs in the Upper Lobby, Main Dining Room or Theatre, please.') Schrempp wore a sports shirt and corduroy trousers for the opening session. A single executive, one of the Germans, sported a tie.

'We must remember that the company's interests must come first,' insisted Schrempp as he opened the key session on management responsibilities. 'Everything we decide here should be decided in the company's interests and not according to our personal agendas.'

The Germans' ears pricked up. Whenever Schrempp started talking about the company's interests, and how they must come before personal agendas, it was a fair bet that individuals would be asked to make sacrifices for the sake of the greater good. And so it proved as Rüdiger Grube produced an organisation chart showing the names of the seventeen board members in separate boxes. The rest of the chart was blank. It was time to haggle, in as polite a way as possible, for the plum jobs. The first decision: financial controllers who had hitherto worked within the individual divisions would be moved to Gentz's department. IT was moved from Tropitzsch to Cordes. Personnel ended up being split between Tropitzsch and Kathy Oswald from Chrysler, much to the Germans' disgruntlement. Throughout the discussion Grube would pop in and out of the room, modifying the slides as he went along. Eventually, he stopped making modifications to the slides; the structure was fixed – as he and Schrempp had agreed it would be before the session.

In another meeting, the Germans and Americans were asked what they thought of each other.

'It is unthinkable for a Chrysler car to be built in a Mercedes-Benz factory,' said one senior DaimlerChrysler executive. 'And for as long as I'm responsible for the Mercedes-Benz brand, only over my dead body will a Mercedes be built in a Chrysler factory.'

'It's not smart to exclude something if it is in the company's interests,' said Eckhard Cordes, diplomatically.

The blunt remark was typical of the Germans' dismissive attitude to Chrysler's engineering. 'It's like we're Mercedes and you're Dodge; we're up here and you're down there,' is how Jim Holden at Chrysler characterised the Germans' attitude. It rankled acutely because the Americans believe they are as good if not better engineers than their Stuttgart counterparts. They are used to being volume producers, rather than luxury car manufacturers. While each Mercedes-Benz car is made in response to an order from an individual customer, Chrysler is used to producing tens of thousands of identical cars. That doesn't make them better or worse engineers – just different. Or at least, so Holden thought.

'When you are trying to compete on price you have to make trade-offs,' said Holden later. 'Mercedes hate that because their brand is not about making trade-offs. We've built our business in the mass market by making choices for our customers in terms of value and style.'

Holden had had a good look at Daimler's engineering in 1995–6 and was particularly dismissive of the A-Class. Chrysler would have built the car in a different way, with a view to keeping costs down. Holden found it amazing that the power train and engine system had been specially developed for just one product.

At Greenbrier, he kept these and other critical observations to himself.

Most mergers fail.

This was the stark message contained in no fewer than three presentations over the course of the retreat. Dr Michael Hammer, author of the influential *Re-engineering the Corporation*, made this point, as did a team from PricewaterhouseCoopers. 'Deal costs are recovered within ten years in only 23 per cent of all transactions,' the PwC consultants declared, somewhat alarmingly. 'In almost 60 per cent of cross-border transactions, the acquiring company does not earn back its cost of capital.'

Rüdiger Grube took up this theme in his presentation on the

morning of the last day. He explained how the Daimler strategy team had looked at 100 recent mergers. Of these, 70 per cent had not accomplished what they set out to achieve. 'They don't exactly fail,' he said. 'They just don't live up to expectations.' A mere 30 per cent had succeeded. What had these companies done right?

The first criterion for a successful merger was sound strategic logic, the research showed. In the case of DaimlerChrysler, there were no doubts on this score. Surprisingly, the other issues that had preoccupied so many of the men in the room for the past few months – effective negotiating, best-structured financing, optimum price – were less critical to the eventual success of the merger than what was ahead of them: the integration of the two companies.

Grube, together with Barry Price, his opposite number from Chrysler, proceeded to spell out a few general principles for successful Post-Merger Integration (PMI). As he explained it, these were:

- Maintain the underlying business while in transition – don't allow the distractions of a merger to destroy what brought you together in the first place.

- Create a 'win-win' situation – in a merger of equals, everyone stands to gain from effective integration.

- Speed! Speed! Speed! From now on, this would be Grube's mantra. The faster you move, the more likely you are to succeed.

- Focus on the value-drivers – i.e. on the factors that you can identify and control and which lead to the creation of maximum shareholder value in as short a period of time as possible. Don't get distracted by the crap!

- Create a strong culture of personal responsibility – the affected parties should also be participating parties, said

Grube. Daimler *Vorstand* members and Chrysler executive vice-presidents would be expected to be directly accountable for the success or failure of PMI projects.

- Remember that the PMI process is temporary – it would last no more than two years.

Every manager involved in implementing the integration would subsequently sign a piece of paper acknowledging these six core principles.

If these were to be the broad guidelines, how would integration be managed in practice? From this point on, Grube's slides became steadily more intricate as he explained the nuances of the process that lay ahead.

He and Price said there were a total of ninety-eight broad topics that needed dealing with: twenty-nine of these had been identified by the two companies' boards, another sixty-nine had emerged as a result of the increasingly close contacts lower down the organisations. These were then winnowed down into fourteen 'issue clusters' – top-line categories into which all individual projects would be bundled. These included: product creation (engineering); volume production (manufacturing); global sales and marketing; procurement and supply; global automotive strategy; human resources; communications; IT and so on.

Dig down below Cluster B (manufacturing) and you found more detailed issues such as increasing capacity for the M-Class or optimising productivity. In Cluster C (sales and marketing) there were plans to develop a common wholesale operation for Thailand or to market a full-size pick-up truck in South America.

One level lower and you came to the individual projects. These were the very specific tasks that needed to be performed in order to deliver the top-line synergies. By the time the PMI process was up and running in late November, there were 1,232 projects. At Greenbrier, Grube and Price briefly talked about just twenty-seven of them.

Number One – named as such because it was big and easily identifiable – was the plan to use surplus production capacity at Chrysler's Jeep plant at Graz in Austria to meet demand for Mercedes M-Class vehicles. Grube demonstrated how the project could save $150 million between 1999 and 2001 by developing a common process for manufacturing vehicle bodies, painting and assembling components. (In deference to purists key elements of the process would of course be kept separate.) Already, there was elaborate detail about the steps required to complete the project: the level of investment required in order to generate the savings; a timetable showing milestones on the road to completion; the names of the board members responsible for the project (Jürgen Hubbert and Dennis Pawley) and an assessment of the probability of success.

With so many projects they had to have clear priorities. In the next few weeks Grube and Price established the criteria for deciding the order in which the projects would be tackled. Top priority were of course those that would have a meaningful impact on the joint company's profits. Also, those that would send strong signals that the merger was on track. Or those 'quick hits' where there was a chance of rapid success. Better to be pragmatic than perfectionist, Grube counselled. Get it 80 per cent right now, rather than spending months trying to get a 100 per cent answer.

In due course, the planning maestro developed a corporate war-room, a real-time management control centre from which he and Schrempp could monitor the exact progress of individual projects. All the information on each individual project was stored on a central computer. The status of each project was colour-coded: those that would definitely meet their objectives were green; those merely likely to meet their objectives were yellow; those falling behind flashed up red. Once the process was up and running, managers responsible for red projects would regularly receive stiff e-mails from Schrempp himself.

The war-room had two crucial effects: it allocated direct

personal responsibility to individual board members for getting things done by a certain date. And it created a healthy competition between board members to exceed expectations and avoid flashing red lights and unpleasant e-mails from the chairman.

Well ahead of 17 November ('Day One' – when the merger was formally completed) Grube and his team had sorted everything out. 'There was not a single outstanding issue,' he said later. Everything had been categorised, coded and boiled down to one piece of paper on which one could read at a glance which were the most important topics, who was responsible for dealing with them and by when. With one click of the button, you could access cascading levels of detailed information on each of the projects.

Shortly before this date, the fifty senior managers responsible for implementing the merger met at the Lämmerbuckel conference centre outside Stuttgart. Schrempp gave each team member one half of a DaimlerChrysler share certificate. The other half would be handed over only when the integration was complete.

The share certificates carried three photos – of Karl Benz, Gottlieb Daimler and Walter P. Chrysler. This was agreed by Eaton and Schrempp on the last night of the Greenbrier retreat.

Kate's Mountain Restaurant, Friday, 28 August 1998

Huddled together in a log cabin in the Allegheny mountains above the hotel, Bob Eaton and Jürgen Schrempp have one last item on the agenda.

Dinner is finished. The atmosphere is jolly, but it is time to get down to business. 'Come on, Bob,' says Schrempp, pulling up a chair. 'I have something to discuss.'

Silence descends on the room. The various board directors from Daimler and Chrysler who have worked night and day on the deal for the past six months want to witness the latest wrangle between the two CEOs.

On the table is a proposal for a share certificate carrying the photos of various historical figures associated with the two companies. From the Daimler side there would be just one person: Gottlieb Daimler.

The Americans wanted two pictures, one of Walter P. Chrysler, the legendary inventor who gave his name to the company he founded in the 1920s. The other was to be of the Dodge brothers, in memory of Horace and John Dodge, founders of the Dodge motor company acquired by Walter Chrysler in 1928.

'We've really got to have Karl Benz's name on there,' insisted Schrempp.

It will be recalled that Daimler came from Stuttgart and Benz from Mannheim. Both cities are in the prosperous south German state of Baden-Württemberg, but they are in many ways as different as New Jersey and Georgia, or California and Wisconsin. Stuttgart is the heart of Swabia, Mannheim is in Baden. Yoked together only since 1952, when the state of Baden-Württemberg was created, Baden and Swabia have strong, distinctive identities.

Swabians are hard-working, pious and thrifty, often referred to as the Scots of Germany. They are independent-minded with a fondness for paradox; Georg Friedrich Hegel, the philosopher who invented dialectical idealism, was born in Stuttgart. They also have a particular gift for mechanical engineering, and Daimler, a restless inventor, was a typical Swabian. Badeners, by contrast, are bons viveurs. Perhaps because this part of the state has so often been ruled by others during the course of history, by France and Austria, they are more relaxed than their Swabian neighbours.

Schrempp, who comes from the beautiful medieval town of Freiburg in the south-west, is an archetypal Badener.

'I promised my father that I'd take care of the Baden heritage,' Schrempp said across the table to Eaton. His beloved father had died the previous year. '*Den Karli muss ich doch d'rauf haben* – I've got to have Karli [Karl Benz] on there!'

'No,' said Eaton, bluntly.

'Come on, Bob, give this one a push,' chipped in Gary Valade, Eaton's mild-mannered chief financial officer and chief negotiator during the merger discussions.

Schrempp then reminded Eaton that he had compromised already on Benz, allowing it to drop from the name of the merged company. The name lives on in the Mercedes-Benz brand, but dropping it from the company name had been more than a formality.

'I have a beautiful car,' said Schrempp. 'You know I have a perfect replica of the very first car made by Karl Benz.'

Eaton, who earlier in the summer had been thrilled to take a spin in a replica of the pioneering three-wheeler, felt he knew where Schrempp was leading.

'Here's my proposal,' continued Schrempp. 'You get the car for your museum [the Walter P. Chrysler museum which Eaton had commissioned at his Auburn Hills headquarters], I get the picture of Benz.'

The American paused for a minute. 'Okay, Jürgen,' he said at last. 'We have a deal.' The Dodge brothers were duly dropped from the certificate and Benz took their place.

'While we're at it, chairman,' chipped in one wag, sensing that Eaton was in a conciliatory mood, 'can we discuss our salaries now please!'

Shortly after the deal is completed, Schrempp is sitting in his office in Auburn Hills together with Eckhard Cordes, Rüdiger Grube and Bill O'Brien, Chrysler's general counsel.

Schrempp is willing to ride roughshod over certain elements of Chrysler culture. He is damned if he is going to abide by Chrysler's rules against smoking and drinking. Hence a bar and humidor have recently been installed in his office. When it comes to jokes, he knows he is on less sure ground.

O'Brien explains to Schrempp that humour is no laughing matter in Auburn Hills. What one person finds amusing, another will deem mortally offensive. People get fired because of their jokes. Better to avoid humour altogether, he counsels.

'Hang on,' says Schrempp. 'Can we not at least try out a few jokes to see what the reaction might be? You can fine me according to how seriously I've infringed the rules.'

'Okay,' says O'Brien.

'I'll start with something inoffensive,' says Schrempp.

His joke concerns a lottery in Calcutta, a famous Indian politician and a T-shirt.

He reaches the punch line. The Germans laugh. O'Brien is silent.

'Okay, so how much do I pay?' asks Schrempp.

'Nothing,' says the lawyer.

'That's good,' says Schrempp, thinking of his next joke.

'It's not good,' says O'Brien. 'You have nothing to pay because you're fired.'

What is culture but the distillation of successful prior experience, expressed as values and manifested as behaviour?

This is how Professor Hammer defined it during one of the Greenbrier sessions. Culture, he said, is built into systems and perpetuated in the way an organisation trains, measures and rewards its people. Culture is bodied forth in touchy-feely concepts such as accountability, control, risk, motivation and individuality. Ignore culture at your peril, he warned. It would be an uphill battle to get people to behave and work in ways that contradicted their values and beliefs. The finest process designs will not be followed unless people believe in them and their goals, he cautioned.

Grube's PMI process was concerned with hard facts. The softer cultural issues were not directly addressed. There was an awkward awareness that there would be cultural barriers, but little systematic attempt to help people overcome them. Insofar as there was formal inter-cultural training, it was regarded with derision.

'We were told that Americans are like peaches,' recalled one

German participant in an acculturation course. 'Soft on the outside and hard on the inside. The Germans were supposed to be like coconuts, hard on the outside but soft in the middle.'

For a time, the Chrysler executives would try playing hardball with the Germans at every encounter. The Germans, who can be formidably emollient when they want to be, were perplexed by this sudden aggressiveness.

This was but one of many mutual misunderstandings. We have already seen how the Germans were horrified at the Americans' refusal to stay up late and socialise with their colleagues from work. As time went on, this broadened into a deeper disillusion with mid-West business culture. Many Germans worked on the naïve assumption that all Americans were like the fiery go-getting New Yorkers they knew from past experience or had encountered during the months of negotiations. The reality turned out different.

After the merger, they found that Chrysler managers often did not have passports. (There was no reason why they would have needed one for business reasons as 95 per cent of Chrysler's turnover was in the US.) They did not like travelling to meetings in Europe. There was no chance of arranging the Day One celebrations for a weekend – the Americans refused point-blank.

They resented giving up a day of the weekend to make the transatlantic trip in time for meetings on a Monday. Some found the trip so stressful that they would demand three days' vacation every time they went to Europe. The Germans got the impression that their counterparts went home on the dot of five o'clock. They drew an absolute distinction between work and family life. The Germans felt they were never invited to American homes, that private contact was discouraged. Displays of affection to colleagues were frowned upon, as Grube found to his cost.

He was saying goodbye to a male colleague with whom he had worked closely for several months. They had become friends. As Grube jumped out of the cab at Detroit International airport, he went over to embrace his friend in a gesture of farewell.

The Chrysler executive recoiled in horror. Looking anxiously around him to check that no one he knew had seen them, he explained to Grube that it was absolutely forbidden to touch colleagues. Whether male or female, it didn't matter, it was a major cultural infringement.

Another time, a senior German executive touched the shoulder of a (female) secretary at Auburn Hills. He asked her politely to go and do some photocopying. She reported him to Kathy Oswald, Chrysler's personnel chief, for alleged sexual harassment. In Germany, as in most of the rest of Europe, some tactile contact between colleagues would not be out of the ordinary.

On yet another occasion, a German executive helpfully brought two chairs into a room where a meeting was about to take place. He had miscalculated, there were three people without a seat, not two. One of the three was an African American lady. She felt snubbed by the fact that there was one fewer chair than there were people. She complained to her superior that she had been the victim of racial discrimination.

For the Germans, such sensitivity smacked of insane political correctness. The Germans are profoundly politically incorrect – and proud of it.

There were further frustrations for the Germans. They had read and heard a lot about Chrysler's freewheeling culture, and yet they were amazed to find that Auburn Hills turned out to be more hierarchical than Stuttgart Möhringen. There were four dining rooms at Auburn Hills, each for a different grade of executive. Chrysler had preserved the kind of many-layered management structure that had been abolished by Schrempp back in 1995–6.

If the Americans were hierarchical, they were far less formal than the Germans when talking to each other at work. As early as Greenbrier, the two sides determined to introduce some of this informality to the new corporate culture. They decided to abolish the use of titles on business cards – a grave disappointment for those such as Professor Hubbert who were proud of such displays of academic distinction. They also resolved to call each other by Christian names, still virtually unheard of when two Germans are talking to each other at work. The rule only applies when people are speaking English so all sorts of amusing anomalies can be observed. The same people who call each other Eckhard and Christoph when speaking English will immediately revert to the formal Dr Walther or Dr Cordes when continuing the same conversation in German.

The final issue was money. American executives get remunerated far more handsomely than their German colleagues doing the same job in Stuttgart. For example, the ten members of the Daimler-Benz management board earned DM20 million ($11 million) between them in the year before the merger. By contrast, Bob Eaton alone made $9.8 million in base salary, bonus and cashing in share options. Bob Lutz earned nearly $16 million. The top five Chrysler managers earned a total of around $35 million in 1997.

Even these numbers would be dwarfed by the payouts received at the time the deal was completed. Chrysler board directors, plus scores of other senior executives at the American company, cashed in prodigious sums. It has never been publicly disclosed how much money they received as a result of exercising their share options. 'North of $100 million', is the steer given by informed insiders. There was no corresponding bonanza for Daimler-Benz executives. Bob Eaton alone is reported to have made $70 million in 1998, compared with Schrempp's E2.3 million package.

The broader theme here is a starkly different compensation philosophy. Eaton, Holden and Gale all point out that they were entitled to most of the money under the terms of their existing option agreements. The merger triggered a change of control clause in their employment contracts which let them get the cash earlier than otherwise. The quantity was not affected, merely the timing. So what if they got vast amounts of money? They feel they deserved it, and, after all, the purpose of business activity is to make money for shareholders, right?

'You guys in Europe have a real problem with this,' says

Bob Eaton. One reason for the success of the North American economy in the last decade has been the broad distribution of incentive compensation. 'Okay, there have been a few successes in Europe, a handful of billion-dollar companies created in the last few years,' Eaton argues, citing the example of SAP, the German software powerhouse. 'But in the US there are literally hundreds and hundreds of companies that have come from nowhere to be worth billions of dollars.'

Schrempp was one of the first German CEOs to recognise the motivational power of share options schemes, introducing a pioneering scheme in 1996. After the merger a lot of work went into creating a level playing field for Chrysler and Daimler executives. The new group's compensation committee found that while lower-level German executives got paid more than their American counterparts, the opposite was true at higher levels of the organisation. German board members and the three grades below that (equivalent to American executive vice-presidents, senior vice-presidents and vice-presidents) received significantly less than their peers in Auburn Hills. It was decided that pay for a small number of top managers – around fifty with international responsibilities – would in time be brought up to US levels. For a broader group of around 3,000 German managers, a growing component of their total compensation would be linked to the company's overall profitability and its share price. The steep decline in the DaimlerChrysler stock price during 1999 has however meant that options packages granted since the merger have yet to come 'into the money'.

Even as pay structures have been harmonised, there remains a more fundamental difference between German and American business culture. Germans are just not motivated by money to the same extent as Americans. They are taxed more highly than Americans and they are less mobile. In the past, a job at Daimler-Benz was a job for life. Ultimately they want different things.

Many American executives came to believe that the prime motivation for German managers is power. Not so much because they want to dominate the world (although that

255

clearly was a factor behind the DaimlerChrysler deal), but in the sense of imposing their will and getting things done. Certainly, Schrempp himself relishes the power to influence events and shape the future of the automotive industry. When asked about his relatively small pay-cheque compared with that of his co-chairman, he dismisses the question with the observation that he is hardly living on the breadline.

Needless to say the Americans had their gripes about the Germans. For example, they bridled at German bureaucracy. The root of this was the Germans' tendency to document every meeting in meticulous detail. A decision is not a decision until it has been minuted and signed off, preferably with two signatures at the bottom (under what the Germans call the *Vieraugenprinzip*, the principle of having two people sign off on a document before it is finalised). By contrast, Americans are more relaxed. Senior managers at Chrysler had got used to working with each other quickly and effectively. A consensus would emerge as a result of a series of meetings. There was no need to compile minutes at every stage of the discussion, nor indeed when a decision was reached.

During the course of 1999 former Chrysler executives found themselves ensnared by the unfamiliar memo-based culture. Either they thought they had reached a decision, and found that they hadn't because they hadn't documented it properly, or, the day after a meeting on a sensitive subject a memo would arrive and they would find themselves bounced into decisions they hadn't realised they had taken. Or again, says Jim Holden, they might have a strenuous argument with their German counterparts, win them over to a different point of view, and then 'by the time the documents come back the decision has morphed its way back to what some committee in Stuttgart wanted in the first place'.

In the early days of the merger, German bureaucracy took many forms, reflects Holden. 'We got frustrated by what appears to be ceremonial, not real work,' he says. 'I put someone on a committee and his counterpart will be eight or nine people.'

Sometimes the results were irritating, as during the planning process when the Germans insisted on obtaining detailed production quotas for 2010 and beyond ('Too far ahead to be meaningful,' is the American view of this), or plain ludicrous, as when Holden received a German study of the North American automotive market which started by chronicling in meticulous detail the number of feet of high-pressure natural gas pipelines in North America, the number of trillion square yards of highway infrastructure, the volume of oil and gas production . . . and so on. It was as if one were visiting the country for the first time. The conclusion, according to Holden, could be boiled down to the following: 'It's a big auto country, you should be there.'

By mid-2000, a compromise has been reached: meetings are minuted, but in less elaborate detail than in the past. And during meetings, Germans are careful to signal when a decision is about to be taken, ensuring that the Americans are aware that the proceedings have reached a critical point. This is the on-the-job development of a new corporate culture.

In April 1999 family-loving mid-Westerners were appalled to read about the break-up of Schrempp's thirty-five-year marriage. 'Merger over marriage' was a typical headline.

'I realised that the challenges of the job at hand were more important to me than anything in the world,' he was quoted as saying. 'My wife is a great person but our goals for life kind of drifted apart. She wanted me to start slowing down. I wanted the merger with Chrysler. Quite simply, the point came when it was no longer possible to reconcile my work with her expectations' (*Automotive News*, 26 April 1999).

The nuances of what Schrempp told Germany's mass-circulation *Bild* newspaper were lost in translation. The way the separation was reported in the US press made him seem chillingly preoccupied with the deal. Here was a man who left his wife to spend more time with his merger.

CHAPTER 17

Cracking the Whip

The Germans take charge

Frankfurt, Friday, 24 September 1999

The darkened amphitheatre slowly fills with powerful men who have flown to Germany from all around the world to DaimlerChrysler's first Global Suppliers Conference. DaimlerChrysler is planning to spend $72 billion with the suppliers gathered in the room during the course of the next year. If it is ever so inconvenient to be there, few have declined the invitation to come and hear Schrempp and Gary Valade talk about the future of the company.

Pop music is pulsing forth from mammoth speakers. Three huge screens loom above the stage, each filled with images of DaimlerChrysler – planes, trains, automobiles and people. At the foot of the amphitheatre, Schrempp stands alone. Smiling and nodding his head as he greets one visitor after another, he looks as if he hasn't a care in the world.

In reality, as he concedes a few minutes later when he mounts the podium to give his speech, it has been one hell of a day. That very afternoon, the supervisory board signed off on a restructuring of the board which has cut the total number of directors from seventeen to fourteen. After weeks of fevered press speculation on both sides of the Atlantic, the axe has fallen. Its victims include Tom Stallkamp, hailed at the time of the merger as a potential successor to Schrempp and a man known and liked by many of the people in the audience. The Germans are cracking the whip.

'We never set out to win any popularity contest,' says Schrempp. 'We set out to run the greatest automotive company in the world.'

Progress towards this ambitious goal is a two-speed process. It is almost as if there were separate mergers going on at the same time. One of these is taking place inside people's hearts and minds, and the pace here is slow. 'It'll take ten years to integrate people's minds,' Schrempp told a reporter from the *Harvard Business Review* at around the same time as Stallkamp's ouster.

The other merger is taking place at the level of the 1,242 individual projects identified by Rüdiger Grube and his team. This one is moving much more rapidly. Its success can be measured in terms of hard facts, of dollars saved, of deadlines met or exceeded. This is a story of Stakhanovite labours from ex-Daimler and Chrysler executives at all levels of the merged organisation, in every discipline from engineering to Information Technology.

Throughout 1999 the board received fortnightly bulletins summarising the progress of PMI. Month by month, the success stories were bundled up into a document that was circulated widely within the organisation, or broadcast on the new internal TV network. Grube and Price themselves became ambassadors for the PMI cause, promising to visit each one of the joint organisation's 196 production locations around the world twice during the course of the year. It was thanks to this undertaking that Grube was at home for only five weekends during the course of 1999.

In early December, Grube makes the last of these presentations, to managers and engineers at the giant Sindelfingen plant near Stuttgart where 30,000 workers manufacture Mercedes-Benz A-, E- and S-Class cars. Gathered in the conference room are around 100 executives who have come to hear Grube's briefing. In a short, punchy presentation, Grube sketches out the by now familiar rationale for the merger before plunging into a number of detailed examples of completed integration.

He explains how Mercedes-Benz diesel engines are now being used inside Jeep Grand Cherokees. How Chrysler's US factories have adopted the powder-slurry paint process developed in the A-Class factory at Rastatt, saving tens of millions of dollars. How the two companies found out they operated through sixty different travel agencies; these had been consolidated down to just two, delivering an annual saving of $45 million. How Mercedes-Benz has adopted Chrysler's world-beating product development technology and as a result has shortened lead times by three months; the reduced time-scale will apply for the new Mercedes-Benz roadster and the successor to the A-Class. How the merged companies have pooled their purchasing of car phones. How they have formed a Corporate University for senior employees. How they have introduced the world's first worldwide business TV network reaching 420,000 employees at more than 460 locations in 40 countries.

Given time, Grube could rattle off hundreds of examples of completed projects. Today he confines himself to the best stories. Eyes shining, his tone is messianic. He explains how PMI has set the standard for other companies that have merged or are thinking about it. Executives from 400 companies have visited Möhringen to learn more about the process. Even Rolf Breuer, chief executive of Deutsche Bank, has taken notice. In the wake of the bank's acquisition of Bankers Trust in June he invited Eckhard Cordes and Grube to come to Frankfurt to give a presentation on PMI. It lasted four hours and as a result

Breuer will model the integration of BT on the DaimlerChrysler merger.

By the end of the year, 80 per cent of the outstanding projects will be complete, Grube proclaims. The task of forging the remaining synergies will be delegated to line management and the $1.4 billion of cost-saving pledged at the time of the merger is secure. PMI will be over after 272 working days – well ahead of schedule. And, Grube says proudly, it has all been done with minimal help from management consultants. Consultants, he explains, were deployed only to help solve very specific technical problems on third-level projects and below. They were not involved in setting strategy or orchestrating the overall plan.

Grube's final announcement concerns his own future. He tells the Sindelfingen managers that he will be leaving DaimlerChrysler at the end of the year. He is leaving to become chief executive of Häussler Holding, a privately owned Stuttgart-based investment company. In due course he will take a major shareholding. He is going to fulfil his lifelong ambition to run his own business. To the cheers of the assembled engineers, he says he is looking forward to spending more time at home.

Rüdiger Grube's career as an independent entrepreneur did not last long – by mid 2000 he returned to the Daimler fold. However, many other senior executives departed in the wake of the merger, including most of the original team who helped revive Chrysler in the late 1980s and 1990s.

Bob Lutz left the still-independent Chrysler on 1 July 1998, as planned. François Castaing stepped down as executive vice-president on 1 January 1998 (staying for two years as a technical advisor), and Dennis Pawley at the end of January 1999. These three left of their own volition, the decision and the timing largely unrelated to the merger.

On the other hand, Barry Price, Grube's Chrysler counterpart in the PMI process, left following the forced exit of Tom Stallkamp.

Stallkamp was described by the *Financial Times* as 'one of the most innovative automotive figures of his generation' (*FT*, 25 September 1999). He made his career in the purchasing function, traditionally an unglamorous part of an auto company's operations but in his hands a source of formidable competitive strength for Chrysler. In the late 1980s and early 1990s he saw how the philosophy of platform teams could be extended to the company's relationship with external suppliers. Castaing and Pawley had created a new collaborative culture *within* the company by smashing down the artificial divisions between production, marketing, design and other disciplines. Stallkamp grasped the opportunity to break down the barriers between Chrysler and the supplier community.

He pioneered so-called 'Extended Enterprise', the system by which Chrysler worked together with manufacturers of components and systems to cut costs. It was based on trust and mutual self-interest. The supplier would be entitled to keep a portion of the cost savings, while Chrysler would eliminate waste. The result: Chrysler's purchasing costs were the lowest in the industry. Stallkamp is reckoned to have saved the company $1.2 billion in 1997 – his last year as procurement chief – and another $2.1 billion in 1998, the year of the merger.

In recognition of his contribution to Chrysler's turnaround, he was appointed successor to Bob Lutz as the company's president – a promotion that signalled Bob Eaton's intention to name him as his successor as CEO. He took up this position on 1 January 1998, so he was only in the job for two weeks and two days before talks with Daimler-Benz were under way. He played an important role in the negotiations but not a central one. At one point the Germans were gratified to hear that Stallkamp was so enthusiastic about the deal that he would even move to Stuttgart to be sure of its success. After the deal was done, he had overall responsibility for integrating the two companies' automotive activities. In the very early days after the merger was completed, Eaton said that he suspected that Schrempp's eventual successor as CEO would come from the Chrysler side of the deal. If that were to be any individual, it would surely be Stallkamp.

Respect for Stallkamp extended beyond Auburn Hills and suppliers. He was liked and admired by Wall Street analysts and investors. In July 1999 Daimler held a badly received press conference in New York for the US financial community. The messages were garbled, the presentation of the half-year figures badly mishandled and the shares fell sharply. The following week, Stallkamp went on a one-man crusade to restore confidence in the merger story, helping to rebuild the company's credibility with the Street.

Investors did not welcome the news of his departure. On Friday, 24 September, the day of the announcement, the share price closed at $68.38, down from its January peak of $108.63 and close to its post-merger low. 'It's crazy,' said John Casesa, the influential automotive analyst at the Merrill Lynch investment bank. 'They need an experienced, well-rounded auto executive to run the North American business. He's one of the most respected auto executives in North America, if not the world.'

Such fulminations were typical of the US response to the announcement. There was widespread disappointment and incomprehension. Stallkamp's exit, trailed in the domestic and international press for weeks beforehand, marked the low point of the merger in people's hearts and minds.

Stallkamp's departure went hand in hand with a restructuring of the top-heavy executive board and a comprehensive reorganisation of the company's operations. Two German board members were forced out at the same time as Stallkamp (Kurt Lauk, head of the trucks division, and Heiner Tropitzsch, who had responsibility for personnel) but the Germans ended up dominating the restructured board.

With the exception of Eaton, who was expected to retire somewhat later than he eventually did, there were just four American directors out of the remaining ten positions. And Chrysler found itself relegated to the status of a division within the group. It was no longer the equal of Daimler-Benz. Rather, it ranked alongside Mercedes-Benz and the global truck business.

It was a good day for Jim Holden. The forty-eight-year-old Canadian was named the new president of DaimlerChrysler Corporation and head of the Chrysler/Plymouth/Jeep/Dodge division. It was also the moment at which the rhetoric of a 'merger of equals' gave way to realpolitik. The Germans were taking charge, and they meant to show it.

Should this have been a surprise? Surely not. The Germans were the dominant party from the very instant the two companies entered into negotiations. They were the bigger of the two companies, the more robust in financial terms and the proud possessor of the most prestigious brand in the automotive industry. True, they had mid-term strategic weaknesses, but which auto company did not? They ran rings round the Americans during the negotiations and ended up with a German AG as a result. They agreed to pay a premium for Chrysler's shares, an obvious if overlooked sign that the German company was the more powerful partner. From day one, Eaton's authority as *primus inter pares* was undermined not merely by the force of Schrempp's personality, but by the simple fact that Eaton had stated he would be stepping down early. That brought clarity to the leadership question, without which there would have been no deal, but it served to emphasise his weaker position *vis-à-vis* Schrempp.

As a result, there was a leadership vacuum in Auburn Hills. Eaton was not a hands-on manager in the style of Lutz. His skill lay in fashioning a powerful, cohesive team out of the bunch of powerful individuals he found in place when he joined the company in 1992. He and the team developed a culture and disseminated it through the entire organisation. He rooted out Chrysler's perennial quality problems. He communicated the rebirth of the company to a sceptical Wall Street. Harrowed by Kerkorian's constant onslaughts, he became acutely sensitised to the need to deliver shareholder value. By doing a deal with Daimler-Benz at $57.50 a share (compared with $8 when he joined), he delivered a spectacular increase in value. At the same time he liberated Chrysler from its endless cycle of boom and bust. He thus fulfilled his ambition to be the first Chrysler CEO since the 1950s not to take Chrysler back from the brink of bankruptcy.

Eaton's effectiveness as a leader was, however, critically dependent on those around him. Lutz stood down from his position as Chrysler president in January 1997, a full year before Stallkamp took over as his successor. Others who had helped to make Chrysler great, such as Castaing and Pawley, were also coming to the ends of their careers with the company. Stepping into these formidable shoes was Stallkamp.

Very little effort went into building a management team around him, and in any case he never got a chance to prove himself. Within a couple of weeks of taking over as president, Chrysler was negotiating the end of its independence. After the deal was done, the job mutated from a straight management challenge into a political nightmare. Eaton grew increasingly detached from day-to-day issues, while Schrempp deliberately stayed away from Detroit. Stallkamp was caught in the middle.

Schrempp wanted to let the Americans get on with running Chrysler. He had at the back of his mind his experiences in South Africa. He expected the Chrysler guys to be fiercely protective of their independence, just as he had been when he was running South Africa. He wanted a healthy degree of antagonism between North America and Stuttgart, just as there had been when he was out in the field. He was surprised that Auburn Hills did not fight harder to take control of its own destiny.

'Tom, you're the boss here [at Auburn Hills],' Schrempp used to say to Stallkamp. 'But why do I read in the [Detroit] newspapers that people are so uneasy?'

'Because you're not coming here enough,' was Stallkamp's standard reply.

'Tom, do me a favour, that makes you look weak. You

don't need me. Jürgen Hubbert [head of Mercedes-Benz] would never say that he had a problem because I wasn't coming more often. In fact he loves me to stay away, unless there is a big challenge.'

Sort it out with Eaton in the next-door office, was Schrempp's advice. But the chemistry between Eaton and Stallkamp deteriorated amid the turf wars that follow a merger as surely as night follows day. In the summer of 1999 it was Eaton who paid a visit to Stallkamp while the latter was on vacation in North Michigan. Eaton had received an ultimatum from the young, ambitious Holden, already disappointed to have been passed over as president in favour of Stallkamp. Holden had said: it's him or me. Eaton decided in favour of Holden, and asked Stallkamp to consider his future. 'Maybe it isn't at Chrysler,' Eaton said.

A few weeks later Stallkamp visited Schrempp in Stuttgart. They had lunch together. Schrempp said bluntly that he agreed with Eaton's decision, but not the way it had been communicated. Stallkamp had been promoted to vice-chairman of DaimlerChrysler Corporation and asked to stay on until the end of the year, even though his career at Chrysler had come to an end in the summer. This was Eaton's way of handling the situation. Schrempp ended up taking the blame for an action conceived in Stallkamp's next-door office – on the fifteenth floor of Auburn Hills, not the eleventh floor of Stuttgart Möhringen.

'Jürgen, this doesn't make any sense.'

Jim Holden told Schrempp how he had got caught up in a fight with Mercedes-Benz bureaucracy. A lot of energy was being wasted squabbling about transfer pricing, a way of shifting costs and profits from one division to another. This has no impact on the company's overall performance, but it makes one division look better than another. Holden wanted to enlist Schrempp's support to sort it out.

'You're right,' said Schrempp after listening to the facts. 'You've got to fight them.'

So Holden decided to take on his Stuttgart counterparts. After several months of what Schrempp might call 'constructive conflict', Holden won through.

'We must not be tentative,' said Holden later, reflecting on the lesson he had learned from this experience. 'We spent the whole year [1998–9] making nice to the in-laws. It's a question of style. Americans will generally try to find their way round controversy, Germans have no problems with it at all.

'Looking back, we were being smothered by lots of little issues. They didn't feel worth fighting for, everyone was busy trying to be nice. I've subsequently discovered that "no" or "go to hell" is a perfectly fine answer. We can't just roll over just because a team from Germany flies over and says: do it this way.

'We need controversy, it's the only way to get best practice.'

There was controversy when he stood up to the Germans over their plans to build a mini-van. 'Okay,' he said. 'It may be that Mercedes-Benz doesn't have a vehicle in this category, but DaimlerChrysler most certainly does. You guys are trying to solve a problem which doesn't exist.' Spend the money somewhere else, Holden counselled. He won the argument.

On one occasion, Holden rang Schrempp on his cell-phone when he was on holiday in Mauritius. The Canadian wanted a quick decision. 'Repeat the case,' said Schrempp. Five minutes later, Schrempp agreed to Holden's request. Holden went back to his meeting in Auburn Hills and said, 'I just phoned Jürgen and it took him five minutes to decide.'

Another time, Holden called Schrempp and told him about the opportunity to hire a talented designer who was being fought over by a number of competitors. Normally, for this level of appointment, board approval would be necessary, but there wasn't time. Within half an hour, Holden had the necessary go-ahead.

Holden is what the Americans call a quick study: he learns and moves fast. He is prepared to be outspoken when necessary, as demonstrated back in 1995 when he recommended cancelling the Q-Star discussions with Mercedes-Benz. Yet he is also capable of being a silver-tongued salesman – much of his varied career was spent on the sales and marketing side of the business. These are some of the qualities that Schrempp and Eaton came to appreciate in their search for leadership at Auburn Hills.

If not quite a Bob Lutz in the charisma stakes, Holden is cast in the same mould. He too is a quintessential car guy. Together with his two sons he reconstructed a 1957 Ford Thunderbird ('the best in Michigan', he says proudly). He owns the sixth Viper GTS ever made, 'the best 440-6 Pack Barracuda Convertible in the world', a 440 Charger/RT and a 1965 Cadillac Convertible – and three other classic cars which he drives around town at weekends. On top of that come the usual half-dozen company cars.

When appointed to the top job at Chrysler, he was in charge of DaimlerChrysler's most profitable business unit. Together with Gale, Hubbert and Zetsche, he was also a member of the powerful Automotive Council whose function is to promote cross-fertilisation between the three automotive divisions.

Holden's tenure at the helm of Chrysler would turn out to be short-lived – the Germans' impatience with the deteriorating performance of the Chrysler unit led to his removal. In late November 2000, he was replaced by Dieter Zetsche, the head of the commercial vehicles division and a veteran Mercedes manager. Much of the responsibility for delivering the potential of the merger now rests on his shoulders.

February 2000

Asked if he has any regrets about selling out to Daimler-Benz, Bob Eaton pauses for a while. Sitting comfortably in a deep leather armchair, his feet propped on the glass table in front of him and his shirt collar undone, Eaton is relaxed, a man with an untroubled conscience. He will be stepping down on 1 April. Retirement beckons, and it will be easeful: at sixty this month he is relatively young and in good health. He also has a very substantial amount of money in the bank. (How many tens of millions, he won't disclose. 'All the reports are out by a factor of 100 per cent,' he says teasingly.) He gazes out over the Auburn Hills complex – the biggest office building in the world after the Pentagon – before answering.

'Unquestionably we did the right thing,' he says, quickly explaining the logic of the deal. He points to the unchallengeable fact of the stock price appreciation during his tenure. 'It would be like taking DaimlerChrysler from $75 today to $600, which I have been telling Jürgen to do,' he says, smiling. 'In fact I think he should take it to $800 a share.'

That won't be his problem, he seems to be indicating. He will be on the golf course or off hunting or driving one of his cars.

Suddenly, he becomes less wistful. He sits up. There is one thing that he would have done differently. He would not have labelled the deal a 'merger of equals'.

'This was a very bad thing.' Eaton drawls. 'It immediately set up score-keeping, it set up something to be challenged. It would have been much better if from the very beginning we had sold it as a merger of two very strong companies.'

That, at least, would have had the merit of being true.

The early emphasis on a merger of equals was well intended. It signified the spirit in which the two sides approached the negotiations and their immediate aftermath. There was mutual respect and a genuine desire to parcel out key appointments as evenly as possible.

'It was not a gimmick,' observes a member of Schrempp's inner circle. 'It was the spirit of the day. Psychologically it was not meant to be a takeover. It just turned out that way.'

PART 5

Some Conclusions

CHAPTER 18

Endgame

*DaimlerChrysler's search for a partner in Asia
and the story of further consolidation
in the automotive industry*

Tokyo, Stuttgart, Tuesday–Wednesday, 9–10 March 1999

For the fourth time in a month, Schrempp is making a day-trip to Japan. As usual, this involves a twelve-hour flight on the company jet, a taxi-ride to a hotel in the centre of Tokyo, a quick shower, followed by a meeting lasting no more than an hour and a half. Afterwards there is just time for a plate of tapanyaki before boarding the plane back to Stuttgart.

Schrempp comes as bearer of bad news. On the flight, he talks to Lydia Deininger, Alex Dibelius and Eckhard Cordes about the message he will be imparting to Yoshikazu Hanawa, president of Nissan Motors.

There had been a long board meeting in Geneva the previous day. It had started with presentations from teams of marketing, finance and engineering experts who looked at the detailed pros and cons of a tie-up with the Japanese company, the world's fifth largest auto manufacturer. Then Schrempp sent the technicians out of the room and asked each one of the seventeen board members to give their views. Only two of the directors had spoken out in favour of a deal. Tom Stallkamp summed up the mood of the meeting when he said: 'It's a great opportunity at the wrong time.'

Ahead of the meeting, Schrempp and Cordes were favourably disposed to doing a deal. The Chrysler merger, completed barely four months before, left a number of big strategic issues unresolved. DaimlerChrysler was still under-represented in Asia: the region accounted for just 4 per cent of the group's turnover. The ideal would be 25 per cent, in line with Asia's share of the world economy. This would provide the proper balance to the company's strong presence in the Americas and Europe.

Another challenge was the lack of a strong small car capability. Strategists from both Daimler and Chrysler agreed that this segment would grow a lot faster than the market as a whole. In most of the developed world the mainstream car business would have trouble growing at more than 2–3 per cent a year. In the developing world, and in Asia in particular, growth had the potential to be a lot bigger. But the great mass of customers would want small cars, not hefty Jeeps or luxurious S-Class Mercedes which would remain the preserve of the elite. In the developed world continuing pressure to reduce fuel emissions would drive demand for small cars.

Schrempp would never have admitted it publicly at the time, but the Smart car was unlikely to cut the mustard on its own. It was open to doubt whether Chrysler's smaller cars would ever take off in the European market. And early estimates suggested it would take the newly merged companies more than $10 billion to build a new small car programme from scratch – a vast investment with no certainty of success.

A deal with Nissan would tackle both these issues at a stroke: it would give DaimlerChrysler small car technology and a 20 per cent share of the Asian market. Schrempp was sorely tempted to seize the opportunity.

The days when the Japanese auto industry inspired the awe of their competitors around the world were long gone. Nissan was heavily indebted and needed the kind of root-and-branch restructuring that Schrempp had implemented at Daimler in 1995–6. Its problems, combined with recession in Asia, opened a window of opportunity that would slam shut if the company turned itself round or if the economy picked up. What's more, Nissan was also talking to Renault. If DaimlerChrysler did not do a deal, the French most certainly would. So, as far as Nissan was concerned, it would be now or never.

On the other hand, Schrempp recognised that it was risky to take on Nissan so soon after the deal with Chrysler. Senior managers were preoccupied with integrating the two companies. Management resource was scarce: where would he find the cadre of forty to fifty top executives needed to knock Nissan into shape?

Schrempp could see the risk that Nissan could turn out to be another Fokker – this time on a far bigger scale and with irreversible consequences for his own position. But he could see that there was a risk in not doing the deal, in missing the opportunity. With the big car groups chasing a diminishing number of Asian opportunities, DaimlerChrysler could end up being permanently lamed.

Ahead of the board meeting, Schrempp had toyed with the idea of pushing the merger through. He took counsel from those who advised caution. As he went round the table asking each board member for their opinion, he came to the view that the risks of doing the deal outweighed those of not doing it.

This, in a nutshell, was the tenor of his short and utterly unexpected message to Hanawa-san. The Japanese had no idea that Schrempp was coming all the way to Tokyo to call off the talks. More likely, they were expecting him to propose some last-minute adjustments to the agreement that they had all but finalised. Schrempp pulled no punches, explaining that the decision to withdraw was due to DaimlerChrysler's own problems and was not to be interpreted as a slight on Nissan. Hanawa-san was visibly stunned. One of the Japanese executives in the room burst into tears. Others were so amazed that they temporarily lost the ability to speak English. Finally, Hanawa-san came over to Schrempp and took his hands. 'I have great respect for the way you handled this,' the Nissan president said.

It was a tough meeting. 'For the first time in my life,' said Cordes to Schrempp on the way out, 'I need a whisky.'

The next step for DaimlerChrysler came almost a year later. It provided Schrempp with the best possible antidote to the disappointing outcome of the Nissan talks.

New York, 7 February 2000

'Schrempp-san,' says Mr Katsuhiko Kawasoe, chief executive of Mitsubishi Motors. 'I know I have to be careful, you have a reputation for being so overwhelming.'

Schrempp smiles. The adjective 'overwhelming' conveys wariness as well as respect. The only response is to be as direct as possible.

'Kawasoe-san, can I be straightforward with you,' says Schrempp. 'If you are interested in doing projects with us I'll hand over to Jürgen Hubbert and Jim Holden, that's their subject.

'If you want to get together permanently, that's my subject. And what I need is at least 34 per cent.'

Now it is the turn of Kawasoe-san to smile. He wants to do a deal, but does not want to let the Germans have more than 20 per cent. The wrangling begins. The negotiations are led by Cordes and Sato-san, his opposite number.

Schrempp and Kawasoe-san meet just once more before finalising the deal, in the Hotel Beau Rivage in Lausanne. The meeting is held at the same time as the Geneva motor show, almost two years to the day since Eaton and Schrempp met in the same hotel and agreed on how to run the new DaimlerChrysler company. For Schrempp, flip-chart at the ready as ever, this is familiar territory.

In late March, Schrempp and Kawasoe-san appear together at press conferences held on two consecutive days in Frankfurt and Tokyo. They announce that they have done an E2.1 billion deal. DaimlerChrysler gets what it wanted: a 34 per cent stake and management control. Mitsubishi is one of the world's leading small car manufacturers. Henceforth a quarter of the German-American group's sales will come from Asia.

For DaimlerChrysler, the Mitsubishi deal was the last piece in the strategic jigsaw. For the auto industry, it was one of a flurry of transactions prompted by the original merger. As Schrempp put it in a speech to American CEOs in April 2000: 'The winds of globalisation and competitive advantage blew through the tree, and more than half the apples fell off.'

The first to fall was Volvo Cars. Shortly after the original DaimlerChrysler deal was announced, the chief executive of the Swedish company gave a presentation in which he spent the best part of an hour explaining to analysts and investors why the big deal would not change the global automotive environment. There was absolutely no reason why Volvo should not remain an independent company, contended Leif Johansson. No reason at all. He was protesting overmuch. Within six months, the car division of AB Volvo was sold to Ford Motor Company for $6.45 billion. Ford thus acquired the premium car company it had wanted to buy when it opened discussions with Daimler-Benz.

The second apple was Nissan. A fortnight after Schrempp's day-trip to Tokyo, Renault spent $5.4 billion to buy a 38 per cent stake in Nissan. The French company then parachuted one of its most aggressive managers into Japan. Carlos Ghosn, nick-named 'le cost cutter', has embarked on a tough restructuring programme. Other Japanese manufacturers, including Mitsubishi, are beginning to follow suit.

The third move took place in March 2000, when General Motors and Fiat Motor Company forged a $2.4 billion strategic alliance. Jack Smith, chairman of General Motors, said explicitly that the deal was a direct response to the merger of Daimler and Chrysler. The two companies agreed to exchange shareholdings and to set up a series of joint ventures. Although both sides are keen to stress that they will preserve their independence, it is not difficult to see the move as the beginning of the Agnelli family's exit from the automotive business.

In the same month that DaimlerChrysler bought 34 per cent of Mitsubishi, BMW finally ended its disastrous six-year engagement with Rover, the last remaining volume manufacturer in the UK. The sale of Rover cars for a nominal £10 and the disposal of Land-Rover constitute a humiliating and costly reversal for the Bavarian car group.

Needless to say, this provoked some *Schadenfreude* among the engineers and strategists of Untertürkheim and Möhringen. In the mid-nineties BMW had openly criticised the Mercedes-Benz decision to go down-market by building the A-Class. It had sought to penetrate the lower segments of the market with the separate Rover brand, thus preserving the exclusivity of the BMW marque.

Now its strategy was in ruins and it would be producing a 2–Series to come in under the 3–Series, an abject volte-face. Despite the protestations of its managers and the Quandt family, owners of a majority stake in the company, the catastrophic Rover investment probably spelled the beginning of the end of BMW's independence too. Over the longer term, it is questionable whether BMW will be able to preserve its market and technological edge without the benefits of far greater scale.

Had Daimler-Benz and the Chrysler Corporation not done the deal they did at the time they did, it is likely that the same questions would have been hanging over their future as now faced by BMW and Fiat. Both would have been 'in play' or

278

might even have fallen victim to unwelcome takeovers. In the event, they had stolen a march on their competitors, putting pressure on everyone else to follow in their footsteps.

CHAPTER 19

The Twelve Laws of
International Mergers

Some lessons learned

T he strategic rationale of the original DaimlerChrysler merger had been vindicated by the actions of the competition within two years of the deal.

But **strategy is not enough.** This is the first clear lesson that emerges from the merger. To ensure that a deal is successfully completed, you have to take strategy for granted. There are so many other stresses and strains when two large organisations come together that **if your strategy isn't right, failure is a foregone conclusion.**

Second, you need to ensure that your own house is in order first. **Operational strength is a precondition for a successfully executed merger.** Daimler-Benz was not healthy enough to merge with Chrysler back in 1995. It was only after three years of restructuring that Daimler was ready to take on Chrysler. Likewise, DaimlerChrysler was not ready to buy into Nissan in March 1999, so soon after completing the merger.

When it comes to the surgery required to get a company into shape, it is a lot easier for the CEO if he knows where he is going. You may not be able to share that vision with more than a handful of trusted colleagues, but it will help you find the energy to do unpopular things.

The third lesson learned is that no matter how compelling the strategic rationale for a deal, **the top executives must trust each other**. Eaton and Schrempp are profoundly different in character, but they trusted each other. The differences in temperament and background helped strengthen their relationship and made them more effective as a team. Frequent and direct contact between the two CEOs helped their companies to defuse the many tricky issues faced during the negotiations.

If trust isn't there, it does not matter how promising a big corporate deal looks, it won't fly – witness the bust-up which led to the collapse of the original merger between Glaxo Wellcome and SmithKline Beecham. Only when there were new CEOs in place could the transaction go ahead.

The fourth lesson: **get the tough issues out of the way as early in the negotiations as possible**. Schrempp and Eaton came to quick agreement on the structure of the transaction: the invention of the first global-registered share, the legal entity and the location of the head office. Crucially, they also agreed how they would divide the leadership of the company.

By staying on together for a certain period of time they ensured that both companies' boards went along with the transaction. To get to this point both Schrempp and Eaton were prepared to put their jobs on the line. Schrempp articulates the fifth lesson thus: '**Never allow egos to stand in the way of a merger which makes economic sense**.'

Of course, not all the sensitive issues were sorted out in the early stages of the negotiations. The name was left until the very last minute. Had the name been brought to the fore too early in the discussions, the deal might have been stillborn. So in such cases one must bide one's time before forcing the issue home.

Here one sees Schrempp's willingness to force a digital decision. It is yes or no. With something as important as the name, there is a line drawn in the sand. Schrempp knew what he wanted and was not bluffing. He was prepared to risk the deal to get it. He judged correctly that the other side had invested too much time, money and energy to let an emotional issue be the downfall of the negotiations.

So here is the sixth lesson: **on important issues be prepared to force a yes or no decision. But before you do this, make sure that the odds are loaded in your favour.**

The seventh lesson: **do your homework.**

Schrempp initiated talks with Chrysler only after thorough preparation. Throughout 1997 he carefully considered all the options to put Daimler-Benz on the path of profitable growth. This led to the decision to concentrate on the automotive industry and to pursue a mould-breaking transaction. Only once the preparation is complete is it time to make a move.

Then move fast: the eighth lesson.

'When people want more time, do it in less time,' says Schrempp. 'It's better to take a decision and be 80 per cent right rather than wasting time trying to make the next step 100 per cent right. With a merger – as with so much of business – speed is critical and there is only one priority: pragmatism before perfectionism.'

Speed becomes more critical after the merger than before. Schrempp notes that the integration programme was completed in just one year, half the time the two companies originally set themselves.

A speedy integration of two companies involves trade-offs. Not everybody is going to be happy with the decisions that are taken, the measures that are forced through or are patently 80 per cent right rather than perfect.

There are plenty of examples of cross-border mergers and takeovers that have slowly died because of what Schrempp calls 'the deadly desire for harmony'. These include Renault's acquisition of American Motors and BMW's purchase of Rover. In Schrempp's universe, there is no point in shilly-shallying around: difficult issues must be identified and dealt with promptly.

So the ninth lesson is: **tolerate, even encourage differences in**

283

style and culture, reap the benefits of 'constructive conflict', manage the tensions.

This thinking underlies the decision to turn Chrysler into a division of the DaimlerChrysler group. While many American managers originally saw this as a form of subjugation, it was intended to be a liberation.

'I'm a hands-on CEO but I want powerful divisions,' explains Schrempp. 'They are responsible for running brands such as Jeep or Mercedes-Benz worldwide. The car guys get together in the Automotive Council and they prepare the board for the decisions that affect the business – you know, how to position the M-Class relative to the Jeep Grand Cherokee, what kind of engines to develop – and so on.

'As a CEO I don't feel above the divisional guys, I'm in the centre. In my former life I was an engineer and I know all about centrifugal forces. I want the divisions to be strong. They have a tendency to be too strong, to pull away from the centre. My job is to hold them at arm's length, to hold them together. I want them to be entrepreneurs but I want to make sure that at the end of the day they make a contribution to the wellbeing of the group as a whole.

'If I manage to stay in the centre and have the strength to hold them,' Schrempp says, arm extended, fist clenched, 'me the guy watching the group's interests and these guys always pulling because they are promoting the division, then we have the optimum set-up.'

The tenth lesson: **keep the negotiating team small.**

The deal was put together by a handful of key executives, strategists and planners from the inside of the company, together with a select team of advisors from the outside. The rationale: to keep the talks as secret as possible.

As Schrempp knew from bitter experience, the more people who know about what is going on, the harder it is to push a merger through. 'It doesn't work when everybody down the line knows what's going on, and you keep reading about your next move in the newspapers,' says Schrempp, reflecting on the circumstances of the painful merger between Mercedes-Benz and its parent company.

The need for secrecy means of course that there is no opportunity to build *overt* consensus for a deal, before the deal is done. Reflects Schrempp: 'We would then have to maintain that consensus – as well as confidentiality – all the way through to the final stage. That would have made things very difficult.'

Note, however, that there *was* broad internal consensus for a deal, even if the specifics were not discussed explicitly until late in the day. The strategic imperative for a merger, as well as the rationale for doing a deal with Chrysler, could be taken for granted. This was the result of careful preparation throughout the course of 1997 and 1998. The Daimler-Benz board knew they needed to do something to guarantee the growth targets they had set themselves. What's more, the automotive executives – Jürgen Hubbert and Dieter Zetsche in particular – knew from the experience of 1995–6 that they could do business with Chrysler. The groundwork had been done.

Schrempp's stealthy style of preparing major transactions has worked well for Daimler; the deal to create the European Aeronautics, Defence and Space group (EADS) was handled in the same way. But it won't work for everybody, as the failure of the attempted merger between Deutsche Bank and Dresdner Bank, its big domestic rival.

In this case, the style of the negotiations owed a lot to the DaimlerChrysler transaction. A handful of senior executives from both these powerful institutions hammered out the broad parameters of a deal. The strategic logic of the merger was compelling. However, there was no fundamental consensus within the two organisations. At least one key issue was not dealt with, namely the fate of Dresdner Kleinwort Benson, Dresdner's investment banking arm. The two sides had not agreed what to do with DKB: whether to sell it off or absorb it into the new entity.

To be more precise, while the two CEOs had agreed on one course of action, they found out only after they announced the transaction that they did not have sufficient internal consensus to go down that route. Hence an outbreak of internal warfare and the talks were killed off. The Deutsche/Dresdner deal died because the banks' two CEOs had not done enough homework.

Once you have completed the transaction, let your own people drive the process of integration: that is the eleventh lesson of the DaimlerChrysler deal. During negotiations, the use of skilled outsiders increases the chances of success. Thereafter, integration was handled entirely by Rüdiger Grube and his team.

As we have seen, external consultants should never be used in the formulation of strategy – strategy is the job of the CEO. Schrempp talks to consultants as part of the information-gathering process, but does not rely on them to tell him what to do.

The twelfth lesson: **if you want to be a global leader in your industry, you have to play by the rules of the international capital markets.** For a German company, that is especially hard – you have to break the mould. Ultimately, as Schrempp has found, only a profitable company can be a social company.

This is a lesson that many other German companies have learned from Schrempp, as we shall see in the next chapter.

CHAPTER 20

RIP Germany AG

The lessons for corporate Germany

In his first five years as CEO of Daimler-Benz and subsequently DaimlerChrysler, Jürgen Schrempp took the company from losses of $3 billion to profits of $11 billion.

The group's market capitalisation rose from E17.6 billion in May 1995 to nearly E65 billion. Formerly a ragbag of mismanaged businesses, it was transformed into a focused automotive company. Schrempp took a weak strategic situation and turned it into a position of strength.

This is a story of leadership. Had Schrempp not known in broad terms what he wanted to do – and then done it against the odds – Daimler-Benz would have entered the twenty-first century nearing the limits of growth. Instead, Daimler transformed its own future and that of the industry in which it operates.

The story goes beyond the achievements of one individual. It symbolises the revival of the German economy in a globalising world.

It is difficult to overestimate the changes that have swept through German industry and finance since the mid-nineties.

Company after company in sector after sector has adopted

the language of shareholder value. A new generation of German CEOs has embraced cost-cutting, adopted Return on Capital targets and started selling off underperforming subsidiaries. RWE and Veba (two big utilities) were among the first, as was Hoechst, a traditional chemicals company which merged with Rhône-Poulenc of France, changed its name to Aventis, and moved its headquarters to Strasbourg.

Even Schrempp's most vociferous critics have come into line. Siemens, for a long time proudly resistant to the shareholder value cause, has embarked on an aggressive restructuring programme. It has disposed of non-core businesses, floated its semi-conductor business on the stock market, introduced tough financial targets for the much-diminished number of divisions, and even adopted American accounting as a prelude to a listing on the New York Stock Exchange. The rhetoric which goes with all these moves is strikingly similar to that of the Daimler CEO back in 1995–6.

Those companies that live by the shareholder value creed must die by it. Mannesmann created tens of billions of value by turning itself from a steel pipes manufacturer to a mobile telephone giant. It then fell to a hostile bid from Vodafone AirTouch of the UK – one of the first forced changes of corporate control in German history. The signal effect was profound. '[It says] "Goodbye Germany AG,"' Rolf Breuer of the Deutsche Bank told the *Wall Street Journal,* 'we are now fully entering international competition' (*WSJ* 28–9 January 2000).

The stock market has boomed, the number of companies seeking a listing has exploded. The Neuer Markt, a new exchange for smaller companies loosely modelled on the NASDAQ market of the US, saw its value treble to DM112 billion in 1999. Private individuals have become enthusiastic buyers of stocks and shares. Hitherto they would have consigned their savings to the relative safety of government bonds. An 'equity culture' has taken root in German soil.

From a macro-economic perspective, these changes are unequivocally good news for Germany. The financial markets are the heart and lungs of an economy. For many decades these organs were underdeveloped in relation to the rest of the body. Europe's strongest economy was depriving itself of the oxygen of capital. The network of interlocking shareholdings – exemplified by the historic ties between Deutsche Bank and Daimler-Benz – further limited circulation of the blood supply. The banks exerted a stranglehold over German industry. The patient was pretty sickly as a result, but felt comfortable. It enjoyed a cosy relationship with organised labour. It was easy to be complacent.

The patient could have lingered on for a few more years, but for a number of profound changes which took place outside the hospital walls. In economists' language, these are exogenous factors – well beyond the patient's control. These have been touched on earlier, but it is worth recapitulating the main points.

The first shock was the elimination of barriers to the international mobility of capital. Capital, which had tended to sit unproductively within the confines of national boundaries, suddenly found itself able to flow around the world in search of the most congenial home. New technology accelerated the flow of information, speeding up the restless circulation of capital.

The second was German reunification. This did not work out as planned. The economy failed to flourish. Instead, reunification dragged Germany into its deepest recession since the war (in 1992–3) and it soaked up capital. Germany's current account surplus swung into deficit. The result: the pool of cheap money traditionally available to industry from banks dried up. Companies had to turn to the international markets for their capital requirements. Then of course they found that they had to compete hard with their international peers. They had to speak the language of those investors. They had to do what those investors wanted. They had to walk the walk and talk the talk.

The third shock came later, in 1995. The German economy was assaulted on three fronts. The Mexico debt crisis destabilised the international financial system and hobbled exports to the developing world. The D-Mark rose 18 per cent against the dollar in 1994–5, punishing Germany's exporters. At the same time, the powerful IG Metall pushed through an irresponsibly high wage settlement.

It was Schrempp, almost alone among German industrialists, who drew the line in the sand. Remember he was at DASA at this time, and the aerospace industry was especially badly affected by the strong D-Mark. Bischoff and Schrempp decided: we cannot use the currency as an excuse, we cannot be passive in the face of these challenges. Hence the Dolores programme. The word means pain in Spanish; for Schrempp it stood for 'dollar low rescue' programme.

By this time, in the last days of the Reuter era, Daimler-Benz had become a machine for misallocating capital. Its massive inefficiencies symbolised the broader problems of German industry.

Then, amid the universal condemnation of its domestic peers, it became the first German company to embrace the international capital markets. Credit is due to Gerhard Liener, Daimler's then CFO, who promoted the company's listing on the New York Stock Exchange in 1993. It is not certain that he or the rest of the Daimler board had a clear idea of the revolutionary consequences for Daimler and for Germany.

It was left to Schrempp to follow through the logic. After Dolores came Stop the Bleeding. The restructuring restored Daimler's finances and revived its profitability. The phase of defensive restructuring was brutally tough. But in some ways, this was the easy bit. Offensive restructuring is trickier.

What do you do when you have taken out the waste, cut costs, restored productivity? How do you promote double-digit growth in a mature industry? The answer is, you leap beyond the boundaries of Germany and of conventional thought. You take steps to become competitive on the international stage.

For Daimler, that meant doing the deal with Chrysler. Other companies followed suit: the Deutsche Bank acquisition of

Bankers Trust is a case in point, or Bertelsmann's acquisition of Random House, and Mannesmann's purchase of Orange. At the time of writing, even the Deutsche Börse – the German Stock Exchange – was getting in on the act, attempting to merge with the London Stock Exchange to create iX in a bid to dominate European share trading. This plan failed, but Germany is becoming more assertive on the world stage.

Back home in Germany, the big banks and insurance companies have been trying to sort themselves out. The creation of a single European currency, coupled with widespread deregulation, has intensified the pressures on German business and finance. The proposed E31 billion ($29.5 billion) merger between Deutsche Bank and Dresdner Bank may not seem the best example of this trend as it ended in embarrassing failure. However, the deal was driven by the logic of globalisation and the imperatives of the international capital markets. It had the blessing of Allianz, the big Munich insurer which has started to become an agent for change in Germany. Get out of domestic banking, deploy your capital where you are at your most competitive on the global stage. That was the plan. The logic was infallible, the failure was in the execution.

Even the German government has helped. It has introduced laws designed to promote efficient capital markets. It has promised to reduce the tax burden on banks and insurance companies when they sell their industrial holdings. Once this happens, the ramparts of the old fortress Germany will crack and crumble. Tens of billions of capital will be liberated. The German economy – and by extension the economy of Europe as a whole – will be further galvanised.

The moral of the tale for Germany? The old consensus surrounding the social market economy is dying. Capital is king. The Anglo-Saxon way has won. And this is for the better. Only a profitable company can be a social company, Schrempp would say. By extension, only an efficient economy can be a social economy.

The trap – and this is true for the rest of continental Europe as well as Germany – is that things have to get worse before they get better. Germany's unemployment hit 13 per cent in early 1998, the worst level since the Weimar Republic of the 1920s. *More* jobs will be lost as a result of restructuring before they will be created in the sectors which benefit from the redeployment of capital to profitable businesses. The transition requires political leadership, a quality in short supply.

The US provides the model. In the early 1990s American companies went through the defensive restructuring phase. Companies cut jobs and strove to restore rates of return on capital. 'The economy expanded while unemployment stagnated, giving rise to "jobless growth",' comments Thomas Mayer, chief economist at Goldman Sachs in Frankfurt. In 1992, for example, US Gross Domestic Product grew by 2.7 per cent while employment grew by just 0.7 per cent. By the middle of the decade, companies embarked on an aggressive search for profitable growth. The US economy metamorphosed into a job machine: in the five years to 1998, it grew by 3 per cent per year with employment rising by an average of nearly 2 per cent.

This is the capitalist's nirvana: simultaneous growth in wealth and jobs; low inflation; perpetual productivity gains, driven by new technology and flexible labour markets; flourishing capital markets which nourish risk-taking and innovation, in turn creating more jobs and wealth. The growth owes a lot to the 'new economy' of Silicon Valley, but the revitalisation of 'old economy' companies like Chrysler played its part.

In Germany, as in much of the rest of Europe, there is reluctance to accept the logic of America's 'new paradigm'. Big business has learned the lessons of globalisation, but powerful interest groups such as the IG Metall union do not see the world in these terms at all. Nor can Gerhard Schröder and his Social Democrats be too overt in their support for capital at the expense of labour. Yet the alliance between capital and labour, sanctified by the laws of co-determination, has become a sham.

On a macro-economic level, the insistence on collective

bargaining for entire industries benefits no one but the unions. It forces companies to deploy capital outside Germany, where labour costs are lower. Siemens, for example, increased employment outside Germany by 50 per cent from 108,000 in 1984–5 to 162,000 a decade later, while employment in Germany fell by 12 per cent. Over the same time-frame, Volkswagen cut domestic jobs by 10 per cent and increased overseas employment by 24 per cent. The same is true of other big German companies such as Bosch, Bayer, BASF, Hoechst, Thyssen, and of course the former Daimler-Benz.

To take another example, the DaimlerChrysler deal was done *despite* worker representation on the supervisory board, not because of it. The only way for German companies to be competitive on the global stage is to work round the workforce representatives, not with them.

German supervisory boards, with ten labour representatives to match ten from capital, are unwieldy and bureaucratic. The process of getting to a decision is baroque. Whether they succeed in creating prosperity depends critically on the relationships between a trio of individuals: between the chairman of the supervisory board, the chairman of the management board, and the senior representative of labour.

When the personal chemistry is wrong, as it was between Hilmar Kopper and Edzard Reuter, the result can be paralysis: necessary reforms are delayed. By contrast, when two men get on as well as Kopper and Schrempp, the conditions are in place for strategic renewal. Likewise, the personal ties between Karl Feuerstein and Schrempp ensured a productive partnership between labour and management through years of difficult restructuring. But this was due to personal chemistry, not the system. It is not good for Germany that so much is left to chance.

Another flaw in the German system of corporate governance is that the representatives of capital on the supervisory board come from old Germany – the big banks and insurance companies – and not the international world which the companies now inhabit. Setting up a special Shareholders' Committee, as DaimlerChrysler has done, is no long-term solution.

The system needs to be reformed if Germany is to carry on being competitive in a ceaselessly changing world economy.

EPILOGUE

Jürgen Schrempp –
The Ten-Year View

London, 27 July 2000

S chrempp is in London for the annual meeting of Vodafone,
the mobile telecoms company where he is a non-executive
director.

This afternoon he is in a reflective mood as he finds himself in
the Dorchester Hotel, scene of many crucial negotiations in the
closing stages of the DaimlerChrysler deal. The place where the
transaction was finalised more than two years ago.

Schrempp is the picture of serene good health, apparently
immune to the stresses of running the global industrial giant
that DaimlerChrysler has become during his tenure at the top.
As he is the first to admit, it has not been an easy ride: the share
price has dropped sharply during the course of 2000 and as a
result Schrempp faces criticism about the logic of the deal and
the way the integration of Chrysler has been managed. Criticism
which Schrempp is happy to address – but first it is time for a
review of his five years as CEO of first Daimler-Benz and then
DaimlerChrysler – and for a look ahead to the next five years.

Schrempp's priority on taking over as CEO in 1995 was to sort out the inheritance bequeathed to him by Edzard Reuter. Only once the legacy of the past had been dealt with, could he begin to implement his strategy.

The first *strategic* objective was to refocus the company on the automotive industry. Accordingly he moved quickly to close down the AEG electricals subsidiary and thereafter to end Daimler's engagement in Fokker, the ailing aircraft manufacturer. By the end of his second year in office he had completed the merger of the Mercedes-Benz subsidiary with its parent company – a necessary precursor to the DaimlerChrysler deal. He also reduced the number of operating units from thirty-five to twenty-three.

In October 1999 the twenty-year dream of ending the fragmentation of the European aerospace and defence industry took a step closer to reality with the creation of the European Aeronautics, Defence and Space group (EADS). In July 2000 this company was floated on the stock market, the last step on Daimler's path to becoming once again a pure car manufacturer.

The second strategic objective was to reduce the group's dependence on Europe and create a truly international automotive business. The DaimlerChrysler deal in 1998 transformed the group's presence in North America. The solution to Asia was found through the strategic alliance with Mitsubishi Motors. A scandal at the Japanese auto manufacturer gave Schrempp the opportunity to renegotiate the original contract in Daimler's favour. On Friday, 8 September 2000 Daimler-Chrysler announced a revised deal. Schrempp secured the right to buy 100 per cent of Mitsubishi after three years – and to tighten his grip on the day-to-day management of the Japanese company through the appointment of a Chief Operating Officer.

On the same day DaimlerChrysler signed off on a deal to buy up to 15 per cent of Hyundai Motors, Korea's largest car manufacturer.

There is more to do in Asia – negotiations are under way to fill the gaps in China and India – but DaimlerChrysler has achieved its aim of becoming a powerful force in the 'triad' markets of Europe, Asia and the Americas. Unlike most of its competitors, DaimlerChrysler is now in a position to hedge the economic and industrial cycles which traditionally play havoc with auto companies' earnings.

The third, closely related objective was for DaimlerChrysler to offer a comprehensive product line-up to every type of customer in every segment of the market – from the smallest passenger vehicle to the biggest truck, from Mercedes-Benz luxury brand to the Smart car. Again, this has been done.

The fourth was to build on Mercedes-Benz' leadership in technology and innovation. It is too early yet to see the tangible fruits of the DaimlerChrysler merger in this respect; the crucial period will be between 2002 and 2005 when the first products overseen by the new management will come to market. The company is spending E50 billion over the next three years to develop sixty new cars, trucks and commercial vehicles. During this time DaimlerChrysler will usher in a new era of mobility, introducing a range of quiet, pollution-free fuel-cell vehicles.

Looking to the future, Schrempp identifies a number of business and cultural challenges.

On the business front, it will be critical for Schrempp to harness the power of new internet-based technologies and thus to prove his assertion that there is no fundamental distinction between the 'old' and 'new' economy – simply a dynamically changing economy. 'It's a tough job for us,' concedes Schrempp. 'We were a little bit asleep because we didn't expect the impact of the new technologies to be so fast and so profound. But we're catching up fast.'

Wherever DaimlerChrysler's strategy takes it, the interests of shareholders will remain paramount. 'But we must never forget social responsibility,' Schrempp cautions. 'We must be at the forefront in training, recruitment, executive development, looking after employees' health. We must be multi-ethnic and multi-cultural. We must balance the interests of shareholders, of those of our employees and customers, of our suppliers and of society at large.'

Lest it be thought that Schrempp is softening, or giving way to uncharacteristic political correctness, he is quick to point out that what he is saying here is not a radical break with the past – his views now are an extension of the philosophy outlined in his speech to the Friedrich Ebert political think tank back in 1997. Self-interest dictates that one should strive to be more altruistic, Schrempp contends, paradoxically. To be really successful in economic terms, a company has to attend to those matters a lot more. If it doesn't keep customers, employees and society happy, it won't be able to satisfy shareholders either.

Keeping shareholders happy is key, but not on a quarterly basis. He finds it difficult to disguise his exasperation with this aspect of Anglo-Saxon short-termism. 'If somebody is off one cent against expectations, all of a sudden the value of the company drops by $10 billion. It's totally ridiculous!'

For the long term, Schrempp believes that he will only deliver value to shareholders if he can instil a common corporate culture in the far-flung DaimlerChrysler empire. 'We need the glue of common values to hold us together,' he insists. 'If you can do that, while tolerating peoples' differences, then you are a fantastic company. I acknowledge that we have a long way to go.'

At this point, Schrempp checks himself: he is alert to the danger of getting carried away by vision and strategy. 'Vision is only 30 per cent of the story,' he says, reiterating one of the central tenets of his business philosophy. '70 per cent is implementation.'

Friday, November 29, 2000

The importance of implementation is brought into sharp relief by events of the last few months of 2000.

On Friday November 17, DaimlerChrysler announced that Dieter Zetsche, then head of the commercial vehicles division, would take over as President and CEO of Chrysler Group with immediate effect. Wolfgang Bernhard, the 40-year old responsible for the successful introduction of the latest S-Class Mercedes, was appointed Chief Operating Officer of Chrysler.

In the same reshuffle, Eckhard Cordes, the main negotiator during the merger with Chrysler, succeeded Zetsche as head of the global commercial vehicle business.

This was the moment that the Germans finally lost patience with the worsening operating performance of the Chrysler unit. Putting aside at last questions of culture and nationality, it was time for Stuttgart to take direct and unequivocal management responsibility for Chrysler. The background: a substantial drop in profitability at Chrysler during the course of 2000 (operating profits were expected to fall from E5.1 billion in 1999 to E2 billion in 2000), and a 20 per cent plus decline in the DaimlerChrysler share price during the course of the year. At around E53 billion, the market capitalisation of the group is little more than that of Daimler-Benz on its own prior to the merger.

(The sharp fall in the share price is one reason why Kirk Kerkorian has launched an $8 billion lawsuit against DaimlerChrysler, alleging inter alia that Daimler-Benz executives wrongfully presented the deal as a 'merger of equals' rather than a pure takeover. His lawyers argued that the decline in shareholder value 'concided with Mr Schrempp's subjugation of Chrysler into a subordinate role'. The company has rejected the claim out of hand.)

The factors behind Chrysler's earnings demise are depressingly familiar for students of the company's history. As so often in the past, Chrylser has proved vulnerable to an intensification of competition in the cyclical US automotive market. Add in the costs of launching new models and Chrysler actually lost E600 million in the third quarter of 2000 – all of which is making analysts nervous about prospects for the coming year. The magic which surrounded the initial merger is long gone – overshadowed by Chrysler's operating problems in North America.

The events of late 2000 beg a number of questions. The most fundamental of these is, did Daimler-Benz do the right thing in merging with Chrysler? Put it another way, would Schrempp have done the deal, had he been able to foresee the condition in which Chrysler would find itself in the latter part of 2000?

Schrempp's answer to the latter question is an emphatic yes:

even if he could have seen what was to come, it was right to do the deal. 'Temporary operational challenges should not be mixed up with the fundamental strategic rationale,' says Schrempp.

Difficult though it is to indulge in the 'what if?' school of analysis, it is unlikely that the old Daimler-Benz would have retained its independence if it had not merged with Chrysler. With Mercedes-Benz as its sole earnings powerhouse, the old Daimler would in all probability have been swallowed up by one of the giants of the industry. Now, notwithstanding the formidable operating difficulties in the US – and the need to turn around Mitsubishi Motors in Japan – DaimlerChrysler has a seat at the top table.

For shareholders, there is little consolation in this: for them, strategy is secondary to earnings. Schrempp, Germany's most powerful advocate of shareholder value, is of course acutely sensitive to this. The challenge is now less strategic than operational – to fight the hard battle to restore Chrysler to robust financial health. This is the mandate entrusted to Dieter Zetsche and Wolfgang Bernhard.

'We have a major task ahead of us and along the way we are sure at times to fall short of people's expectations,' says Schrempp.

'The thing is to stay firm. Mentally you have to be able to face up to all the criticism that inevitably comes in your direction. You have to listen, but you mustn't let it overwhelm you when you are convinced you are on the right track. Say to yourself: "I'm going my way. I'm going my way." Because you have a responsibility to the next generation and you know it is the right thing to do.

'I often say this to people when they are being scrutinised by the media or by the financial markets. They ask me whether they should change course or carry on and argue the case. I always say, just stand there. As long as I am the captain of this ship, this is the way we go. End of story.'

SELECT BIBLIOGRAPHY

The History of Daimler-Benz AG

Appel, Holger and Hein, Christoph, *Der DaimlerChrysler Deal*, DVA, 1998

Barthel, Manfred and Lingnau, Gerold, *Daimler-Benz die Technik*, von Hase & Koehler, 1986

Eglau, Hans Otto, *Edzard Reuter*, Econ Verlag, 1992

Gregor, Neil, *Daimler-Benz in the Third Reich*, Yale University Press, 1998

Kruk, Max and Lingnau, Gerold, *Daimler-Benz das Untérnehmen*, von Hase & Koehler, 1986

Niemann, Harry, *Wilhelm Maybach, The Father of Mercedes*, Motorbuchverlag, 1996

Reuter, Edzard, *Schein und Wirklichkeit – Erinnerungen*, Siedler, 1997

Töepfer, Armin, *Die A-Klasse, Elchtest, Krisenmanagement, Kommunicationsstrategie*, Luchterhand, 1999

Töepfer, Armin, *Die Restructurierung des Daimler-Benz Konzerns 1995–1997*, Luchterhand, 1999

The History of Chrysler Corporation

Flammang, James M. et al., *Chrysler Chronicle – An Illustrated History of Chrysler, De Soto, Dodge, Eagle, Jeep, Plymouth,*

Publications International, 1998

Iacocca, Lee, with Novak, William, *Iacocca, an Autobiography*, Bantam Books, 1984

Levin, Doron P., *Behind the Wheel at Chrysler: The Iacocca Legacy*, Harcourt Brace, 1995

Lutz, Robert A., *Guts, the Seven Laws of Business That Made Chrysler the World's Hottest Car Company*, John Wiley, 1998

The Automotive Industry

Halberstam, David, *The Reckoning*, Transworld, 1986

Keller, Maryann, *Collision*, John Wiley, 1993

Womack, James P., Jones, Daniel T. and Roos, Daniel, *The Machine that Changed the World*, Rawson Associates, 1990

German Industry

Eglau, Hans Otto, *Wie Gott in Frankfurt – Die Deutsche Bank und Die Deutsche Industrie*, Econ Verlag, 1990

Gall, Lothar et al., *Die Deutsche Bank 1870–1995*, C.H. Beck, 1995

The Macro-Economic Picture and Shareholder Value

Black, Dr Andrew, Wright, Philip, Bachman, John E. (Price Waterhouse), *In Search of Shareholder Value – Managing the Drivers of Performance*, Financial Times Pitman Publishing, 1998

Charles Leadbetter Centre for European Reform, *Europe's New Economy*, 1999

Mayer, Thomas and Rauh, Joshua, *Europe's Restructuring Trap* (Global Economics Paper No 10), Goldman Sachs, 24 March 1999.

Other

Machiaveli, Niccolo, *The Prince*, Penguin, 1961

Acknowledgements

Special thanks are due to Jürgen Schrempp, who gave me many hours of his time. These meetings were stimulating and highly entertaining. Hilmar Kopper was very helpful and forthright. Christoph Walther and Roland Klein opened many doors within DaimlerChrysler. Eckhard Cordes, Rüdiger Grube, Hartmut Schick and Lydia Deininger all took time out from their busy schedules to answer my barrage of questions.

Many other people helped to get the book on the road. I would like to thank in particular: Manfred Bischoff, Maya Breichlin, Werner Breitschwerdt, Alexander Dibelius, Sezin Dormuss, Silke Diener, Bob Eaton, Tom Gale, Manfred Göbels, Prof. Victor Halberstadt, Keith Hayes, Jim Holden, Terri Houtman, Jürgen Hubbert, Susan Hullin, Vernon Jordan, Herbert Kauffmann, Gershon Kekst, Matthias Kleinert, Steve Koch, Michael Kuhn, Gary Lapidus, Marc Lemcke, Steve Lipin, Bob Lutz, Peter Matson, Thomas Mayer, Tim Metz, Prof. Garel Rhys, Harry Niemann, Bill O'Brien, Heinz Prechter, Andreas Richter, Sebastian Richter, Michael Schell, Christiane Schwarzkopf, Leighton Smith, Nick Snee, Christian Strenger, Mike Taylor, Georg Thoma, Gary Valade, Yvonne Walther, Helmut Werner, Markus Will, Jim Wolfensohn, Philip Wright and Dieter Zetsche.

Anita Greiner was a superlative research assistant – diligent, fast and accurate.

Roland Phillips and Roseanne Boyle at Hodder & Stoughton

and Margit Ketterle and Heike Gronemeier of Econ Verlag had the good sense to buy the book and leave me in peace to go away and write it. Bill Hamilton, my agent, was a welcome voice of calm during the entire process.

My partners Mike Prest and Richard Spiegelberg and colleagues at Chancery Communications allowed me a sabbatical at a critical stage of the company's development. Michaela Davison-Jenkins and Rowena Merrick were especially tolerant of my day-by-day accounts of the book's progress.

My sister Jane and her husband Walter Wager had me to stay many times when I was in Stuttgart and explained what it means to be Swabian.

Duncan Campbell-Smith helped me develop the idea and read an early draft of the book. He is a good friend and a sharp-eyed reader who made many trenchant comments on an early draft of the book. Other members of the Weald of Kent Book Club permitted me to talk about the book at length and have promised to buy two copies each.

Jane, my beloved wife, lived with the book – from idea to completion – for years. She now knows more about the automotive industry than she ever thought possible – or desirable. She was wonderfully supportive throughout, even though she saw a lot more of me than usual.

Finally, Max and Pippa were a constant source of welcome distraction.

David Waller

INDEX

Abbreviations are used as follows:

BE Bob Eaton; C Chrysler; D-B Daimler-Benz; DC DaimlerChrysler; JS Jürgen Schrempp; M-B Mercedes-Benz

305

Index

Index

Index